MACHINE LEARNING FOR MALWARE DETECTION

MACHINE LEARNING FOR MALWARE DETECTION

Editors

Edward Raff
CrowdStrike, USA

Charles Nicholas
University of Maryland, Baltimore County, USA

Robert J Joyce
University of Maryland, Baltimore County, USA

World Scientific

NEW JERSEY • LONDON • SINGAPORE • BEIJING • SHANGHAI • HONG KONG • TAIPEI • CHENNAI • TOKYO

Published by

World Scientific Publishing Co. Pte. Ltd.
5 Toh Tuck Link, Singapore 596224
USA office: 27 Warren Street, Suite 401-402, Hackensack, NJ 07601
UK office: 57 Shelton Street, Covent Garden, London WC2H 9HE

Library of Congress Control Number: 2026013722

British Library Cataloguing-in-Publication Data
A catalogue record for this book is available from the British Library.

MACHINE LEARNING FOR MALWARE DETECTION

ISBN 978-981-12-6203-6 (hardcover)
ISBN 978-981-12-6204-3 (ebook for institutions)
ISBN 978-981-12-6205-0 (ebook for individuals)

For any available supplementary material, please visit
https://www.worldscientific.com/worldscibooks/10.1142/13017#t=suppl

Desk Editors: Soundararajan Raghuraman/Steven Patt

Typeset by Stallion Press
Email: enquiries@stallionpress.com

https://doi.org/10.1142/9789811262043_fmatter

Preface

Artificial Intelligence and Cybersecurity are two of the hottest topics in Information Technology, and that seems unlikely to change in the foreseeable future. AI covers a lot of topics these days, and our particular interests are in machine learning. Likewise, cyber covers a lot of topics, and we focus on malware detection and analysis. The intersection between machine learning and malware analysis is the topic of this book.

The volume begins with a detailed introduction to the topic of malware analysis. This chapter is intended to serve as a tutorial, rather than original research, and is based on our several years of experience in teaching the topic to graduate and undergraduate students at our university. The more technical chapter by Daniel Gibert continues in this vein, with his emphasis on the use of machine learning in the detection of malicious PE files. Much of the work in malware analysis, with or without discussion of machine learning, has focused on static analysis. Erick Galinkin contributes a chapter on dynamic malware analysis, explaining tools and techniques, along with the advantages and disadvantages of the dynamic approach.

In the next chapter, Jonathan Jiang and Mark Stamp present some of their original research on multi-modal ML as applied to the detection of malicious executables. Artificial intelligence has on occasion been accused of producing results that may seem reasonable but come without any explanation. Hence, the interest in the field of Explainable AI, or XAI for short, and this is the topic of the chapter by Giuseppina Andresini, Annalisa Appice, and Donato Malerba.

The cat-and-mouse nature of malware creation and malware detection is well understood. The same can be said for machine learning applications that involve two or more actors with antagonistic goals. Adversarial ML in the context of malware is the topic of the chapter contributed by Luca Demetrio and Battista Biggio. The volume concludes with more original research by Derek Everett, Edward Raff, and James Holt, in which they discuss the automatic discovery of regular expressions that can be used to identify malicious files.

The chapters can be read in any order, although we do suggest that reading the first chapter will be helpful in understanding and appreciating the others. Each chapter is otherwise self-contained, hence our decision to gives its chapter its own bibliography.

On behalf of ourselves, as well as the international set of authors, we take this opportunity to thank our students, past and present, for both motivating us and working with us to achieve a better understanding of this vital area of research.

https://doi.org/10.1142/9789811262043_fmatter

About the Editors

Charles Nicholas is a Professor in the Department of Computer Science and Electrical Engineering at the University of Maryland, Baltimore County, where he has been a faculty member since 1988. He served as Department Chair from 2004 to 2010. His research areas lie at the intersection of data science and cybersecurity. He received his BS degree from the University of Michigan – Flint, and the MS and PhD degrees from The Ohio State University.

Edward Raff has been a Senior Director of Data Science at CrowdStrike since 2025, where he leads Artificial Intelligence and Machine Learning research. Drawing on areas such as adversarial machine learning, high-performance computing, reproducibility, and related fields, he works with others to develop holistic, novel approaches to challenging problems in the scale and asperity of cybersecurity data. Previously, Dr Raff served as a Director at Booz Allen Hamilton, where he founded its machine learning research group. A senior member of the Association for the Advancement of Artificial Intelligence and the Institute of Electrical and Electronics Engineers, he has won six best paper awards and over 100 peer-reviewed articles. Dr Raff received his BS and MS from Purdue University, his PhD from the University of Maryland, Baltimore County, and his MBA from Syracuse's Whitman School of Management.

Robert J. Joyce is an Assistant Teaching Professor in the Computer Science and Electrical Engineering department at the University of Maryland, Baltimore County, where he also received his PhD. Formerly, Robert was a malware researcher in the machine learning research group at Booz Allen Hamilton. Robert's research focuses on aggregating and labeling malware datasets, studying antivirus detections, and statically analyzing malware.

https://doi.org/10.1142/9789811262043_fmatter

Contents

https://doi.org/10.1142/9789811262043_0001

Chapter 1

Encountering Malware Analysis

Charles Nicholas and Robert Joyce
University of Maryland, Baltimore County, USA

1.1 Introduction

With the exponential growth of the malware industry in recent years has come a similar growth in the amount of malware and related data that can be collected. Individual malware specimens can be analyzed, and textbooks (such as Sikorski and Honig, 2012) cover this topic. Since Fall of 2012 our university has used Sikorski's book **Practical Malware Analysis**, hereafter often abbreviated PMA, to teach our combined graduate/undergraduate Malware Analysis course. PMA remains a comprehensive introduction to malware analysis, and the concepts, techniques, and labs it provides continue to be relevant. We still regard it as the best available textbook for this subject, although other books on this subject have appeared since its publication, and several features of PMA have become outdated as time has passed:

- Several malware analysis tools in PMA have fallen out of favor, including ApateDNS, INetSim, and OllyDbg, and some new tools need to be addressed.

- Several versions of Windows have come and gone since PMA was published. PMA focuses on Windows XP, which is now used by only a small fraction of all Windows users.[1,2]
- The malware ecosystem has changed drastically. Attacker tradecraft has evolved, ransomware and cryptocurrency miners have become cybercriminal staples, and malware is increasingly targeting Android and Linux devices.

It is our purpose in this chapter to present a primer on malware analysis, supplementing PMA with malware analysis concepts, resources, and tools that have emerged in the years since its publication. We include several tools that increase analyst productivity via automation or artificial intelligence. The intended audience is the undergraduate or graduate student of cybersecurity or computer science. We assume working knowledge of a high-level language such as C or C++, up to the level of an undergraduate course in data structures. Knowledge of assembly language is quite helpful, but not necessary for the concepts discussed in this introductory chapter. We further assume that the reader is familiar with Windows at the user level. Knowledge of the internals of Windows can be acquired as needed. Basic knowledge of computer networks is assumed, and again additional knowledge can be acquired as needed.

1.2 A Safe Environment for Malware Analysis

To begin, we need to discuss the malware analysis environment, which we define as a hardware platform, a suite of software tools, and other resources of use to the malware analyst. A rudimentary malware analysis environment can be built from the items below:

- A virtualization environment such as VirtualBox or VMWare.
- A virtual machine (VM) with an appropriate operating system for analyzing a particular type of malware.
- A suite of malware analysis tools installed on the VM.
- One or more files to analyze.

[1]Throughout this volume, we sometimes use footnotes to lead the reader to web sites, rather than placing links in the main body of the text, or the references.

[2]https://www.bleepingcomputer.com/news/microsoft/its-windows-xps-20th-birthday-and-way-too-many-still-use-it/.

Access to a virtualization environment is critical to malware analysis. We begin by explaining some terminology. The host (or base layer) refers to whatever operating system is running on "bare metal". The virtualization environment, whether it be VirtualBox, VMWare, or perhaps some other hypervisor, runs on top of that base layer. The virtualization environment can run several guests, or virtual machines, at the same time if there are sufficient compute resources available.

Running malware specimens inside of a virtual machine safeguards the host from any damaging behavior. Furthermore, most virtual environments offer snapshot capabilities. A snapshot captures the state of a virtual machine in such a way that the VM can be restored to that state in a few seconds. Snapshots are essential for malware analysis, so that after running a malware specimen, the VM can be reverted back to a "clean" state with ease.

A free version of VMWare is used in PMA, and there may be times when VMWare is the best choice. However, since PMA came out, VirtualBox[3] has become widely used, and we likewise use it throughout this chapter. VirtualBox is available for Windows and Linux, but support for Apple Silicon devices may be limited. We will not review the steps required to install VirtualBox on the reader's computer, but the VirtualBox website has ample documentation, and helpful tutorials and demos are available on the Internet.[4]

Once VirtualBox has been installed, the next step is to install a virtual machine. The reader is free to fashion their own malware analysis environment, and there are advantages in doing so. Like PMA, we focus on malware that targets a modern Windows computer; a different analysis environment would be needed to analyze malware that targets other platforms. For this, we strongly recommend setting up a Virtual Machine with a licensed version of Windows 10[5] or higher and installing FLARE-VM[6] on it. Using FLARE-VM, analysts no longer have to individually locate, download, and install every malware analysis tool they plan to use. FLARE-VM provides access to an extensive suite of malware analysis tools, and manages

[3]https://www.virtualbox.org/.
[4]https://www.virtualbox.org/manual/topics/installation.html.
[5]https://www.microsoft.com/en-us/software-download/windows10.
[6]https://github.com/mandiant/flare-vm.

the installation of any tools selected by the user. In our opinion, it is the most streamlined way to create a Windows malware analysis environment.

The reader who attempts to use the various tools available to them will soon realize that a powerful computer is of great help when doing malware analysis. More memory is better than less. Additional monitors make a surprising difference, given that the analyst may need to have a web browser, a disassembler, a debugger, a text editor, and several other tools open at the same time. An external hard drive may be useful for storing large Virtual Machines and collections of malware specimens. The environment we just described might represent a significant expense, especially on a student's budget. Labs provided by their department or university may provide such an environment, but many students may not have access to such labs. The last section of this chapter describes how to create a malware analysis environment in the cloud, which a student may be able to set up and use from even a modest laptop.

1.3 Accessing Malware Specimens to Analyze

There is no shortage of malware specimens to analyze. The collection of labs[7] provided in PMA is of great help to the novice student, especially since detailed solutions to those labs are given in the back of that book. Samplepedia[8] provides malware analysis labs of varying difficulty, and each has a written or video solution. Vx Underground[9] and SecRepo[10] are massive repositories of malware specimens.

For the purpose of demonstrating several malware analysis tools and concepts, the remainder of this chapter will feature a file named EncounteringLab.exe. The program is not malicious, but it performs potentially-unwanted behaviors that are frequently exhibited by malware. As we will learn by analyzing it, EncounteringLab.exe copies itself to another location, makes a system configuration change so that it runs on startup, creates a mutex (a shared resource object),

[7]https://github.com/mikesiko/PracticalMalwareAnalysis-Labs.
[8]https://samplepedia.cc/.
[9]https://www.vx-underground.org/.
[10]https://www.secrepo.com/.

and makes a DNS request. It also uses a few anti-analysis techniques. If the reader wishes to follow along, EncounteringLab.exe is available for download as an encrypted 7zip file.[11] The password to the 7zip file is `infected`. It is best practice to treat EncounteringLab.exe as if it were live malware—this file, and all such files, should only be downloaded and executed in a safe malware analysis environment.

1.4 Malware at a Glance Using VirusTotal

The quantity and variety of tools available for the malware analyst may seem intimidating at first. Some tools focus on aspects of the malware specimen as a file, while others focus on aspects of the specimen's execution. This is a quick description of the difference between static and dynamic malware analysis, and each has its place in the malware analyst's toolbox. Some tools are used to take a "quick-and-dirty" look at a file, while others are used to fully understand a file inside and out. Some tools (whether static or dynamic) are run locally, while others are hosted on various websites.

In some instances, the analysis objective is simply to answer the question "Is this file malicious?" For this, we introduce VirusTotal,[12] a web-based malware analysis platform that happens to have both static and dynamic analysis capabilities. VirusTotal can scan suspected files or URLs with a large collection of security products, making it an excellent way to make quick determinations about a suspect file. Each security product then outputs whether it believes the input to be malicious or benign. Some may take a while to return a decision, while others scan files or URLs quickly. VirusTotal accepts submissions of any file type, including executable binaries, scripts, and documents. The set of security products used to scan a file depends on its file type.

Most anti-virus products in the VirusTotal ensemble scan files using a combination of signatures and heuristics. Signatures attempt to match patterns of bytes known to appear in a particular type of malware, while heuristics look for file attributes or behaviors that

[11] https://drive.google.com/file/d/1k18axSmxSbM_lZySiadtbP1mwKLxFOVS.
[12] https://www.virustotal.com/gui/home/upload.

are associated with maliciousness. Anti-virus products are increasingly incorporating (or in some cases, exclusively employing) machine learning to identify malware.

If a file or URL is flagged by enough security products, it's typically safe to assume that it is malicious. Likewise, when no security products flag a file or URL, it's most likely benign. However, be aware that security products can make mistakes and newly-emerging malware may evade detection. The analyst's interpretation of these detection results depends on the situation and the user's tolerance for risk.

EncounteringLab.exe is not malware, but in many aspects it certainly looks like it. The program is not one that any normal user would want to run. When uploaded to VirusTotal, EncounteringLab.exe appears suspicious enough to be flagged by 35 of the 71 security products that scanned it. Some of the detection results are shown in Figure 1.1.

Files known to VirusTotal can be queried by their hash digests, which are presumably unique numeric values generated from a file's contents. Malware reports share the hashes of malicious files so that others can check if their networks have been compromised by those files. Clicking the "Details" tab in VirusTotal shows the file's MD5, SHA-1, and SHA-256 hashes, among others (Figure 1.2).

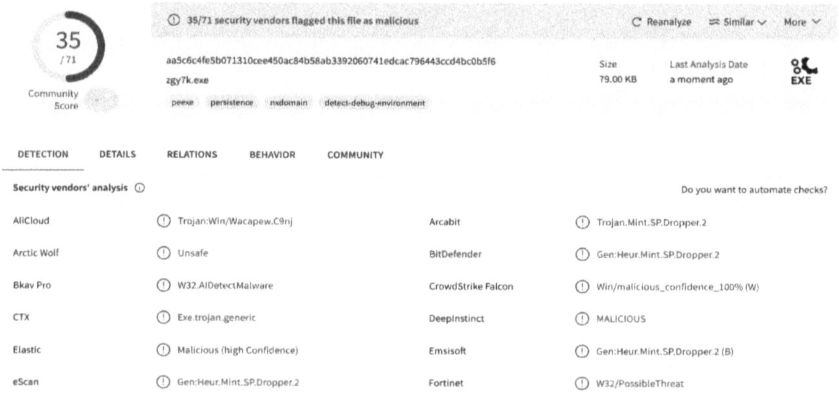

Fig. 1.1. Detection results showing that 35 of 71 anti-virus products in VirusTotal detect EncounteringLab.exe as malware.

Fig. 1.2. The MD5, SHA-1, and SHA-256 hashes EncounteringLab.exe shown in VirusTotal.

It must be noted that some malware analysts work in sensitive environments where online analysis tools like VirusTotal should not be used. Uploading a file, or even one of its hash values, to some external web site is proof that you, the malware analyst, have access to that file. An attacker becoming aware of this could ruin an investigation.

1.5 Automating Malware Analysis Using Sandboxes

Once it is known that a file is malware, the next question to be asked might be "What malicious things can this file do?" The simplest way to attempt to answer this question is to run the malicious file in a sandbox. A sandbox is a virtual environment for safely running programs and monitoring the behaviors they exhibit. A sandbox may be hosted as a web service or on an analyst's own virtual machine. VirusTotal supports several in-house and external sandboxes.[13] Cuckoo Sandbox is perhaps the most well-known sandbox software that can be hosted locally.[14] In recent years, Platform for Architecture-Neutral Dynamic Analysis (PANDA) has also gained a following as a locally-hosted whole-system dynamic analysis engine.[15]

Hybrid-Analysis[16] is a notable example of a web-based sandbox. When we submit EncounteringLab.exe to the Hybrid-Analysis sandbox, we receive the report shown in Figure 1.3, as well as a longer PDF file with more details. Among other actions that the malware performs, Hybrid-Analysis shows that the malware writes

[13] https://docs.virustotal.com/docs/in-house-sandboxes.
[14] https://cuckoosandbox.org/.
[15] https://github.com/panda-re/panda.
[16] https://www.hybrid-analysis.com/.

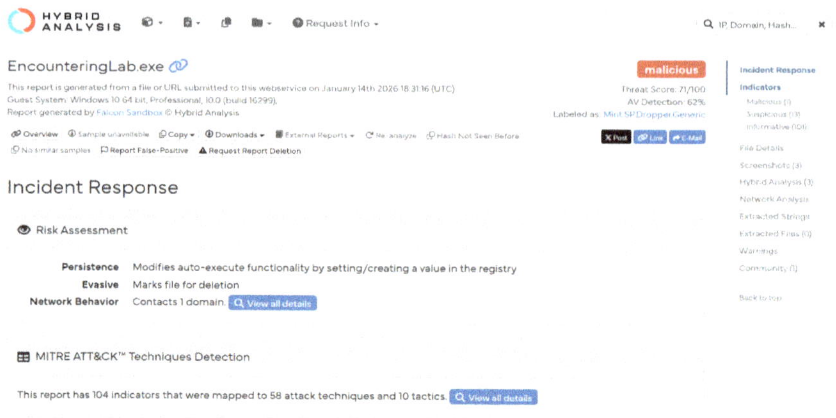

Fig. 1.3. The Hybrid-Analysis sandbox analysis for EncounteringLab.exe.

Fig. 1.4. Hybrid-Analysis shows that EncounteringLab.exe writes to a file in the `%WINDIR%\SysWOW64\` folder and makes that file persistent.

to a file and creates a registry key, as shown in Figure 1.4. First, the malware writes a new file to `%WINDIR%\SysWOW64\EncounteringLab.exe`. `%WINDIR%` is an environment variable that typically has the value `C:\Windows\`. Further analysis will show that the malware is copying itself to the `SysWOW64\` folder. Then, the registry key `HKCU\Software\Mi- crosoft\Windows\CurrentVersion\Run\Encounter` is created and assigned the value `%WINDIR%\SysWOW64\EncounteringLab.exe`. Malware often interacts with the Windows Registry to make configuration changes, and there are several registry keys that grant a program the ability to run

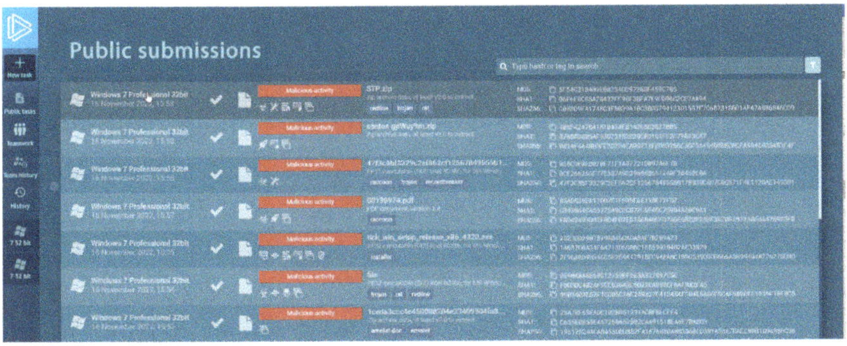

Fig. 1.5. An excerpt from the archive of reports generated by ANY.RUN.

automatically when a computer boots up. This is known as a "persistence mechanism". Of the many persistence mechanisms malware is known to use on Windows, the `Run` key used by EncounteringLab.exe is perhaps the most common.

As another example of online sandbox services, we include ANY.RUN (Figure 1.5). Like Hybrid-Analysis, ANY.RUN supports analysis of suspicious URLs and files of all kinds.[17] With an appropriate license, ANY.RUN will also make the submitted specimens and the corresponding reports available to other users, with the submitters' consent. The submitted specimens include many files found to be benign, as well as specimens that are suspicious, and others that determined to be malicious. The number of specimens available is on the order of hundreds of thousands.

1.6 Utilities for Basic Static Analysis

Although automation can accelerate malware analysis, it has limits. Malware might detect that it is running in a virtual environment, causing a sandbox run to fail. It may exhibit certain behaviors only under specific conditions, such as receiving commands from an attacker via a network connection. In such cases, the analyst will have to get their hands dirty. This often begins by investigating the

[17]https://app.any.run/. For a time, ANY.RUN made enterprise-level access to their site available to the authors for research and educational use, including the preparation of this chapter.

file's contents and attributes, a stage referred to as basic static analysis. This process heavily depends on the type of file being analyzed, and the scope of this chapter is limited to Windows malware in the Portable Executable (PE) format, a file format that includes EXEs, DLLs, and device drivers.

One of the first steps to be taken in basic static analysis is to scan the suspect binary for readable strings. A non-obfuscated binary, that is, one where the executable has not been packed, encrypted, or in some other way made difficult to read, should have several such strings. The first string in most PE files will be the `This program cannot be run in DOS mode.` message, which is an error message to be printed if the file is run on DOS rather than Windows. Other common strings are other error messages, the names of imported functions, and the names of DLLs. One should be particularly interested in any strings that were defined in the malware's source code and that suggest behaviors the malware might take—for example, if one encounters the string `C:\Windows\System32\evilfile.exe`, they should check whether the malware creates or interacts with that file during later analysis. Other types of strings to pay particular attention to include IP addresses, URLs, user agent names, registry keys, and mutexes. Analysts should also be on the lookout for unique strings that could be used to signature the malware or assist in attribution.

The `strings` command in UNIX, and the utility of the same name in the Sysinternals Suite for Windows, can be used for this. It is often useful to limit the output to strings of at least a certain length using a command such `strings -n 8 EncounteringLab.exe`. This is because printable characters may occur next to each other by chance, causing short "junk" strings. The `strings` output in Figure 1.6 reveals the mutex `Global\EncounteringLab_Mutex`, the file path `C:\Windows\System32\En- counteringLab.exe`, the partial registry key `Software\Microsoft\Window- s\CurrentVersion\Run`, and the random-looking domain name beginning with `ae503`.

The `floss` command-line utility will produce a list of readable strings, in addition to searching for certain types of obfuscated strings. `floss` will, for example, identify strings that are encoded with a simple cipher or constructed on the stack at runtime. Its command-line arguments are very similar to those of `strings`. As shown in Figure 1.7 there are five "stack strings" found by `floss` but

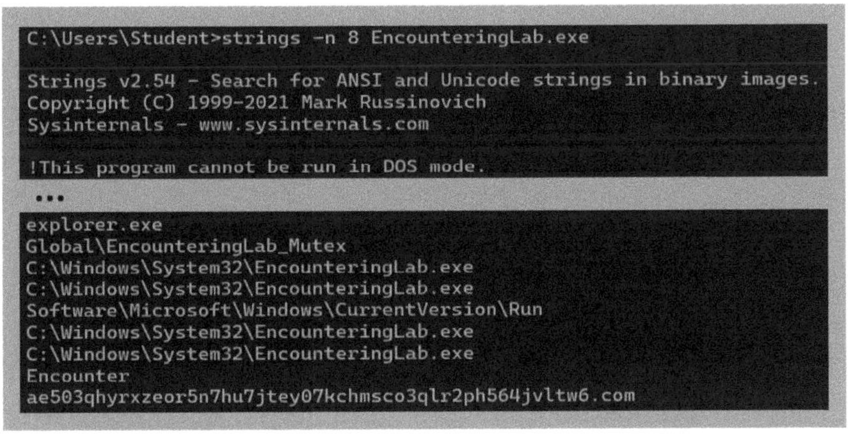

Fig. 1.6. The output of `strings -n 8 EncounteringLab.exe`.

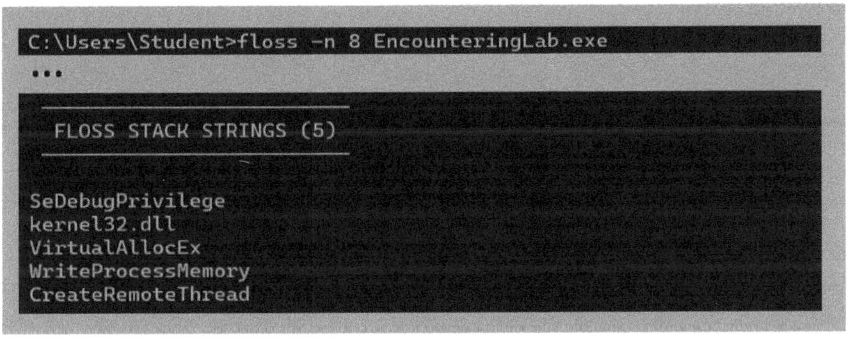

Fig. 1.7. The output of `floss-n 8 EncounteringLab.exe`.

not by `strings`. The first, `SeDebugPrivilege`, is a Windows privilege that allows a program to read and modify the memory of any other process. The second, `kernel32.dll`, is the name of a legitimate dynamic-link library file that contains numerous functions for interacting with the Windows operating system via the Windows API. Following that, we see the names of three Windows API functions that appear within kernel32.dll—we will return to these shortly.

Scrutinizing the functions that an executable file imports is another important aspect of basic static analysis, especially those functions that enable the malware to interact with the victim's computer (e.g., Windows API functions). For PE files, imported functions are listed in the Import Address Table (IAT). Seeing particular functions, or combinations of functions, in a file's IAT can point to specific behaviors the file might perform. For example, the combination of `VirtualAllocEx`, `WriteProcessMemory`, and `CreateRemoteThread` (in addition to the `SeDebugPrivilege` string from Figure 1.7) indicates that EncounteringLab.exe may try to execute code in the address space of another process. This technique is called process injection.

There are several tools that can display the functions in a PE file's IAT, including PEStudio and Detect It Easy. Here, we use PE-Bear, which shows that EncounteringLab.exe imports 81 functions from three DLL files. One notable inclusion is `IsDebuggerPresent`, which EncounteringLab.exe may use to check whether it is being debugged. The combination of `ToolHelp32- Snapshot`, `Process32First`, and `Process32Next` would allow EncounteringLab.exe to inspect which programs are currently running. Other imports suggest that it can interact with the filesystem and registry, make network connections, and create mutexes. We note that `VirtualAllocEx`, `WriteProcessMemory`, and `CreateRemoteThread` do not appear in the IAT of EncounteringLab.exe (Figure 1.8). Several techniques can prevent functions from appearing in the IAT, and we will revisit how EncounteringLab.exe achieves this later.

Offset	Name	Func. Count	Bound?	OriginalFirstThun	TimeDateStamp	Forwa
1185C	WS2_32.dll	3	FALSE	125EC	0	0
11870	ADVAPI32.dll	6	FALSE	124AC	0	0
11884	KERNEL32.dll	72	FALSE	124C8	0	0

KERNEL32.dll [72 entries]

Call via	Name	Ordinal	Original Thunk	Thunk	Forwa
D024	IsDebuggerPresent	-	1268A	1268A	-
D028	CloseHandle	-	1269E	1269E	-
D02C	GetLastError	-	126AC	126AC	-
D030	CreateMutexA	-	126BC	126BC	-
D034	GetCurrentProcess	-	126CC	126CC	-
D038	FreeLibrary	-	126E0	126E0	-
D03C	GetModuleFileNameA	-	126EE	126EE	-
D040	GetProcAddress	-	12704	12704	-
D044	LoadLibraryA	-	12716	12716	-
D048	CopyFileA	-	12726	12726	-
D04C	CreateToolhelp32Snapshot	-	12732	12732	-
D050	Process32First	-	1274E	1274E	-
D054	Process32Next	-	12760	12760	-

Fig. 1.8. A few of the imports from EncounteringLab.exe's IAT.

1.7 Basic Dynamic Analysis on a Virtual Machine

At this point, basic static analysis has given us an understanding of EncounteringLab.exe's capabilities, and running it in the Hybrid-Analysis sandbox has revealed some of its behaviors. Using a sandbox is one form of basic dynamic analysis; the other is to run malware on a VM and manually investigate its behavior. There are a host of tools for performing basic dynamic analysis on a VM. Several tools recommended in the Practical Malware Analysis textbook remain relevant at the time of writing:

- Process Monitor, which captures Windows events related to the filesystem, registry, processes, and threads.
- Process Explorer, which is can be used to list and inspect all currently-running processes.
- Regshot, which identifies changes to the filesystem and registry after running a malware specimen.
- Netcat, which lists information about all current network connections.
- Wireshark, which captures and visualizes network traffic.

Before running malware in a virtual machine, it is important to take a snapshot of the VM. This allows the VM to be restored to a clean state after it has been infected. It is also crucial to ensure that the VM cannot make external network connections. For this, we want to highlight FakeNet-NG,[18] a tool that was released after the publication of PMA. Fakenet-NG spoofs network connectivity on a VM, tricking a malware specimen into believing it is connected to the Internet, when it is, in fact, running in an isolated environment. Fakenet-NG redirects external network traffic to a set of listeners for common network protocols.

Figure 1.9 shows an example of this network redirection. If we try navigating to a webpage, FakeNet-NG's HTTPListener intercepts our web browser's HTTP request and sends a fake response back. This keeps malware running just a bit longer—without FakeNet-NG, a large portion of malware specimens would simply exit when they discover that they cannot reach the Internet.

[18]https://github.com/mandiant/flare-fakenet-ng.

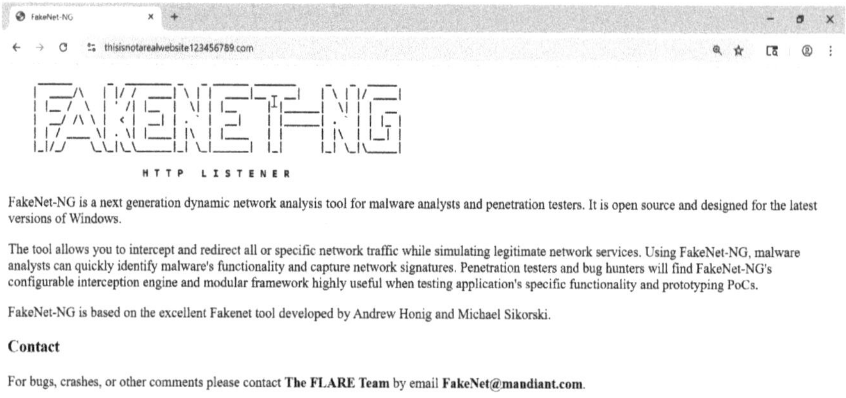

Fig. 1.9. Making a HTTP request while FakeNet-NG is running. The FakeNet-NG HTTPListener intercepts our request and makes this response.

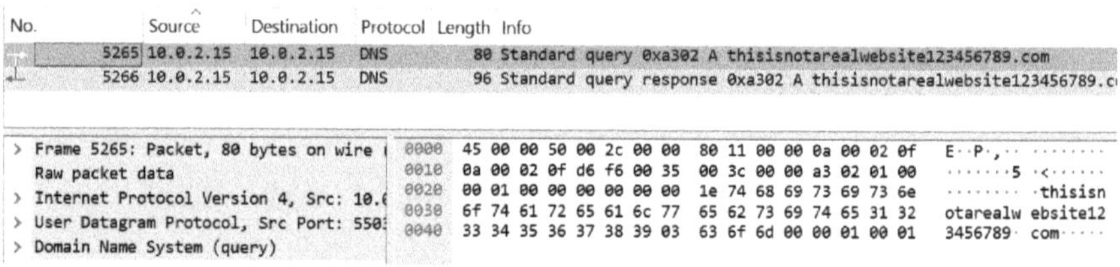

Fig. 1.10. A DNS request from EncounteringLab.exe and the DNS response by FakeNet-NG's DNSListener shown in WireShark.

Continuing our analysis of EncounteringLab.exe, we take a snapshot of the analysis VM and run FakeNet-NG. We can confirm that FakeNet-NG is running properly by attempting to make a ping request or by navigating to a webpage in a browser (Fig. 1.10). We could also run any basic dynamic analysis tools with which we wish to monitor the malware's behavior. Finally, we execute the malware.

FakeNet-NG saves all captured network traffic to .pcap files. With FLARE-VM, these are saved in the `fakenet_logs\` folder on the VM's desktop by default. Double-clicking the .pcap file for the current FakeNet-NG session opens WireShark. Filtering for DNS packets shows that EncounteringLab.exe tried to make a DNS request to the domain `ae503qhyrxzeor5n7-hu7jtey07kchmsco3qlr2ph564jvltw6.com`. We leave investigating EncounteringLab.exe's other behaviors using basic dynamic analysis tools as an exercise for the reader.

1.8 Utilities for Advanced Static Analysis

For a long time, the most important tool available to the malware analysts was the Interactive Disassembler, or IDA. IDA is a commercial product with many useful reverse engineering features. The student malware analyst may be glad to learn that a freeware version of IDA is available.[19] The free local installation of IDA supports only disassembly, but its cloud version offers free decompilation of some architectures.

In addition to IDA, we must mention Binary Ninja,[20] which is functionally similar to IDA and (as we shall see) Ghidra. In addition to having a similar user interface as the former tools, Binary Ninja can also be used from the command line, and from inside Jupyter Notebooks, which is an intriguing vehicle for simultaneously performing analysis and writing a report.

1.8.1 Using Ghidra

The release of Ghidra was one of the most important events in the malware analysis field in recent years. Ghidra is a free, open-source tool that can disassemble, decompile, and debug programs. One can download Ghidra from its web site.[21] The reader may wish to view any of the several Ghidra tutorials available on the Internet, especially YouTube. Serious users of Ghidra may want to acquire the Ghidra Book (Eagle and Nance, 2020). Our purpose here is not to duplicate those efforts, so we focus on the Ghidra decompiler. Decompiled C code is much easier to interpret than assembly language, and if we can figure out what is going on in some portion of a binary by looking at C code (even if it doesn't exactly match the original source code) then that's an advantage. We still have the option of drilling into the assembly code if needed.

To begin analyzing a file in Ghidra, create a new project using "File" -> "New Project" and import the file using "File" -> "Import File". As shown in Figure 1.11, Ghidra then prompts the user to begin

---

[19]https://hex-rays.com/ida-free/.
[20]https://binary.ninja/.
[21]https://ghidra-sre.org/.

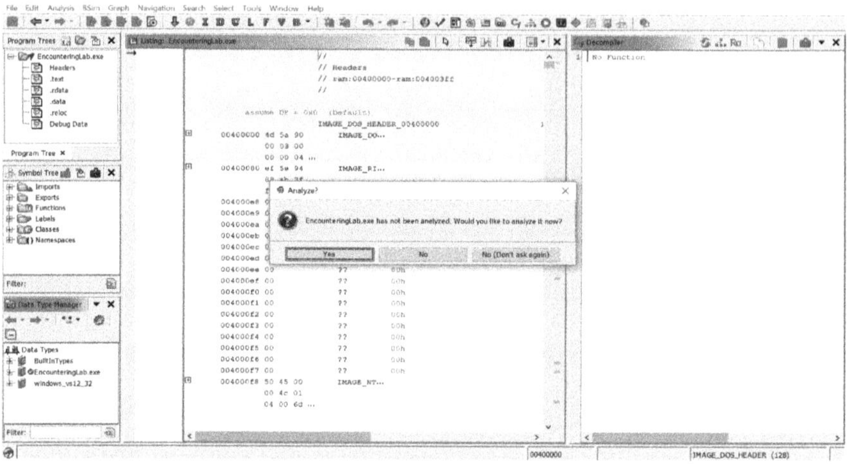

Fig. 1.11. Importing EncounteringLab.exe in Ghidra.

auto-analysis and select which analysis options to apply. In addition to the default analysis options, we recommend selecting "WindowsPE Propagate External Parameters".

Once a PE file has been analyzed, Ghidra places the Listing and Decompilation views at the file's entry point. Although it is possible to reverse engineer a file from start to finish, this is often wasteful. A large portion of functions in a PE file are often boilerplate added by the compiler or functions from statically linked libraries. To avoid wasting analysis time, a better approach is to begin with functions that contain notable strings or Windows API functions identified during prior analysis.

Importing and analyzing EncounteringLab.exe in Ghidra and then navigating to "Window" -> "Defined Strings" displays the file's strings and the addresses at which they appear. Some of the more notable strings are shown in Figure 1.12. One could begin with any of these, but we will start by investigating `Global\EncounteringLab_Mutex`, which is defined at the address 0x00413010. Double-clicking this address in the Defined Strings view will update each of Ghidra's other views to show that address. Alternatively, "Navigation" -> "Go To" will achieve the same result.

00413000	explorer.exe	...
00413010	Global\EncounteringLab_Mutex	...
00413030	C:\Windows\System32\EncounteringLab.exe	...
00413058	C:\Windows\System32\EncounteringLab.exe	...
00413080	Software\Microsoft\Windows\CurrentVersion\Run	...
004130b0	C:\Windows\System32\EncounteringLab.exe	...
004130d8	C:\Windows\System32\EncounteringLab.exe	...
00413100	Encounter	...
0041310c	ae503qhyrxzeor5n7hu7jtey07kchmsco3qlr2ph564jvltw6.com	...

Fig. 1.12. The Defined Strings view in Ghidra. **`Global\EncounteringLab_Mutex`** appears at the address 0x00413010.

```
                     s_Global\EncounteringLab_Mutex_00413010      XREF[1]:     FUN_00401000:00401004(*)
00413010 47 6c 6f        ds          "Global\\EncounteringLab_Mutex"
         62 61 6c
         5c 45 6e ...
0041302d 00              ??          00h
0041302e 00              ??          00h
0041302f 00              ??          00h
```

Fig. 1.13. Information about **`Global\EncounteringLab_Mutex`** in Ghidra's Listing view, including an XREF at 0x00401004.

Switching to the Listing view, shown in Figure 1.13, there is one "XREF" to `Global\EncounteringLab_Mutex` at the address 0x00401004. An XREF, or cross-reference, denotes where one part of the program references another part of the program. Here, the XREF is the result of the program using the string. Navigating to the address 0x00401044 updates the Listing and Decompilation views in Ghidra to show FUN_401000.

FUN_401000, displayed in Figure 1.14, calls three Windows API functions: `CreateMutexA`, `GetLastError`, and `CloseHandle`. When coming across an unfamiliar function, a great first step is to read its documentation. For example, according to the Microsoft Learn documentation for `CreateMutexA`,[22] its third parameter is a pointer to a string containing the name of the mutex to create. Investigating the arguments passed to `CreateMutexA` in EncounteringLab.exe shows that this function attempts to create the mutex `Global\EncounteringLab_Mutex`. The documentation also states that `CreateMutexA` returns a handle to the created mutex object,

[22]https://learn.microsoft.com/en-us/windows/win32/api/synchapi/nf-synchapi-createmutexa.

```
undefined4 FUN_00401000(void)

{
  HANDLE hObject;
  DWORD DVar1;
  undefined4 uVar2;

  hObject = CreateMutexA((LPSECURITY_ATTRIBUTES)0x0,1,s_Global\EncounteringLab_Mutex_00413010);
  DVar1 = GetLastError();
  if (DVar1 == 0xb7) {
    if (hObject != (HANDLE)0x0) {
      CloseHandle(hObject);
    }
    uVar2 = 0;
  }
  else {
    uVar2 = 1;
  }
  return uVar2;
}
```

Fig. 1.14. The Ghidra Decompilation view for FUN_401000.

or NULL if the function call failed. If the mutex already existed before `CreateMutexA` was called, the error `ERROR_ALREADY_EXISTS` is set. The next line in FUN_401000 is a call to `GetLastError`, which returns the most recently set error code. This is stored in a local variable automatically named `DVar1`.

It is good practice to rename variables and function names in Ghidra throughout the course of analysis. To do this, right-click the item and select "Rename Variable" or "Rename Function". A descriptive new name for `DVar1` would be `DLastError`.

After the call to `CreateMutexA` in FUN_401000, an if statement checks if `DLastError` is equal to 0xb7. This happens to be the hexadecimal value of `ERROR_ALREADY_EXISTS`.[23] If the mutex `Global\EncounteringLab_Mutex` already exists, FUN_401000 attempts to close the handle to that mutex and sets the value of another local variable, `uVar2`, to 0. The function returns uVar2, so an appropriate new name might be `uReturnValue`. If the mutex did not already exist, the function sets `uReturnValue` to 1. Finally, the function returns `uReturnValue`.

In summary, FUN_401000 returns 0 if the mutex `Global\EncounteringLab_Mutex` already exists, and 1 if it does not.

[23]https://learn.microsoft.com/en-us/windows/win32/debug/system-error-codes–0-499-.

```
undefined4 CheckForMutex(void)

{
  HANDLE hObject;
  DWORD DLastError;
  undefined4 uReturnValue;

  hObject = CreateMutexA((LPSECURITY_ATTRIBUTES)0x0,1,s_Global\EncounteringLab_Mutex_00413010);
  DLastError = GetLastError();
  if (DLastError == 0xb7) {
    if (hObject != (HANDLE)0x0) {
      CloseHandle(hObject);
    }
    uReturnValue = 0;
  }
  else {
    uReturnValue = 1;
  }
  return uReturnValue;
}
```

Fig. 1.15. The Ghidra Decompilation view for FUN_401000 after renaming the function and two local variables.

A descriptive new name for FUN_401000 would be `CheckForMutex`. Figure 1.15 shows FUN_401000 after it and two of its local variables have been renamed.

An appropriate next step for analyzing EncounteringLab.exe is to investigate how the `CheckForMutex` function is used within the file. To do this, XREFs are once again helpful. The Listing view shows that `CheckForMutex` has three XREFs, though only one occurs due to other code in EncounteringLab.exe calling the function. This XREF occurs at the address 0x4018f3 inside of `FUN_004018f0`, shown in Figure 1.16. At the top of `FUN_004018f0` is a call to `CheckForMutex`, which stores its return value in `iVar2`. If `iVar2` is 0 (which occurs when `Global\EncounteringLab_Mutex` already exists), the local variable `uVar3` is set to 1 and then the function returns `uVar3`.

The remainder of `FUN_004018f0` has calls to seven other functions, and only executes if the mutex did not already exist prior to `CheckForMutex` being called. This is a common behavioral pattern in malware that wishes to avoid re-infecting a computer. First, the malware checks if a unique mutex exists on the computer it plans to infect. If it does, the malware determines that it has already infected that computer and exits. Otherwise, it creates the mutex and performs its malicious behavior.

```
undefined4 FUN_004018f0(void)

{
  bool bVar1;
  int iVar2;
  undefined4 uVar3;
  undefined3 extraout_var;
  undefined3 extraout_var_00;

  iVar2 = CheckForMutex();
  if (iVar2 == 0) {
    uVar3 = 1;
  }
  else {
    FUN_00401050();
    FUN_004010d0();
    bVar1 = FUN_00401160();
    if (CONCAT31(extraout_var,bVar1) == 0) {
      uVar3 = 1;
    }
    else {
      bVar1 = FUN_00401200();
      if (CONCAT31(extraout_var_00,bVar1) == 0) {
        uVar3 = 1;
      }
      else {
        FUN_004013f0(s_explorer.exe_00413000);
        FUN_00401220();
        FUN_004014b0();
        uVar3 = 0;
      }
    }
  }
  return uVar3;
}
```

Fig. 1.16. The contents of FUN_004018f0 in Ghidra's decompilation view.

1.8.2 Automating Reverse Engineering with GhidraMCP

Machine learning is being increasingly utilized to automate malware analysis tasks. Large language model (LLM) copilots show immense promise for streamlining the reverse engineering process. One such tool is XRefer,[24] a plugin for the professional version of IDA. XRefer

[24]https://github.com/mandiant/xrefer.

uses Google Gemini to automatically analyze, identify, and group the functions in an executable file.

We will continue our analysis of EncounteringLab.exe using GhidraMCP,[25] a plugin that allows Ghidra to communicate with a LLM via the Model Context Protocol (MCP). GhidraMCP allows a connected LLM to interact with a program being reverse engineered in Ghidra, and it provides nearly two dozen built-in commands. The GhidraMCP installation page has instructions for connecting the plugin with Claude Desktop, so we will use it as well. Specifically, the malware analysis tasks performed below were performed using Claude Opus 4.5.

Claude was instructed to reverse engineer FUN_004018f0 (the function we began analyzing at the end of Section 1.8.1) using the following prompt: "In Ghidra, analyze FUN_004018f0 and the functions it calls. Output a report about this code's functionality." The beginning of its response is shown in Figure 1.17. After this,

Malware Analysis Report: FUN_004018f0

Executive Summary

FUN_004018f0 is the main initialization routine for a malware sample that exhibits multiple characteristics of sophisticated malicious software, including persistence mechanisms, anti-analysis techniques, and code injection capabilities.

Function Overview

The function serves as an orchestration routine that performs a series of malicious initialization steps. It returns 0 on success or 1 on failure.

Detailed Analysis

1. Mutex-Based Singleton Check (CheckForMutex)

The malware creates a named mutex `"Global\EncounteringLab_Mutex"` to ensure only one instance runs at a time. If the mutex already exists (GetLastError returns ERROR_ALREADY_EXISTS: 0xb7), the function returns 0, causing the main function to exit. This is a common technique to prevent multiple infections and avoid detection through resource consumption.

Fig. 1.17. The beginning of a report about FUN_004018f0 in EncounteringLab.exe, created by interfacing Claude with Ghidra using GhidraMCP. It correctly identifies the mutex check we found in our own analysis.

[25] https://github.com/LaurieWired/GhidraMCP.

```
undefined4 MalwareInitialization(void)

{
  bool checkResult;
  int mutexCheckResult;
  undefined4 returnValue;
  undefined3 extraout_var;
  undefined3 extraout_var_00;

  mutexCheckResult = CheckForMutex();
  if (mutexCheckResult == 0) {
    returnValue = 1;
  }
  else {
    InstallToSystem32();
    CreateRegistryPersistence();
    checkResult = CheckC2ServerReachable();
    if (CONCAT31(extraout_var,checkResult) == 0) {
      returnValue = 1;
    }
    else {
      checkResult = CheckDebuggerPresent();
      if (CONCAT31(extraout_var_00,checkResult) == 0) {
        returnValue = 1;
      }
      else {
        FindExplorerProcess(s_explorer.exe_00413000);
        ObtainDebugPrivilege();
        LoadProcessInjectionAPIs();
        returnValue = 0;
      }
    }
  }
  return returnValue;
}
```

Fig. 1.18. The contents of FUN_004018f0 in Ghidra's decompilation view, after Claude has renamed each variable and function using GhidraMCP.

we prompt Claude one more time: "In Ghidra, rename all functions and variables in FUN_004018f0. Give each a descriptive new name". Using GhidraMCP, Claude was able to modify the contents of FUN_004018f0 in Ghidra, making the function much easier to understand. The modified function is shown in Figure 1.18.

Claude's report contained detailed and (mostly) correct analysis of each function while drastically reducing the time it would have taken to reverse engineer them. XRefer, GhidraMCP, and similar tools have massive potential in aiding malware analysts. At the same time, it is important to keep in mind that these tools are not infallible, and malware analysts must be diligent about how these tools are applied and how their outputs are interpreted. We encourage the reader to reverse engineer these functions themselves and compare their own analysis to that of a LLM. Below, we provide brief summaries of each remaining function called inside FUN_004018f0.

- **FUN_00401050**. This function uses `GetModuleFileNameA` and `str- icmp` to check whether its current path is `C:\Windows\System32\Enc- ounteringLab.exe`. If not, it copies itself to that location. It is common for malware to copy itself to a system folder, where it may blend in with other legitimate programs.
- **FUN_004010d0**. This function uses `RegOpenKeyExA` to get a handle to the registry key `Software\Microsoft\Windows\CurrentVersion- \Run`. It creates the subkey `Encounter` with the data entry `C:\Win-dows\System32\EncounteringLab.exe` using `RegSetValueExA`. Then, it closes the handle to the registry key. This makes the copy of EncounteringLab.exe persistent.
- **FUN_00401160**. This function makes a DNS request to `ae503qhyr- xzeor5n7hu7jtey07kchmsco3qlr2ph564jvltw6.com` using `gethost- byname`. If the DNS request is successful, the function returns 0. If it fails, it returns 1. Claude's report speculates that this function "likely serves as a kill-switch or verification that the C2 server is reachable". It ultimately renames the function `CheckC2ServerReachable`, when its true purpose is the former. This function is an imitation of the WannaCry ransomware's "kill switch domain" anti-analysis check.[26] It makes a DNS request to a domain that is unregistered at the time of writing. If EncounteringLab.exe is run while a tool like FakeNet-NG is answering all DNS requests, it determines that it is being analyzed and the rest of FUN_004018f0 is skipped.
- **FUN_00401200**. This function checks whether EncounteringLab is running in a debugger using `IsDebuggerPresent`. It returns 0 if the program is being debugged and 1 if it is not. If the function returns 0, the rest of FUN_004018f0 does not run.
- **FUN_004013f0**. This function takes a pointer to a string as an argument. FUN_004013f0 calls `CreateToolhelp32Snapshot`, which creates a list of processes that are running at that moment. The function then calls `Process32First` and `Process32Next` in a

[26]https://www.checkpoint.com/cyber-hub/threat-prevention/ransomware/wannacry-ransomware/.

loop over those processes. It compares the name of each process to the string argument using the case-insensitive compare function `stricmp`. If any process' name matches that string, the function returns 1. Otherwise, it returns 0. Searching through processes is a common behavior in malware, and one that may have a multitude of purposes. Malware may be checking if it is running in a VM, searching for the presence of a security product, or searching for another process to inject into. When called in FUN_004018f0, its parameter is `explorer.exe`, which manages the Windows File Explorer and Windows GUI, and is a common target of process injection. Similar functions often return a handle for the process the malware plans to inject into, rather than a boolean value.

- **FUN_00401220**. At the beginning of this function, the string `SeDebugPrivilege` is created by individually copying each character to a location on the stack. Ghidra's Decompilation view abstracts this by defining a function named `builtin_memcpy`, but the behavior is visible in the Listing view's disassembly. As discussed in Section 1.6, this causes `SeDebugPrivilege` to not appear in the output of `strings`, but it is still found by `floss`. As we mentioned earlier, `SeDebugPrivilege` is a Windows privilege that allows a program to read and modify the memory of another process. The function uses a combination of `OpenProcessToken`, `LookupPrivilegeValueA`, and `AdjustToken Privileges` to grant itself this privilege. When running as a normal user, malware needs this privilege to perform process injection.
- **FUN_004014b0**. This function begins by constructing four more stack strings: `kernel32.dll`, `VirtualAllocEx`, `WriteProcessMemory`, and `CreateRemoteThread`. It then calls `LoadLibraryA` with the parameter `kernel32.dll`, causing `kernel32.dll` to be loaded into EncounteringLab.exe's address space. Next, `FUN_004014b0` calls `Get- ProcAddress` three times, getting pointers to the functions `VirtualAllocEx`, `Write ProcessMemory`, and `CreateRemoteThread` in `ker- nel32. dll`. The combination of `LoadLibraryA` and `GetProcAddress` allows access to any function from any DLL on the computer. This technique is called runtime linking, and it allows EncounteringLab.exe to keep`VirtualAllocEx`, `WriteProcessMemory`, and

`CreateRemote- Thread` from appearing in its IAT. These three functions can be used to reserve memory in another process' address space, write code and/or data to that memory, and start a thread inside of another process. Their presence is rare in typical executable files, and would likely cause a program to get flagged by a security product due to the program's ability to perform process injection.

1.9 Analyzing Malware with a Debugger

The fact that malware is often complex and attempts to hide its behavior should not come as a surprise to the reader. Frequently, analysts are faced with code that is difficult to understand or whose behavior cannot be determined without first running the program. Often, the best approach is to use advanced dynamic analysis—running the program in a debugger and investigating exactly how the registers, stack, and other memory are affected. Debuggers also allow an analyst to control a program's execution, forcing execution to take a code path it may not have ordinarily followed.

We assume the reader is familiar with debuggers from other courses in programming. We recommend x32dbg and x64dbg, open-source debuggers for both both 32- and 64-bit applications respectively. EncounteringLab.exe was compiled for a 32-bit architecture, so we make use of x32dbg in this chapter, but both debuggers are functionally identical. Be cautious when debugging malware—like basic static analysis, it should be done inside of a safe environment with external network connectivity disabled. It is good practice to take a snapshot prior to debugging malware and restoring to a clean state afterwards.

Upon opening EncounteringLab.exe in x32dbg, execution is shown paused in `ntdll.dll`. Like similar debuggers, x32dbg begins execution outside of the debugged program and attempts to place a one-time breakpoint at its entry point. Selecting "View" -> "Breakpoints" shows that there is indeed a breakpoint placed at 0x00E51DA0. Clicking "Debug" -> "Run" (or Run icon) once causes execution to reach this breakpoint and pause. Figure 1.19 shows execution paused at the entry point.

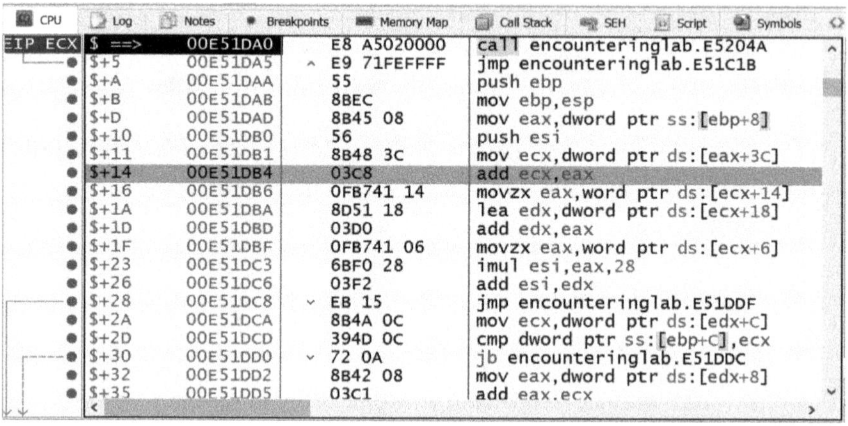

Fig. 1.19. Execution paused at the entry point of EncounteringLab.exe in x32dbg's CPU view.

Comparing the program's entry point in x32dbg to the entry point reported by any static analysis tool would reveal a discrepancy: The entry point is located at 0x00E51DA0 in x32dbg, but the entry point is listed as 0x00401DA0 in EncounteringLab.exe's PE header. The reader who follows along may see the entry point in x32dbg at a different address than either of the above. This is due to relocation, which presents an issue if trying to debug a program while simultaneously referencing a tool such as Ghidra, since addresses between the two will not match. The issue must be resolved in the disassembler/decompiler tool.

The image base of the program can be found in x32dbg using "View" -> "Memory Map". In our debugging session, the entry for EncounteringLab.exe lists the address of the image base as 0x00E50000. Ghidra allows the image base to be changed by navigating to "Window" -> "Memory Map" and clicking the "Set Image Base" icon that appears as a house (see Figure 1.20). Setting the image base in Ghidra to match that of x32dbg allows addresses to match again.

The function previously at 0x00401200 in Ghidra has been remapped to the address 0x00E51200. This address can be navigated to in x32dbg by right-clicking the upper-left pane of the CPU view, selecting "Go to" -> "Expression", and entering 0x00E51200. To set a

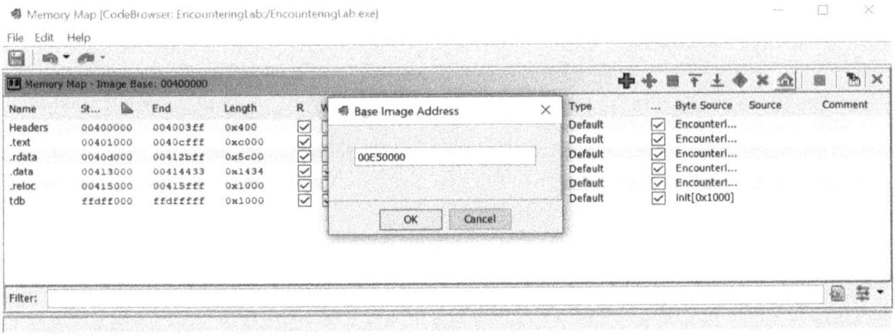

Fig. 1.20. The assembly contents of FUN_00401DA0, which was relocated to 0x00E51200.

breakpoint at 0x00E51200, right click the address and select "Breakpoint" -> "Toggle". Finally, selecting the "Run" icon allows execution to reach 0x00E51200.

Be cautious when attempting to run code to a breakpoint. Malware may be able to take several code paths, and execution will not necessarily take the code path that reaches a given breakpoint. However, in this instance, the program's execution does pause at the desired address.

Figure 1.21 shows the assembly code of the function at 0x00E51200. Recall that this function checks whether the program is being debugged by calling `IsDebuggerPresent`. The function returns 0 if a debugger was detected and 1 otherwise. In assembly, the RAX register stores the function's return value, and at the address 0x00E51211 we see assembly instruction `MOV EAX, 1`. This instruction executes if `IsDebuggerPresent` detects that the program is being debugged, and would cause EncounteringLab.exe to exit early. One way to circumvent this is to patch the assembly instruction in a way that forces the function to return 0 regardless of whether a debugger is in use.

The assembly instruction `MOV EAX, 1` can be patched by right-clicking it in x32dbg, selecting "Assemble", and entering `MOV EAX, 0`. EncounteringLab.exe can be permanently patched using "File" -> "Patch file". The patched function is shown in Figure 1.22. Stepping to the "RET" instruction shows that the EAX register is 0, even though the program is being debugged. This nullifies the debugger check, and we are free to continue debugging the program further.

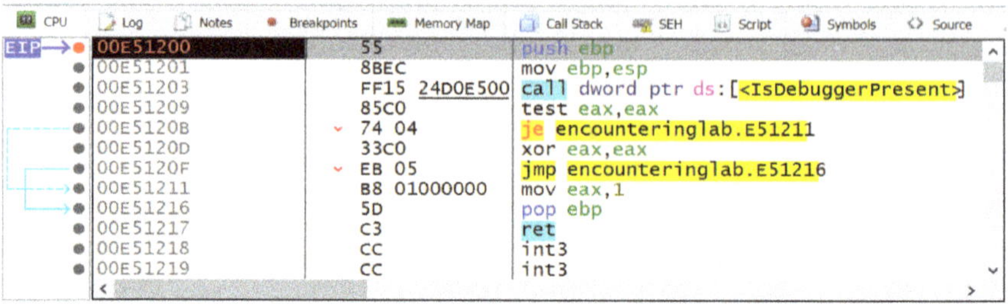

Fig. 1.21. The assembly contents of FUN_00401DA0, which was relocated to 0x00E51200.

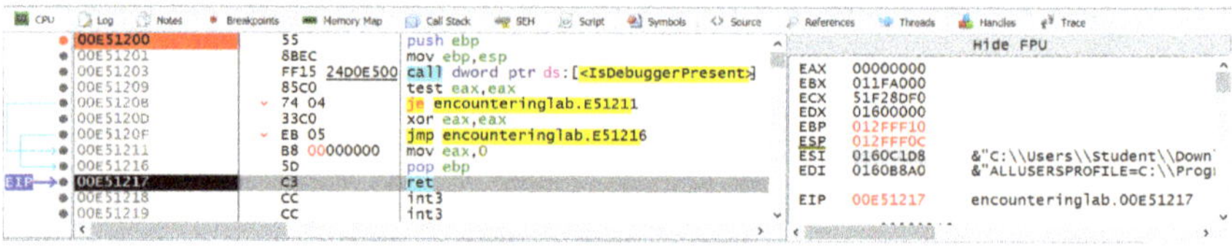

Fig. 1.22. The assembly contents of FUN_00401DA0 after being patched to ignore the debugger check.

The reader is encouraged to try patching other parts of EncounteringLab.exe themselves, including the function containing the "kill switch" DNS request.

1.10 Using the Cloud for Malware Analysis

Before concluding this chapter, it seems appropriate to admit that tools we've described so far, including disassemblers, debuggers, not to mention virtualization environments running different operating systems, may put quite a load on an ordinary laptop. Indeed, there may be several reasons to use a cloud service as a platform for malware analysis:

(1) The user's own laptop (or desktop) computer may not have enough CPU power, or memory, to run several VMs at once.
(2) The user's computer may not support virtualization, and therefore not be able to run VMWware or VirtualBox at all.
(3) The user may want to analyze malware in the cloud in order to conform to policy that forbids the presence of malware on their computer, even if virtualization is used.

(4) The user may want to have access to the same malware analysis environment from a variety of physical locations, such as home, work, or when on travel.

Cloud service providers, or CSPs, offer their customers access to a variety of virtual machines. This variety may include a choice of operating systems, number and type of CPUs, memory, disk storage, and software configurations. Selecting the right configuration is mostly a trade-off between capability and budget. Many CSPs offer a free tier of services, and charge more depending on the size of the virtual machine, and the level of access desired. For the student malware analyst, free or at most "pay as you go" is probably the best choice.

Before describing how to set up a Windows desktop suitable for malware analysis using a particular cloud service, we need to discuss nested virtualization. Nested virtualization can be described as the ability to run a virtual machine inside another virtual machine. If one acquires a Windows or Linux desktop running in the cloud, that desktop is actually a VM running under the control of a hypervisor (such as Xen), and it's the hypervisor that is running on real, bare metal hardware. Cloud service providers vary in the extent to which, and at what cost, they make nested virtualization available.

Whatever CSP we use, we intend to connect to the cloud platform using a virtual network controller, or VNC. Several VNC servers are freely available on the Internet. The Remote Desktop Protocol, or RDP, would be an option were we to connect to a Windows VM from a Windows PC. For the sake of licensing if no other reason, Linux VMs seem to be the more common CSP offering. In what follows, we describe the creation of an Ubuntu VM, and how to connect to it using VNC. We caution the reader that details in what follows may change at any time.

1.10.1 Google Compute Engine

The Google Cloud Platform (GCP), and the Google Compute Engine in particular, is the example we use. The place to start is the GCP Console, accessed at https://console.cloud.google.com/, as shown in Figure 1.23.

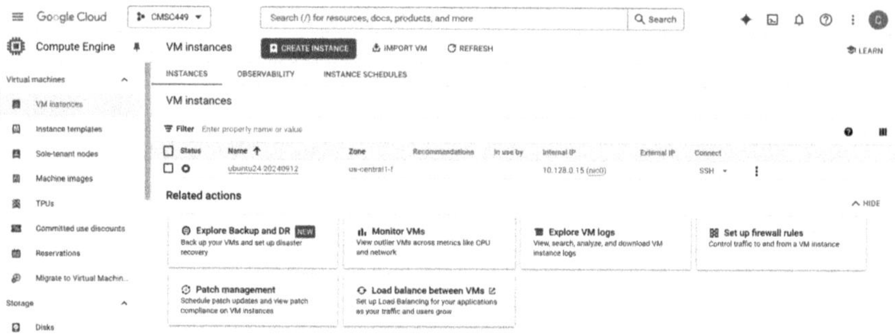

Fig. 1.23. Google Compute Engine Console, showing a single VM instance. Note the "CREATE INSTANCE" button highlighted in blue.

The GCP console may look different at your institution. We again caution the reader that systems change, and what worked for us as we were preparing this chapter may not work for you. Details large and small may need to be updated.

From the Console, use the "Create Instance" button to bring up a menu, allowing you to create a new VM instance, with many possible configurations. For malware analysis, which may require running one or two virtual machines, as well as the host operating system, choose a configuration with at least 16GB of RAM. Each of those VMs will require a couple of processor cores at least, so choose a configuration with at least eight cores. Adjust the size of the boot disk to at least perhaps 200 GB, since OVA files, VMs, and snapshots can use a lot of disk space!

Referring back to the matter of nested virtualization: The GCP documentation suggests that a chip such as the Intel Haswell, or better, is required. In the example in the figures, the machine type we've selected is "n2-highcpu-16", running on an Intel "Cascade Lake" or better, which meets GCP's requirement (see Figure 1.24).

We will need more than the default disk configuration, so scroll down to the Boot disk area. Select "CHANGE", and note the various Boot disk options. We've selected the Ubuntu version 24.04, and a size of 200 GB, as shown in Figure 1.25. Press "SELECT" to return to the Machine Configuration Menu, and press the "CREATE" button at the bottom.

After a few moments, an updated list of VM instances appears, as shown in Figure 1.26. The default name for a VM is based on

Fig. 1.24. Machine configuration menu. We need a machine that has several cores, sufficient RAM, and support for nested virtualization.

its creation timestamp. The green circle with a check mark indicates that the new VM is already running. Take note of its "External IP", which will change each time the instance is started.

We can start using this VM by connecting to it with ssh. Press "SSH" on the far right. By default, an ssh client built into the browser is used, and we see no reason to change that. The first action is an exchange of ssh keys, and no password is needed—or allowed. The default user has sudo access. After a moment, a new shell appears, as shown in Figure 1.27.

To see that our shell has sudo access, see if the command `sudo whoami` replies with "root". Now, running a shell is a good start, but we need to do some additional setup to use this VM as a remote desktop. From among several options, we've chosen to use the xfce4 desktop, a well-known and quite suitable window manager. To install

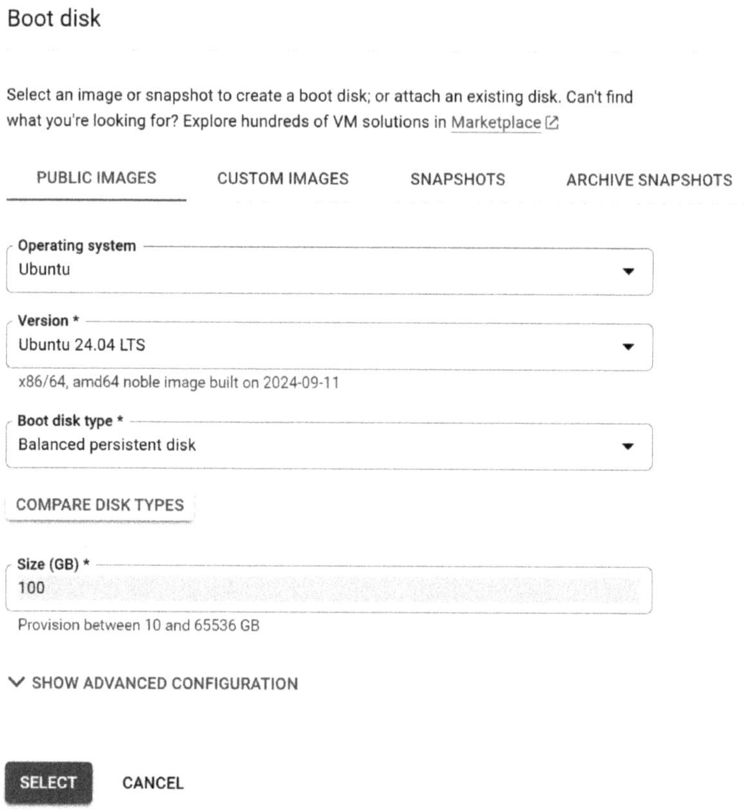

Fig. 1.25. Selecting the OS and boot disk capacity.

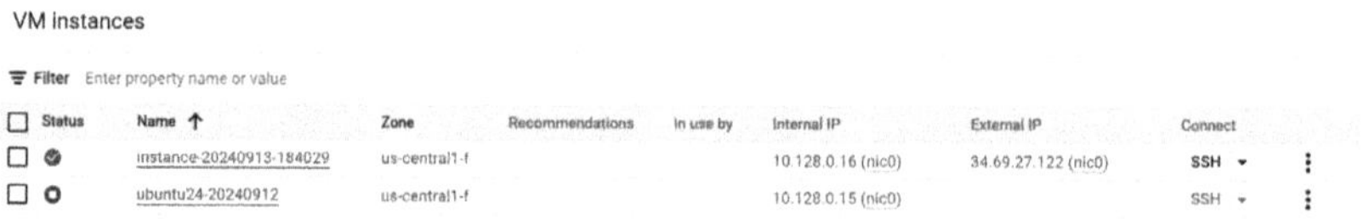

Fig. 1.26. Listing of VM instances, with the VM we just created at the top.

xfce4, we first need to install the tasksel utility, as shown below. Installing tasksel make take a few moments, but it makes installing xfce4 much easier.

```
sudo apt-get update && sudo apt-get upgrade
sudo apt install tasksel -y
sudo tasksel
```

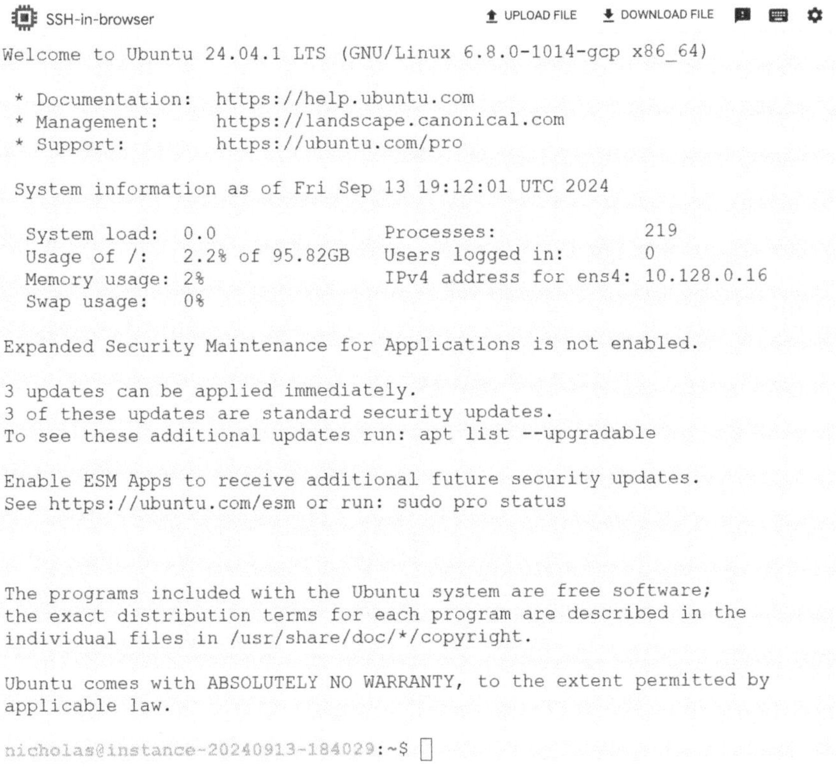

Fig. 1.27. A new SSH session, using the in-browser client. Note the icons for uploading and downloading files.

Invoke tasksel as shown above, select the Xfce option, tab down to the bottom, and press "Okay", as shown in Figure 1.28.

Once xfce is installed, we'll install a VNC server as shown below. This too will take a few minutes. Once all this is done, we can invoke the vncserver. This last command will prompt for a password. Use the command "lsof -i :5901" to see that the Xtightvnc process is listening to port 5901. If that succeeds, kill the server because some additional configuration work needs to be done. The process is summarized here:

```
sudo apt install tightvncserver
sudo apt-get install autocutsel
sudo apt-get install dbus-x11
vncserver
(prompts and confirms a password)
```

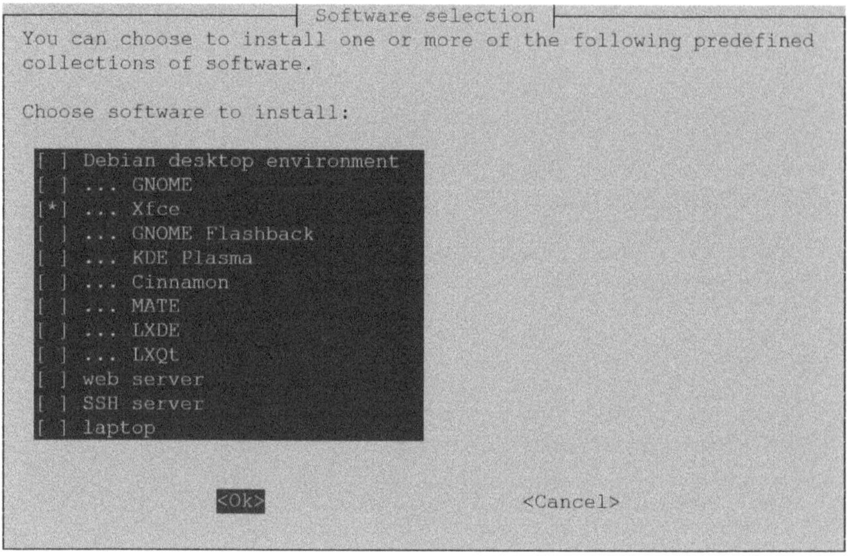

Fig. 1.28. Use tasksel to install the Xfce window manager.

```
lsof -i :5901
(see if the VNC server is listening on port 5901
vncserver -kill :1
```

Now use a text editor such as `nano` to modify the file `.vnc/xstartup` as shown:

```
#!/bin/sh
xrdb $HOME/.Xresources
startxfce4 &
```

Issue the command `vncserver` and, having done so, verify that our VNC Server is listening on port 5901 using the command `lsof -i :5901`. Feel free to specify a window size, e.g. `vncserver -geometry 1600x1200`. we should now be able to connect to our new Ubuntu VM using a VNC client of our choice. We happen to prefer Remote Ripple, from the same people who wrote Tight VNC. Scale the VNC window as you wish (see Figures 1.29–1.31).

In the GCE version of Ubuntu, VirtualBox is not installed by default. Instructions for installing VirtualBox are available on the

```
nicholas@instance-20240913-184029:~/.vnc$ cat xstartup
#!/bin/sh

xrdb "$HOME/.Xresources"
startxfce4 &
nicholas@instance-20240913-184029:~/.vnc$ vncserver

New 'X' desktop is instance-20240913-184029.us-central1-f.c.cmsc449.inter
nal:1

Starting applications specified in /home/nicholas/.vnc/xstartup
Log file is /home/nicholas/.vnc/instance-20240913-184029.us-central1-f.c.
cmsc449.internal:1.log

nicholas@instance-20240913-184029:~/.vnc$ 
```

Fig. 1.29. Start the VNC server.

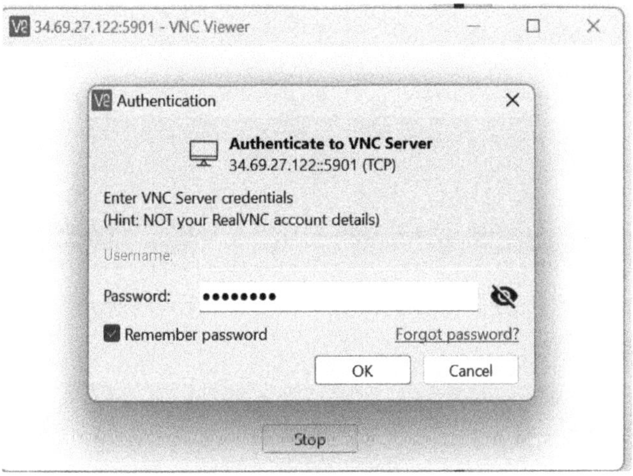

Fig. 1.30. Enter a password to connect the VNC session.

web, and there are several ways of doing it, so we omit such instructions here. The instructions will likely describe adding an appropriate repository, adding security keys, and running `sudo apt-get update` followed by `sudo apt-get install virtualbox`. To actually run VirtualBox, however, it turns out that nested virtualization needs to be explicitly enabled for the Ubuntu instance using the Cloud Shell. Stop the newly created Ubuntu instance, and give it time to shut down gracefully. (Feel free to refer to the GCP documentation.[27])

[27]https://docs.cloud.google.com/compute/docs/instances/nested-virtualization/overview.

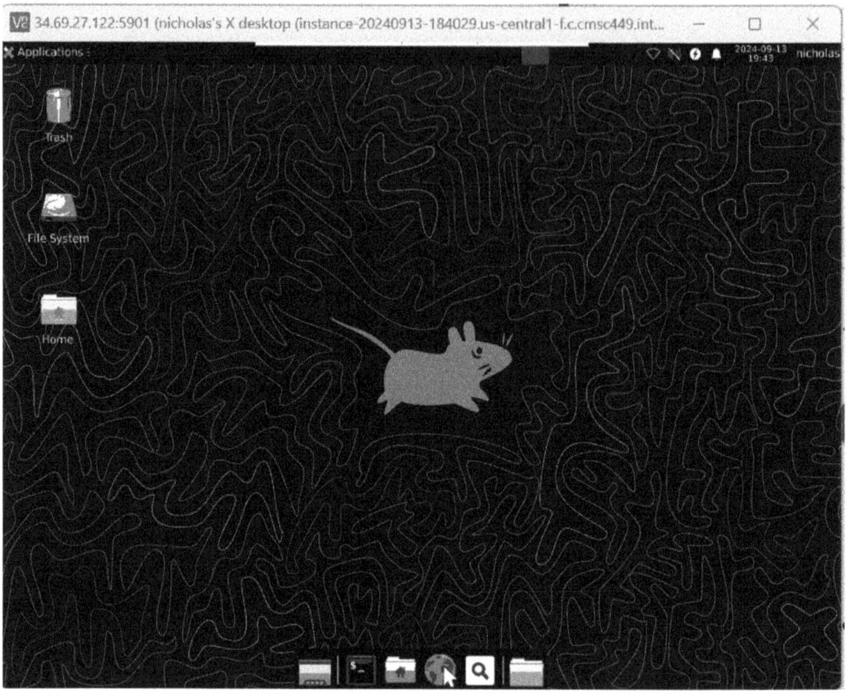

Fig. 1.31. We've connected to a new Ubuntu VM!

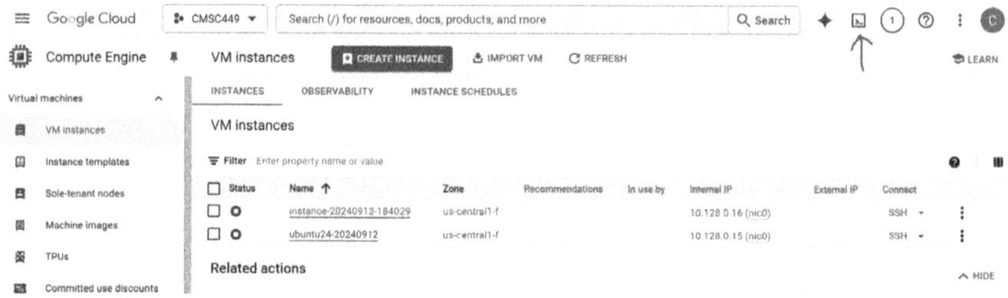

Fig. 1.32. The icon used to activate the cloud shell.

Invoke the Google Cloud shell, by tapping the ">_" icon at the upper right, indicated in Figure 1.32.

The new Cloud Shell session may take a moment to start, but you'll soon see a shell prompt. Have the shell write a configuration file to "yaml.txt", and then edit that file to include the parameter setting to enable nested virtualization, as shown below.

```
nicholas@cloudshell:~ (cmsc449)$ gcloud compute instances \
export instance-20240913-184029 --destination=yaml.txt \
--zone="us-central1-f"
Exported [instance-20240913-184029] to 'yaml.txt'.
nicholas@cloudshell:~ (cmsc449)$ nano yaml.txt
nicholas@cloudshell:~ (cmsc449)$ tail -3 yaml.txt
advancedMachineFeatures:
  enableNestedVirtualization: true
```

Now, upload the edited configuration file.

```
nicholas@cloudshell:~ (cmsc449)$ gcloud compute instances \
update-from-file instance-20240913-184029 --source=yaml.txt \
--most-disruptive-allowed-action=RESTART --zone="us-central1-f"
Updated [.../us-central1-f/instances/instance-20240913-184029].
nicholas@cloudshell:~ (cmsc449)$
```

We then start the Ubuntu instance, connect to the machine using ssh, and confirm that the command `grep -cw vmx /proc/cpuinfo` returns something non-zero. (As we mentioned earlier, the GCP documentation says to make sure the VM is running on an Intel Haswell or later.)

1.10.2 Connecting to the New GCE Instance

Once the virtual machine has been created as described above, we need to install VirtualBox and start running virtual machines. It's usually a good idea to do an update and upgrade, especially if the VM has not been used for a while. Issue the command `vncserver` after the updates, and use your VNC Client to access the VM. If you've forgotten the password for your VNC Server, remove the file `.vnc/passwd` and restart vncserver. It may prompt for a new password.

Before doing much more, we need to get a web browser working. Ubuntu comes with Firefox, which can be launched from the Applications menu under Internet, or by creating a desktop launcher. If Firefox doesn't seem to come up right away, use the command "xhost +localhost" from a shell and try again.

1.10.3 Installing VirtualBox and Virtual Machines

Much of the rest of the setup for VirtualBox can be done from a shell and a browser running on the Ubuntu instance. Instructions for installing VirtualBox on Ubuntu are available on the Internet, so you need not follow the instructions given here. From a shell, enter "sudo apt install virtualbox". There will be several lines of output, and then the shell prompt returns. To see if it worked, try the command "VirtualBoxVM –help" to see version information and the command line options. Use the command "virtualbox" in the usual way.

Since we have a browser, you can visit whatever web site you wish to find OVA files available for download. We have OVA files for Kali Linux and Windows Server, among others. Download the OVA files, use the VirtualBox File menu to import the new appliance(s), and see if they work!

We now have the ability to run virtual machines, using VirtualBox, but those machines will not be able to access the Internet until they can acquire IP addresses. So, from a shell on the Ubuntu instance, issue the command `VBoxManage list vms` to see the names of the VMs, and then enter `VBoxManage modifyvm aNewVM -natdnsproxy1 on` where "aNewVM" is replaced with that VM's name in VirtualBox (Figure 1.33). This will allow the guest operating systems to go out to the Internet for updates, and web browsers running on the guest will be able to reach the Internet.

Some helpful hints:

- Before starting a newly-imported VM, check the settings. Both Kali and Windows Server will run with 2 gigs of RAM, but 4 gigs is better (Figures 1.34 and 1.35).
- When interacting with Windows, ctrl-alt-del is used a lot. Don't do this with your physical keyboard—use the VirtualBox menu Input; Keyboard; Insert Ctrl-Alt-Del instead.
- If you find a virtual machine taking control of your mouse, pressing Right-Ctrl may help.
- When booting Kali Linux, and if it hangs, check the Settings. Under System;Processor, check both Extended features.
- VirtualBox usually selects reasonable defaults. For example, set paravirtualization to default, unless experience indicates otherwise. Linux prefers KVM, while Windows prefers Hyper-V.

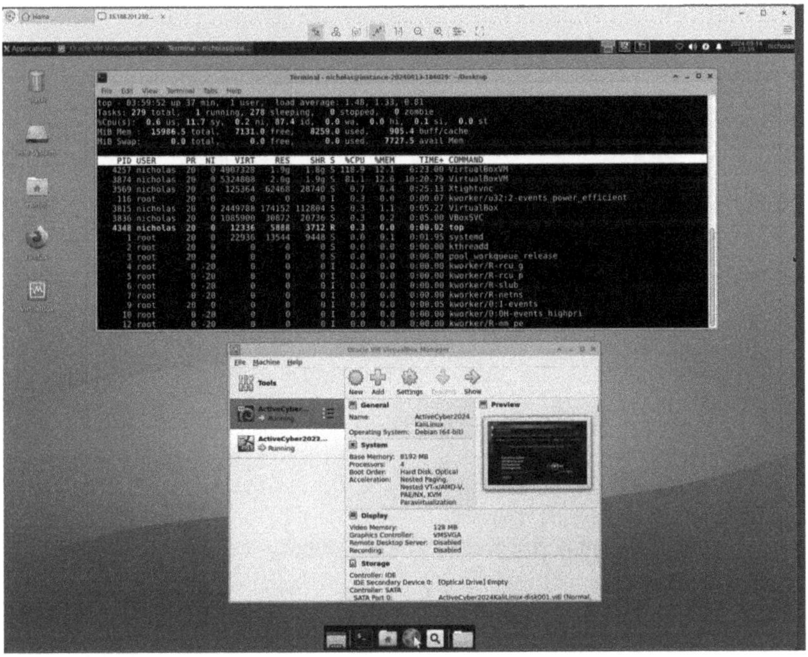

Fig. 1.33. Running a shell and the VirtualBox GUI on our Ubuntu instance.

- We found it convenient to use the Workspaces provided by the Ubuntu desktop. For example, run a shell in one workspace, Firefox in another, Kali in the third, and the Windows Server OS in the fourth.
- When building a new VM, whether from an ISO image or an OVA file, it's probably better to build the new VM on an ordinary (non-cloud) desktop. Let it do updates there. Once the new system is updated and stable, create an OVA file and move that up to the cloud, where it can be unpacked and used.

1.10.4 Optional Setup: Disks in the Cloud

Given the size of OVA files, and that we may need several of them, we might want to add a standard disk, which we need to format. The GCP console has links to instructions. In some earlier work of this sort, we set up the disk /dev/sdb to be mounted at /mount/disks/disk1, with fstab configured to mount it automatically at boot

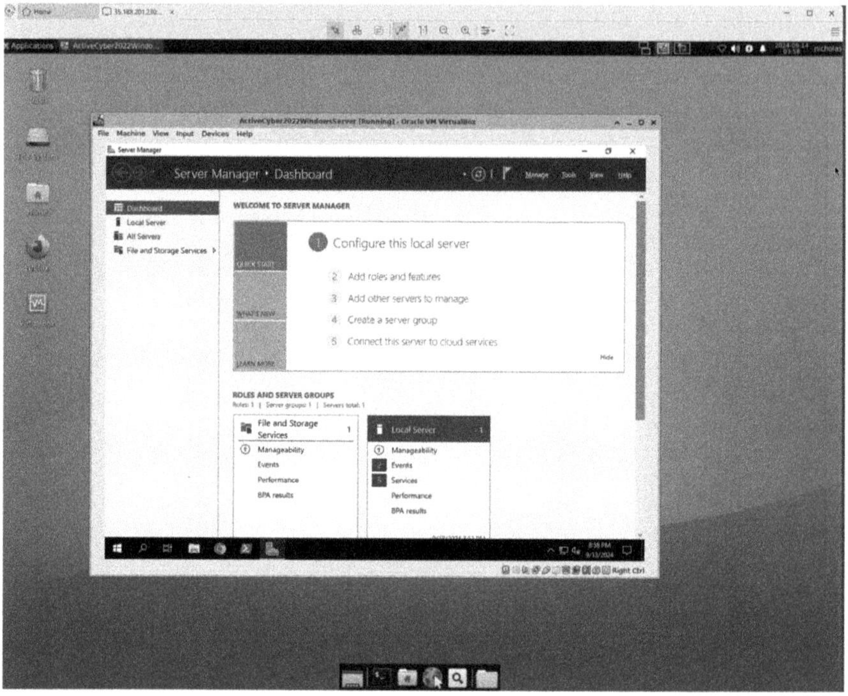

Fig. 1.34. Running Windows Server as a guest on the Ubuntu instance.

time. (In a situation where several students in the same class may need read-only access to a set of ISO or OVA files, the disk can be shared between virtual machine instances belonging to the same GCP project.)

Once the various guest systems are updated and stable, it's not a bad idea to export them as VirtualBox appliances, that is, as OVA files. Likewise, once the GCP instance is able is able to support VNC connections and run VirtualBox successfully, creating an image of that VM instance as a backup is appropriate.

The process of starting a VM, connecting to it with VNC, and using VirtualBox to create virtual machines can be summarized as follows:

- Go to the GCP Compute Engine VM Instances page
- Select the VM instance to be started, and start it
- Note the external IP address `nnn.nnn.nnn.nnn`

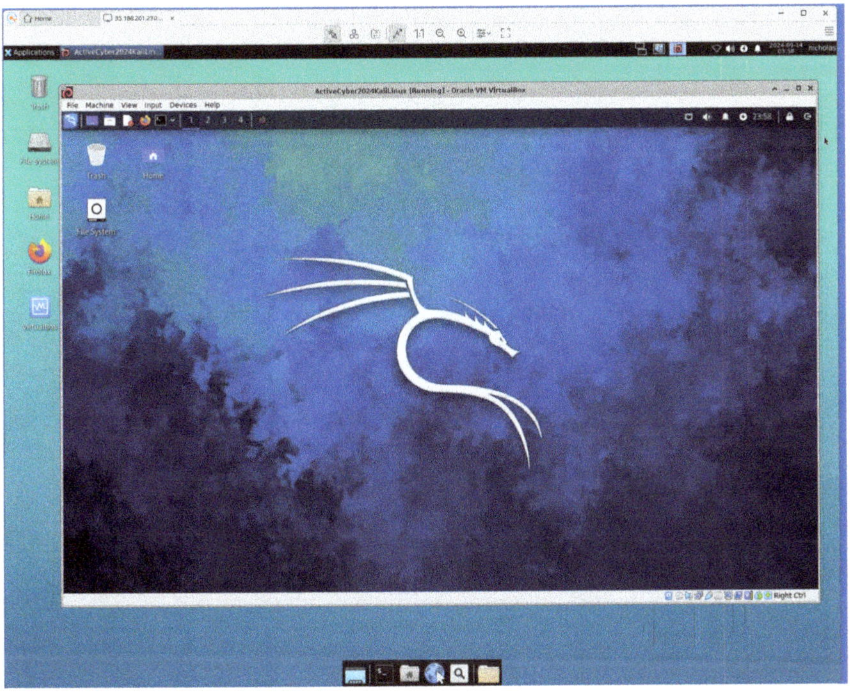

Fig. 1.35. Running Kali as a guest on the Ubuntu instance.

- Use SSH (right menu) to connect to that VM once it has started
- From that shell, run `vncserver`
- Use a VNC client to connect to `nnn.nnn.nnn.nnn:5901`
- When the remote desktop appears, zoom to your level of comfort
- Invoke VirtualBox from the new desktop
- If creating or importing a new VM into VirtualBox, issue the VBoxManage modifyvm command as shown above
- Keep the CPU and memory configuration minimal, e.g. one CPU and four GBs of RAM. More can be added later, once the new VirtualBox VM is stable
- Network should be NAT, cable connected
- Install Guest Additions as desired
- Do whatever you need to do...take snapshots as desired
- Shut VirtualBox down cleanly
- Close the VNC client session
- If desired, run `vncserver -kill :1` to stop that server

- **MAKE SURE** to shutdown the VM instance on the Instances page—or it will cost more money!

1.11 Conclusion and Lessons Learned

In this work we have tried to summarize the tools and techniques that have become part of malware analysis over the last several years. We have made some observations of a more general nature during that same time:

- Malware analysis is a field where details matter. But when it comes to instruction sets, system calls, and vulnerabilities, it's much easier to look things up as needed rather than to try to remember it all.
- The tools we use, such as Ghidra and x64dbg, are powerful and complicated. They can be intimidating for the beginner, and the cure for that is experience.
- Since the publication of PMA, relevant blogs and social media are among the best ways to keep up with the latest and greatest developments and trends.

Given this chapter's place in this volume, we obviously appreciate the importance of machine learning, now and in the future, in the field of malware analysis. The anti-virus vendors have long been making use of machine learning when applied to malware detection. Analyst-assistant tools will reshape the traditional reverse engineering process and only continue to improve. The malware analyst's time is valuable, and tools that use ML to assist in triage, classification, or in-depth analysis will continue to gain importance.

Bibliography

Eagle, C. and Nance, K. (2020). *The Ghidra Book: The Definitive Guide* (No Starch Press).

Sikorski, M. and Honig, A. (2012). *Practical Malware Analysis* (No Starch Press).

https://doi.org/10.1142/9789811262043_0002

Chapter 2

Machine Learning for Windows Malware Detection based on Information Extracted from Static Analysis

Daniel Gibert

Artificial Intelligence Research Institute (IIIA-CSIC), Barcelona, Spain

In this chapter, we delve into the application of machine learning to detect malware based on information that can be statically extracted from Portable Executable files. We begin by introducing the Windows Portable Executable file format. We continue by describing how machine learning has become a powerful, complementary tool for malware detection. We then examine the variety of learning-based detection systems that have been proposed, categorizing them based on the input representation upon which they rely.

2.1 Malware Detection and Classification

Malicious software, known as "malware", has long posed a serious and increasingly widespread problem. As society becomes more and more dependent on computer systems for communication, commerce, healthcare, and critical infrastructure, the impact of malware continues to grow. The widespread reliance on digital technologies means that disruptions caused by malicious software can have far-reaching consequences, ranging from personal data breaches and financial losses to threats against national security and public safety. For instance, in 2017 NotPetya, a file wiper disguised as ransomware, entered the computer systems in Ukraine via a compromised update of the software M.E.Doc.[1] Once inside the network, they exploited the EternalBlue vulnerability, developed by NSA and disclosed by the hacking group ShadowBrokers, and employed credential-stealing tools like Mimikatz to rapidly propagate across systems. However, NotPetya ended up spreading to hundreds of organizations worldwide (including the Danish shipping giant Maersk, the pharmaceutical company Merck, FedEx subsidiary TNT Express, and the French construction materials company Saint-Gobain, among others), exposing how vulnerable our interconnected digital systems are. In 2021, the Health Service Executive (HSE) in Ireland was compromised by the Conti ransomware, forcing a nationwide shutdown of HSE's IT systems, cancellation of hospital appointments, and widespread disruption of healthcare services.[2] These are only two of countless attacks targeting critical infrastructure that put public safety, economic stability, and national security at risk.

Given the rapid digitalization of our society, the economic cost of malware is expected to continue to rise, with projections estimating that global ransomware costs could reach approximately $275 billion annually by 2031.[3] Therefore, it is necessary to develop better tools to detect malware and aid security analysts and professionals.

Current malware detection methods typically fall into three categories:

- Signature-based approaches, which rely on the creation and maintenance of a database of unique "signatures". These signatures are typically derived from distinct features of computer programs,

[1]https://www.sipa.columbia.edu/sites/default/files/2022-11/NotPetya%20Final.pdf.

[2]https://about.hse.ie/publications/conti-cyber-attack-on-the-hse-independent-post-incident-review/.

[3]https://cybersecurityventures.com/global-ransomware-damage-costs-predicted-to-reach-250-billion-usd-by-2031/.

such as file hashes or specific byte patterns within the executable. During analysis, to determine if a file is malicious, its signature is compared against the signature database. Signature-based detection is quite effective for identifying previously encountered malware. However, it can easily be bypassed by obfuscation techniques that alter the structure and appearance of the code, such as packing and encryption. Consequently, maintaining the effectiveness of these approaches requires significant effort in analyzing and extracting new signatures to continuously update the signature database.
- Behavior-based approaches, which analyze the actions of computer programs at runtime to flag potentially malicious behavior. These approaches look for activities that typically raise alarms such as unusual system calls, abnormal memory usage, or attempts to escalate privileges. However, these methods can generate a high number of false positives, burdening security analysts. Furthermore, these approaches require executing the program in a controlled environment, which can be time-consuming and computationally expensive. In addition, sophisticated malware specimens incorporate evasion techniques designed to detect sandbox environments or delay the execution of the malicious actions, thereby avoiding detection.
- Machine learning-based approaches, which leverage large datasets of benign and malicious samples to automatically learn complex patterns that distinguish malware from legitimate software. These approaches have experienced significant growth over the last decade due to advances in computational power and the availability of large malware datasets. As a result, ML approaches have been widely adopted by security companies such as Sophos[4] and Crowdstrike,[5] among others, for fast detection of previously unseen malware variants and to complement signature-based detection.

This chapter centers on Windows malware detection, and specifically, malware detection approaches that use machine learning. As far as the desktop and laptop market is concerned, Windows remains the most commonly used operating system and, as a result, the most

---

[4]https://www.sophos.com/.
[5]https://www.crowdstrike.com/en-us/.

frequently targeted by cybercriminals.[6] In the following, we formalize the task of malware detection and classification, describe the format of executable files in Windows, and present a taxonomy of the detection methods proposed so far.

2.1.1 Malware Detection and Classification

The task of malware detection involves determining whether a given file is benign or malicious. Formally, this can be expressed as a binary classification problem where each file $x \in \mathbf{X}$ (represented either as raw bytes, extracted features, or behavioral traces) is mapped to a label $y \in \{0, 1\}$, with $y = 0$ indicating benign and $y = 1$ indicating malicious. The objective of a malware detector is therefore to learn a function

$$f_\theta : \mathbf{X} \to [0, 1],$$

where $f_\theta(x)$ represents the estimated probability parameterized by θ, or confidence score, that file x is malicious. The final decision is obtained by thresholding

$$\hat{y}(x) = 1\{f_\theta(x) \geq \tau\}$$

with threshold $\tau \in [0, 1]$ chosen to meet a specific level, such as a desired false positive rate.

In addition to detecting whether or not a file is malicious, another relevant task is malware classification. Malware classification goes a step further by assigning a detected malware sample to a specific family. This task is important because determining whether a sample belongs to a known malware family (e.g., Zeus, NotPetya, Emotet, among many others) helps analysts understand its propagation methods and capabilities. The task of malware classification can be formally expressed as a multi-class classification problem where each file $x \in \mathbf{X}$ is associated with a label $z \in \mathcal{F} \in \{1, 2, ..., \mathcal{K}\}$, where $\mathcal{K}$ denotes the number of malware families. The objective of a malware classifier is to learn a function

$$g_\theta : \mathbf{X} \to \mathcal{F}$$

[6]https://gs.statcounter.com/os-market-share/desktop/worldwide/.

that assigns each malicious file to its corresponding family. In practice, classification models often produce a probability distribution over families

$$p_\theta(z \mid x) = \frac{\exp(h_z(x))}{\sum_{j=1}^{K} \exp(h_j(x))},$$

where h_j is the score associated with family j. The predicted family is then obtained from

$$\hat{z}(x) = \arg\max_{k \in \mathcal{F}} p_\theta(k \mid x).$$

2.1.2 Portable Executable File Format

Windows executables follow the Portable Executable (PE) format. This format is used by .exe, .dll, .sys, and similar files. The PE file format, summarized in Figure 2.1, consists of several parts that encapsulate all the information the OS requires to load and run the program:

- **DOS Header + Stub:** The DOS header and stub are components kept only for backward compatibility purposes. Historically, these components allowed the executable to print "This program cannot be run in DOS mode" if run in DOS. The DOS header also contains a pointer (e_lfanew) to the next component, the File header.
- **File Header:** The File header, also known as the COFF header, is a structure of fixed size (20 bytes) that contains metadata about the file, including the target CPU architecture, the number of sections, a timestamp for when the file was created or linked, the file offset of the COFF symbol table (PointerToSymbolTable), the number of entries in the symbol table, the size of the following Optional Header, and bit flags that describe the attributes of the file.

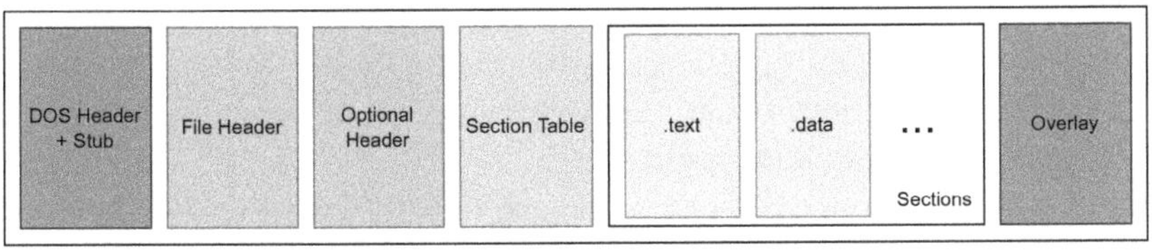

Fig. 2.1. Representation of the Windows Portable Executable file format.

- **Optional Header:** The Optional header provides important information to properly load, map, and execute the program, such as the entry point address (where the execution starts), the starting relative virtual address (RVA) of code and data sections, the alignment of sections in the file, the required OS version, and the data directories. The data directories are tabulated in an array that points to key tables such as the Import Table, Export Table, Resource Table, and Certificate Table.
- **Section Table:** The Section Table immediately follows the PE Header (File Header + Optional Header), and contains as many entries in the table as indicated by the **NumberOfSections** field in the File Header. Each entry describes one section of the executable, including where it is in the file, where it should be mapped in memory, its size, and certain of its characteristics e.g., whether the file is readable, writable, or executable.
- **Sections:** Next come the Sections, with the actual code, data, and resources of the program, organized according to the Section Table.
- **Overlay:** Lastly, we find the overlay space, which refers to extra data located at the end of the PE file. Since the overlay isn't mapped into memory by the Windows loader, malware frequently uses the overlay space to hide payloads, configuration data, or unpacking stubs.

2.1.3 Taxonomy of Detectors

Figure 2.2 illustrates a taxonomy of static machine learning-based malware detection methods. These static approaches can be broadly divided into two categories, depending on the type of input representation: the binary program or its assembly language counterpart.

The binary program refers to the compiled executable file, e.g., a PE file on Windows, in its machine code (binary) format. This is the form loaded into memory by the OS for direct execution. Binary-based detectors can be further divided into four subcategories: raw byte sequence analysis, image-based detectors, structural entropy–based approaches, and feature-based detectors. On the other hand, the assembly language source code refers to the disassembled representation of the binary generated by disassemblers such as IDA

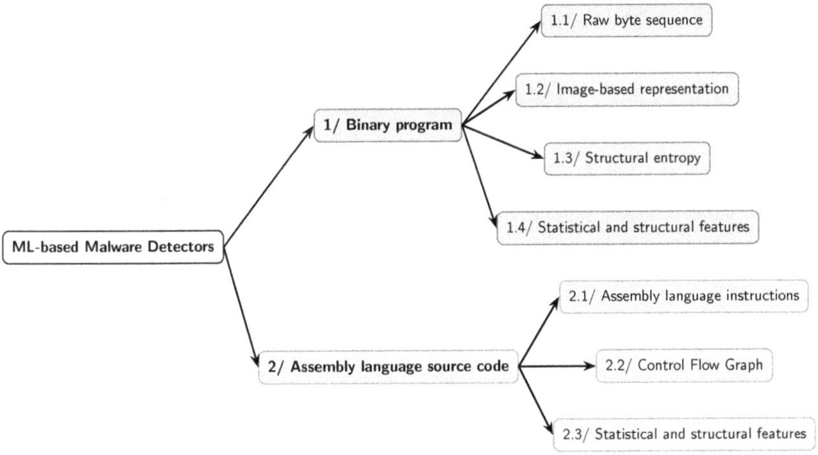

Fig. 2.2. Taxonomy of ML-based malware detectors.

Pro,[7] Ghidra[8] or Radare2.[9] Similarly, assembly-based detectors fall into three main subcategories: assembly instruction-based detectors, graph-based approaches, and feature-based detectors.

2.2 Binary-based Malware Detectors

Binary-based detectors analyze the executable file in its compiled machine code form, extracting information directly from raw bytes, a compressed representation of those (e.g., image-based representation or structural entropy), or statistical characteristics and structural properties of the binary.

2.2.1 Binary-based Feature Extraction

Feature-based detectors extract a set of features from files (e.g., PE Headers, imported functions, section entropy) and train a machine learning model to classify the files as malicious or benign.

[7]https://hex-rays.com/ida-pro.
[8]https://github.com/NationalSecurityAgency/ghidra.
[9]https://github.com/radareorg/radare2.

2.2.1.1 *EMBER Features*

We now describe the features provided by the well-known EMBER malware dataset (Joyce *et al.*, 2025). The EMBER features, updated in 2024, consist of twelve groups[10] extracted with `pefile`[11] that include both parsed features and format-agnostic histograms and counts of strings.

General file information: This set of features include basic information obtained from the PE header, including the file size, the Shannon entropy of the entire file (a real value in the range 0-8 bits/byte), a binary flag which indicates if the parsed object is a PE file or not, and the first four bytes of the file.

Header information: This group of features includes information extracted from the COFF, OPTIONAL, and DOS headers, including the timestamp of file creation, the target machine architecture, a list of image characteristics, a list of DLL characteristics, target subsystem, major and minor image versions, major and minor linked versions, size of code, size of headers, size of initialized data, size of uninitialized data, number of sections, number symbols, the address of the entropy point, etc.

Rich header information: This feature set include information extracted from the Rich Header, an officially undocumented structure that is only present in executables built using Microsoft Visual Studio. The Rich Header encodes the toolchain "component IDs" (compiler/linker/product+build) and counts the objects produced by each component. This set of features is created by counting how many (ID, count) pairs are found in the Rich Header and then producing a 32-dimensional vector using the hashing trick.

Authenticode signature information: This set of features consists of the following: the number of certificates embedded in the file; whether the certificates, if any, are self-signed; whether the signature's "program name" description field has empty values; whether there is a timestamp proving when the file was signed; whether the

[10]https://github.com/FutureComputing4AI/EMBER2024.
[11]https://github.com/erocarrera/pefile.

Authenticode structure couldn't be parsed cleanly; the longest certificate chain length seen across all signature blobs; the most recent timestamp found among the certificates; and the difference between the most recent timestamp found among the certificates and the PE headers timestamp.

Imported functions: This feature set is created by extracting the set of unique libraries and functions imported in the Import Address Table and then using the hashing trick to scatter these sets into 256 and 1024 bins, respectively. In addition, this feature set also includes the total number of imported functions and the number of unique imported DLLs. Because libraries and functions imported vary across samples, feature hashing is used to map them into fixed-dimensional vectors, thereby ensuring a constant input size across samples.

Exported functions: This set of features is created by extracting the set of exported functions and then using the hashing trick to produce a 128-dimensional vector from the exported functions.

Section information: This collection of features includes information about the section names, the amount of raw data, entropy, virtual size, the size ratio of the section compared to the total size of the file, the size ratio of the raw data compared to its virtual size, and characteristics of the section. This information is summarized into a fixed-length vector using the hashing trick.

Data directories information: This feature set includes the size and virtual address of the first 15 data directories.

Byte histogram: This collection of features consists of a 256-bin count of byte values (0-255) in the file, normalized to a probability distribution.

Byte-entropy histogram: This feature set, loosely based on Saxe and Berlin (2015), constructs a 2-D byte-entropy histogram (16×16) by sliding a 2,048-byte window across the file with a 1024-byte step. For each window, the Shannon entropy (a value between 0 and 8) is computed and binned into 16 levels to populate the 2-D histogram, which is finally flattened into a 256-dimensional vector.

String information: This group of features consists of simple statistics about printable ASCII bytes (0x20-0x7f) of length ≥ 5. In particular, a record is made of the number of strings, their average length, a 96-bin histogram over characters 0x20-0x7f, the total count of printable characters across all strings, and the entropy of characters across all printable strings. In addition, this feature set includes regular expressions that match strings indicative of file paths, URLs, registry keys, and embedded PE executables.

PE format warnings information: This set of features consists of 88 features for tracking various errors and warnings generated during the parsing of the file.

2.2.1.2 *Training Your Own Feature-based Detector*

One can use the following CLI wrapper to train a LightGBM classifier on the EMBER2024 (vectorized) features using the thrember package. The CLI arguments are:

(1) `data_dir`: The path to the directory containing the pre-vectorized data.
(2) `model_path`: Where to write the trained LightGBM model.
(3) `-config_file` (optional, default `lgbm_config.json`): JSON with LigthGBM training parameters (e.g., objective, metrics, num_boost_round, early_stopping_rounds, learning_rate, num_leaves, etc.).

This wrapper calls `thrember.train_model(args.data_dir, params=fit_params)` to handle loading datasets and fitting a LightGBM booster under the provided parameters. Afterwards, it saves the model to `model_path`.

```
import os
import json
import thrember
import argparse
import lightgbm as lgb
from sklearn.model_selection import train_test_split


if __name__ == "__main__":

    parser = argparse.ArgumentParser()
    parser.add_argument("data_dir", type=str,
                        help="Path to the directory containing the
                        ↪  EMBER2024 dataset.")
```

```
    parser.add_argument("model_path", type=str,
                        help="Path to save the trained model.")
    parser.add_argument("--config-file", type=str,
    ↪   default="lgbm_config.json",
                        help="Path to LightGBM config file.")
    args = parser.parse_args()

    # Validate data directory and config file
    if not os.path.isdir(args.data_dir):
        raise ValueError("Not a directory:
        ↪   {}".format(args.data_dir))
    if not os.path.isfile(args.config_file):
        raise ValueError("Not a file: {}".format(args.config_file))

    # Parse LightGBM config file
    fit_params = json.load(open(args.config_file, "r"))

    # Load data and train model
    model = thrember.train_model(args.data_dir, params=fit_params)

    # Save model
    model.save_model(args.model_path,
    ↪   num_iteration=model.best_iteration)
```

Once the LightGBM model has been trained, the model can be used to predict the maliciousness score of new, unknown samples as follows:

```
def predict_sample(lgbm_model: lgb.Booster, file_data: bytes) ->
↪   float:
    """
    Predict a PE file with an LightGBM model
    """
    extractor = PEFeatureExtractor()
    features = np.array(extractor.feature_vector(file_data),
    ↪   dtype=np.float32)
    predict_result: np.ndarray = lgbm_model.predict([features])
    return float(predict_result[0])
```

2.2.1.3 *Byte N-Gram Features*

N-Grams are contiguous sequences of n items from a larger sequence. In malware analysis, these items are typically bytes or instruction opcodes. A byte n-gram feature thus represents a specific sequence of n bytes (e.g., 0xDE 0xAD 0xBE 0xEF as a 4-gram). The use of n-grams for malware detection has a long history, dating back to early the 2000s: in a preliminary study Abou-Assaleh *et al.* (2004) showed the potential of using the most frequent n-grams, with $n \in \{1, ..., 10\}$, with their normalized frequencies representing a class profile (benign/malicious) and using the k-nearest neighbors algorithm for classifying unknown samples. Around the same time, Kolter and Maloof (2004) applied machine learning to distinguish malware from benign programs based on byte 4-gram feature vectors. In their method, each binary was converted into a feature vector where each position indicates the presence or absence of a particular byte n-gram (ignoring the frequency) and then used feature selection to retain only the top 500 n-grams.

Since these early works, n-gram features have become a fundamental tool in static malware analysis, with numerous studies using n-grams of various lengths (n=2 up to n=6 or higher) as input to classifiers ranging from k-nearest neighbors to support vector machines, random forests, and neural networks (Jain and Meena, 2011; Raff *et al.*, 2018b; Reddy and Pujari, 2006; Tang *et al.*, 2023; Zak *et al.*, 2017). Despite capturing only short local patterns, n-grams have shown surprising effectiveness in classifying malware. Byte n-grams can capture recurring code motifs or stylistic fingerprints of malware authors and toolchains. For example, malware created using the same tooling tend to share certain byte sequences in their payload. Another advantage is that n-gram features are extracted automatically from the data, which makes it hard for an attacker to craft malware that systematically avoids detection, since no analyst needs to manually define a signature in advance. This automation contrasts with traditional signature-based detection, where handcrafted rules can be circumvented once discovered by the adversary.

The process of extracting n-grams from a file is straightforward to implement:

(1) Read the file's bytes as an array of values $b[0 \ldots m-1]$.
(2) For each index i from 0 to $m - n$, form the n-gram $(b[i], b[i+1], ..., b[i+n-1])$. This sequence can be stored as a byte string of length n or converted to an integer ID.
(3) Count the occurrences of each n-gram across the file (if using frequencies) or mark its presence.

Below is a Python snippet illustrating byte n-gram extraction and vectorization for a single file, using 4-grams as an example:

```
from collections import Counter

# Read binary file as bytes
with open("sample.exe", "rb") as f:
    data = f.read()

n = 4  # for example, 4-byte $n$-grams
ngrams = Counter()

# Slide a window of length n over the byte sequence
for i in range(len(data) - n + 1):
    gram = data[i:i+n]                # extract n contiguous bytes
    ngrams[gram] += 1

# Example: print the 5 most common 4-grams in hex format
for gram, count in ngrams.most_common(5):
    print(gram.hex().upper(), ":", count)
```

Feature representation for byte n-grams typically adopt the bag-of-words (BoW) model from text classification. In this framework, each distinct n-gram observed in the training set is treated as a "word" in a very large vocabulary, and each file is represented as a vector of counts or frequencies of those n-grams. The challenge is that the potential vocabulary grows exponentially with n (e.g., $256^2 = 65{,}536$, $256^3 = 16{,}777{,}216$, $256^4 = 4{,}294{,}967{,}296$), quickly making explicit representations infeasible. In practice, the number of distinct n-grams observed in real programs levels off because executables use only a small subset of all possible byte sequences (Kolter and Maloof, 2004). Even so, dimensionality reduction is essential. Two common strategies for dimension reduction are feature selection and feature hashing. Feature selection retains only the top k n-grams based on criteria such as information gain, chi-square, or mutual information, discarding the rest. Feature hashing (the "hashing trick" mentioned earlier) instead maps each n-gram to a fixed-size vector via a hash function, accumulating counts at the corresponding index. This removes the need for a massive dictionary, though collisions can occur when different n-grams map to the same index. Fortunately, because n-gram frequencies in malware follow a Zipfian distribution, where a few n-grams are very common and most are rare, collisions rarely distort the truly frequent patterns.

Building on this, Raff and Nicholas (2018) introduced Hash-Grams, a method to approximate the top-k n-grams far more efficiently than exact counting on massive datasets. Hash-Grams hash each n-gram into one of B buckets using a rolling hash, then identify the top-k buckets via QuickSelect in O(B) time. This yields near-identical classification performance at a fraction of the cost. The major limitation, however, is that the original n-grams are lost due to the hashing function, preventing analysts from inspecting the selected features. Moreover, even with these techniques, practical applications typically constrain $n \leq 6$ due to the computational overhead.

Yet, there has long been an intuition that larger values of n are necessary to capture the semantics of executable code. For example, a single x86 instruction can be up to 15 bytes long, requiring at least a 16-gram for full context. Early studies found that large values such as $n = 15$ performed best (Abou-Assaleh *et al.*, 2004), but were practical only on small corpora (e.g., 36.9Mb). Goldberg *et al.* (1998) advocated for 20-grams, citing that malware detection signatures in 1998 averaged 20 bytes in length. The BitShred clustering framework also used 16-grams but required a 64-machine cluster to scale beyond 60,000 files, and because it relied on feature hashing, true features were lost (Weinberger *et al.*, 2009). Today, the Anti-Virus (AV) industry routinely works with corpora of tens of millions (Li *et al.*, 2017) if not hundreds of millions (Spafford, 2014) of files, far beyond what these methods can handle. To address this challenge, Raff *et al.* (2019) proposed KiloGrams, an algorithm that extends the Hash-Gram approach with a two-pass procedure and a hashing-stride mechanism, enabling the efficient extraction of top-k n-grams even for very large n (up to 1024 bytes) on multi-terabyte corpora. Unlike Hash-Grams, KiloGrams preserves the actual n-gram identities, making the features interpretable for analysts while still achieving orders of magnitude speedups over traditional methods.

2.2.2 Learning from Raw Bytes

Bytes are the lowest-level and most direct representation of a program that can be used for detection. Motivated by the success of deep learning in computer vision and natural language processing, several methods have been proposed that operate directly on the sequence of bytes that constitute an executable. These methods, typically based on Convolutional Neural Networks (CNN) and Recurrent Neural Network (RNN) architectures, learn discriminative features directly from raw byte sequences to distinguish malicious from benign programs, eliminating the need for manual feature engineering.

Raff *et al.* (2017) explored the feasibility of using a fully-connected neural network (FCNN) and a recurrent neural network to detect malicious files by taking as input a portion of the Portable Executable file header. In particular, only the MS-DOS, COFF, and Optional Headers of the PE file are considered, excluding the Sections Table, the Import Address Table (IAT) and the Export Address Table (EAT). Per the PE specification (Microsoft, 2018), the first 64 bytes of a program correspond to the MS-DOS header while the COFF and Optional Header information is contained in the next 248 or 264 bytes following the offset at byte 0x3C. Therefore, they took the 264 bytes for safety and concatenated them with the bytes of the MS-DOS header, resulting in a sequence of 328 bytes.

The fully-connected neural network (Figure 2.3) takes as input the sequence of 328 bytes, with each byte converted to a feature vector using an embedding layer. After each byte is embedded, the 328 feature vectors are concatenated into a large feature vector $\mathbb{R}^{5248}$, followed by four fully connected hidden layers and a softmax layer.[12]

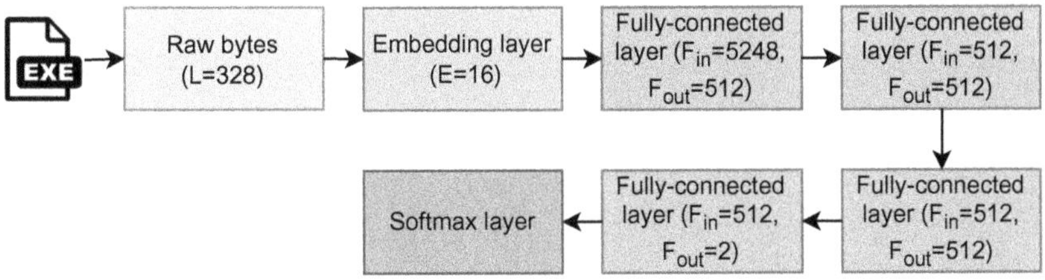

Fig. 2.3. Fully-connected neural network for malware detection based on the PE Headers bytes.

[12]Note that if the output layer has two neurons, you can apply a softmax layer to obtain the probabilities of the input x being benign or malicious. If the output layer has only one neuron, use a sigmoid function instead.

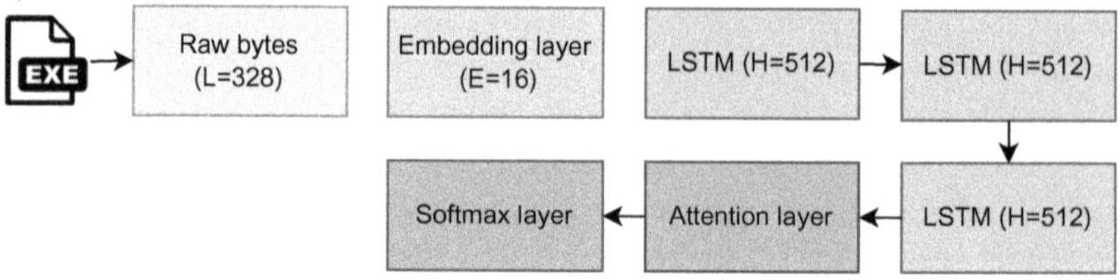

Fig. 2.4. Recurrent network for malware detection based on the PE Headers bytes.

The recurrent neural network (Figure 2.4), similarly to the FCNN, embeds the 328-byte sequence into a feature vector using an embedding layer. Afterwards, it is followed by three long-short term memory (LSTM) layers, an attention layer and a softmax layer.

The PE Headers contain only a small fraction of the content of an executable file. To process far more of the file, later works (Coull and Gardner, 2019; Gibert *et al.*, 2021; Krcál *et al.*, 2018; Raff *et al.*, 2018a) switched to convolutional neural networks with one or more convolutional layers followed by a global max-pooling or average-pooling layer. Convolutions help reduce memory requirements due to reusing a small set of weights over the whole sequence. In the following we estimate the memory requirements associated with the parameters of the network (M^P), the training activations saved for the backward pass (M^{TR}), and the inference activations (M^I) for each type of layer considering a sequence length L = 1,000,000, an embedding size $E = C_{\text{in}} = 16$, and a batch size $B = 1$, assuming FP32 precision (4 bytes per parameter):

Fully-connected (FC) layer: The input of the fully-connected (dense) layer has shape $[B, L, E]$, which flattens to $[B, L \times E]$. In our example, the input is [1, 16000000]. A fully-connected layer with H units has $(L \times C_{\text{in}}) \times H + H$ parameters. Therefore $P_{FC} = (1{,}000{,}000 \times 16) \times 512 + 512 = 8{,}192{,}000{,}512$ and $M^P_{FC} = P_{FC} \times 4 \approx 32.768\ GB$. During training and inference, only the input and output are saved. Thus, $P^{TR}_{FC} = P^I_{FC} = B \times (L \times E) + B = 16{,}000{,}512$ and $M^{TR}_{FC} = M^I_{FC} = 16{,}000{,}512 \times 4 \approx 64.002\ MB$.

LSTM layer: The input of the LSTM layer has shape [B, L, E], with no flattening. A LSTM layer with hidden size H has $4(d \times H + H^2 + H$ parameters, where $d = C_{\text{in}}$. In our example, $P_{LSTM} = 4(16 \times 512 + 5122 + 512) = 1{,}083{,}392$ and $M^P_{LSTM} = 1{,}083{,}392 \times 4 = 4.3336\ MB$.

Unfortunately, for a LSTM layer, the number of activations saved for backward propagation explodes with the sequence length L. A LSTM layer computes 4 gate activations and 2 states, resulting in $4H \times 2H = 8H$ values. This results in storing a total of $B \times L \times 8H$ floats per layer/direction, which results in $M^{TR}_{LSTM} = (1 \times 1{,}000{,}000 \times 8 \times 512) \times 4 \approx 16.384\ GB$ per layer. The output of the LSTM layer has shape [B, H]. Therefore, $M^{I}_{LSTM} = (B \times (L \times E) + B \times H) \times 4 \approx 64.002\ MB$.

Convolutional layer: The input of a convolutional layer has shape $[B, E, L]$. A 1-D convolution with kernel size K, $C_{\text{in}} \rightarrow C_{\text{out}}$ channels has $K \times C_{\text{in}} \times C_{\text{out}} + C_{\text{out}}$ parameters. If $C_{\text{out}} = 100$ it results in $M^{P}_{C} = (512 \times 16 \times 100 + 100) \times 4 \approx 3.28\ MB$. The output of a convolution depends on the stride s, the padding p, and the dilation space d and is defined as $L_{\text{out}} = \frac{L+2p-d(k-1)-1}{s} + 1 = 999{,}489$. During training, it is stored $B \times (C_{\text{in}} \times L + C_{\text{out}} \times L_{\text{out}})$ activations, which results in $M^{TR}_{C} \approx 463.8\ MB$.

As has been shown, the memory footprint of a convolutional layer is minimal compared to a fully-connected or LSTM layer, which scale with the sequence length. Furthermore, these convolutional neural network architectures designed for malware detection use global max-pooling and global average-pooling layers to reduce the entire temporal dimension $B \times C_{\text{out}} \times L_{\text{out}} \rightarrow B \times C_{\text{out}}$, making the downstream classifier length-invariant. Global max-pooling takes the maximum response over the entire length, which can be seen as a saliency detector for strong byte patterns. On the other hand, global average-pooling aggregates all responses.

Following this discussion, we will present several representative CNN architectures for malware detection, highlighting their design choices and pooling strategies.

MalConv (Figure 2.5), proposed by Raff *et al.* (2018a), is a shallow convolutional neural network that takes as input sequences up to 2,000,000 bytes ($\approx$ 2MB) and consists of a 8-dimensional embedding layer, a gated convolutional layer with kernel size of 512, followed by a global max-pooling and a feed-forward layer.

AvastConv (Figure 2.6), proposed by Krcál *et al.* (2018), is a convolutional neural network that takes as input sequences of up to 512,000 bytes ($\approx$500KB) and consists of a 8-dimensional embedding layer, two convolutional layers, followed by a max-pooling and two

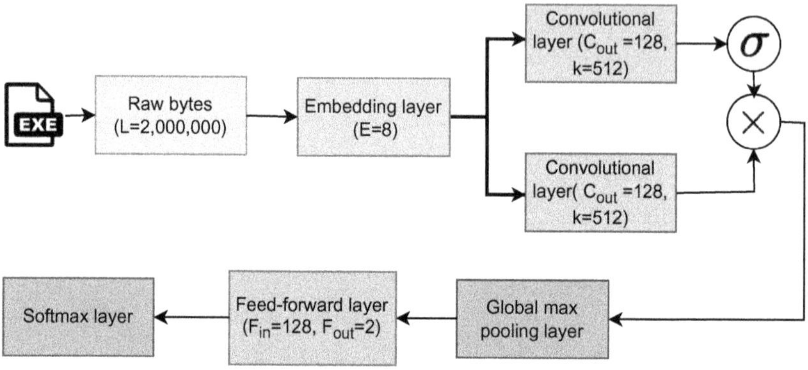

Fig. 2.5. MalConv architecture.

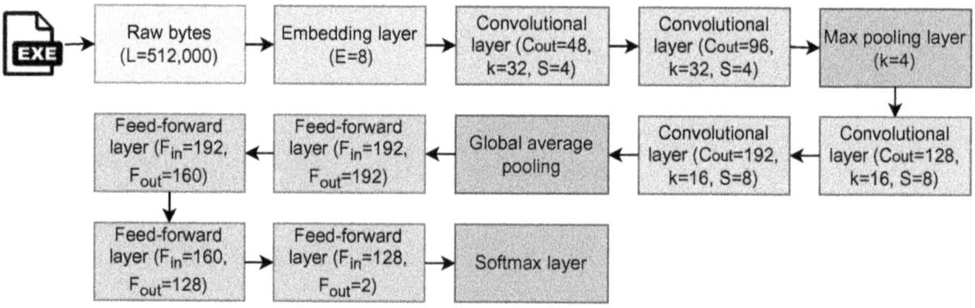

Fig. 2.6. AvastStyleConv architecture.

more convolutional layers, a global average-pooling layer, and four feed-forward layers.

BBDnn (Figure 2.7), proposed by Coull and Gardner (2019), is a convolutional neural network that that takes as input sequences up to 102,400 bytes, and begins with a 10-dimensional embedding layer and then applies five blocks, each containing a convolutional layer followed by max-pooling. After these blocks, both global max-pooling and global average-pooling are applied and the resulting pooled outputs are then passed to a feed-forward layer.

NGramConv (Figure 2.8), proposed by Gibert *et al.* (2021), is a shallow convolutional neural network that processes input sequences of up to 512,000 bytes ($\approx$ 500KB) and approximates n-gram extraction using convolutions. It employs an embedding layer, a single convolutional layer with a small kernel size, a global max-pooling layer, and finally a feed-forward layer.

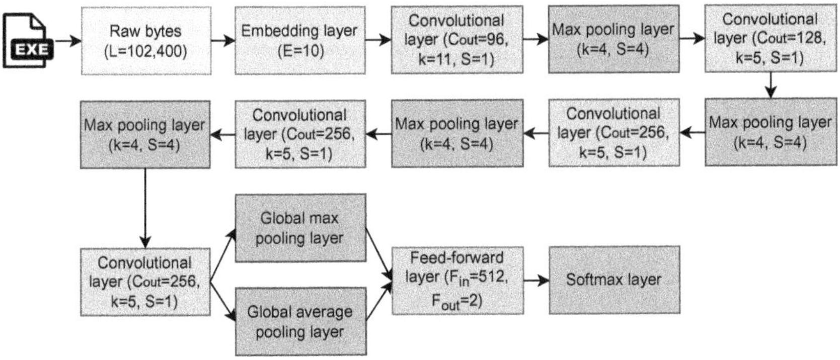

Fig. 2.7. BBDnn architecture.

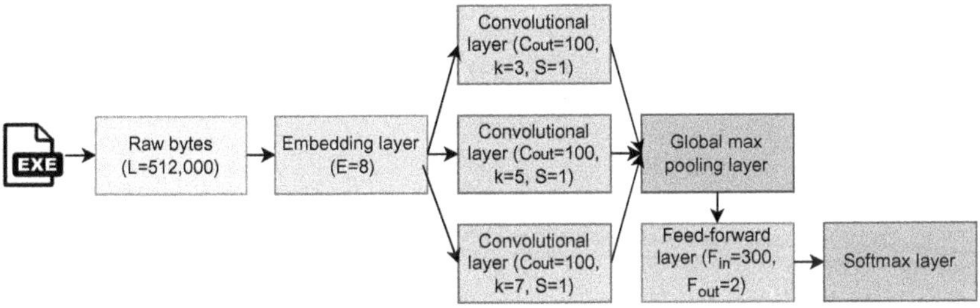

Fig. 2.8. NGramConv architecture.

Malware detection from raw byte sequences can require analyzing files over 100 MB in size, corresponding to sequences of up to 100 million steps. However, existing deep learning models such as MalConv are constrained to inputs of approximately 2 MB, since the memory requirement grows linearly with the sequence length L. Specifically, a convolutional layer with C channels and an input length L must store $C \times L$ activations, resulting in an overall memory cost of $O(L)$.

To overcome this limitation, Raff *et al.* (2021) introduced a new method that renders memory consumption invariant to L by exploiting the sparsity of gradients in global max pooling. The central observation behind this method is that max pooling produces sparse gradients: for each channel, only a single value (the maximum) contributes to the gradient, while the remaining $C \times L$ activations are unused during backpropagation. Their approach leverages this property to reduce the memory complexity from $O(L) \to O(1)$ by

(1) turning off gradient tracking and splitting the sequence into overlapping chunks;
(2) computing the maximum value and its index for each channel within each chunk;
(3) keeping track of the global winners across all chunks (one per channel);
(4) retaining only those C winning values rather than the full $C \times L$ activations;
(5) and recomputing the convolution and pooling at the selected positions with gradients enabled.

This strategy achieved 116× reduction in memory usage and up to 25.8× improvements in training speed, thereby enabling byte-based malware detectors to be trained on commodity hardware.[13]

2.2.2.1 *Training your own Byte-based Detector*

Most of the neural network architectures described in Section 2.2.2 are implemented inside the maltorch library,[14] a Python library for testing the security of AI-based Windows malware detectors. This library is based on secML-Torch,[15] which provides a PyTorch native toolkit for evaluating PyTorch models.

In the following we showcase how to train your own byte-based malware detector using MalConv's architecture. Below is the MalConv class that implements this architecture in PyTorch: it embeds the byte tokens, applies a gated pair of 1-D convolutions (ReLU × sigmoid), performs global max-pooling over time, and feeds the resulting 128-dimensional vector to a feed-forward layer.

```
import torch
import torch.nn.functional as F
from torch import nn
from maltorch.zoo.model import EmbeddingModel
```

[13]This optimization is specific to *global max-pooling* layers, as it relies on the sparsity of gradients. This property is not shared by global average pooling because all activations contribute to the gradient.
[14]https://github.com/zangobot/maltorch.
[15]https://github.com/pralab/secml-torch.

```
class MalConv(EmbeddingModel):
    """
    Malware Detection by Eating a Whole EXE
    Edward Raff, Jon Barker, Jared Sylvester, Robert Brandon,
↪   Bryan Catanzaro, Charles Nicholas
    https://arxiv.org/abs/1710.09435
    """

    def __init__(self, embedding_size: int = 8,
                 max_len: int = 2**20,
                 min_len: int = 512,
                 threshold: float =0.5,
                 padding_idx: int = 256,
                 kernel_size=512,
                 stride=512):
        super(MalConv, self).__init__(
            name="MalConv",
            ↪   gdrive_id="1Uk7QHjjXMEy-RADX5kHD9vIYk6UT2nii",
            ↪   max_len=max_len, min_len=min_len
        )
        self.embedding_1 = nn.Embedding(
            num_embeddings=257, embedding_dim=embedding_size,
            ↪   padding_idx=padding_idx
        )
        self.conv1d_1 = nn.Conv1d(
            in_channels=embedding_size,
            out_channels=128,
            kernel_size=(kernel_size,),
            stride=(stride,),
            groups=1,
            bias=True,
        )
        self.conv1d_2 = nn.Conv1d(
            in_channels=embedding_size,
            out_channels=128,
            kernel_size=(kernel_size,),
            stride=(stride,),
            groups=1,
            bias=True,
        )
        self.dense_1 = nn.Linear(in_features=128,
        ↪   out_features=128, bias=True)
        self.dense_2 = nn.Linear(in_features=128, out_features=1,
        ↪   bias=True)
        self.embedding_size = (embedding_size,)
```

```
        self.max_len = max_len
        self.threshold = threshold
        self.invalid_value = padding_idx

    def embedding_layer(self):
        return self.embedding_1

    def embed(self, x):
        emb_x = self.embedding_1(x)
        emb_x = emb_x.transpose(1, 2)
        return emb_x

    def _forward_embed_x(self, x):
        conv1d_1 = self.conv1d_1(x)
        conv1d_2 = self.conv1d_2(x)
        conv1d_1_activation = torch.relu(conv1d_1)
        conv1d_2_activation = torch.sigmoid(conv1d_2)
        multiply_1 = conv1d_1_activation * conv1d_2_activation
        global_max_pooling1d_1 = F.max_pool1d(
            input=multiply_1, kernel_size=multiply_1.size()[2:]
        )
        global_max_pooling1d_1_flatten =
        ↪   global_max_pooling1d_1.view(
            global_max_pooling1d_1.size(0), -1
        )
        dense_1 = self.dense_1(global_max_pooling1d_1_flatten)
        dense_1_activation = torch.relu(dense_1)
        dense_2 = self.dense_2(dense_1_activation)
        return dense_2

    def embedding_matrix(self):
        return self.embedding_1.weight
```

To train MalConv, we need to implement our custom Dataset method in the torch.utils.data class for processing the executable files. A custom Dataset class must implement three functions: `__init__`, `__len__`, and `__get_item__`.

The `__init__` function is run once when instantiating the Dataset object, named BinaryDataset. The function takes three input parameters:

- csv_filepath: path to a CSV file that indexes your dataset.
- max_len: optional cap on how many bytes you'll keep per file (saved for later use).

- min_len: optional cap on the minimum number of bytes a file must have (saved for later use).
- padding_idx: the token used later for padding/EOF (saved for later use).

and reads the CSV into a pandas DataFrame, which later iterates over each row and appends [row["path"], row["label"]] to self.all_files. The function doesn't load any file bytes yet but simply builds an index of (filepath, label) pairs from the CSV and stores the configuration values (max_len, min_len, padding_idx) for later use in __get_item.

```
class BinaryDataset(Dataset):
    def __init__(self, csv_filepath: str = None, max_len: int =
    ↪   None, min_len: int = None, padding_idx: int = 256):
        self.all_files = []
        self.max_len = max_len
        self.min_len = min_len
        self.padding_idx = padding_idx

        rows = pd.read_csv(csv_filepath)
        # Ensure required columns are present
        required_columns = {"path", "label"}
        if not required_columns.issubset(rows.columns):
            raise ValueError(f"CSV file must contain the following
            ↪   columns: {required_columns}")
        for _, row in rows.iterrows():
            self.all_files.append([row["path"], row["label"]])
```

The `__len__` function returns the number of samples in our dataset

```
    def __len__(self) -> int:
        return len(self.all_files)
```

The `__get_item__` method retrieves the sample at index `idx`. This method resolves the corresponding file path on disk, loads the executable via `load_single_exe` to obtain a byte tensor, and returns a tuple (EXE,label). The helper `load_single_exe` reads up to `max_len` bytes and right-pads the tensor when its length is below `min_len`. This padding is required for architectures such as BBDnn and AvastConv, whose convolutional layers expect a minimum input length; otherwise, shape mismatches can cause convolutional errors.

```
    def __getitem__(self, index) -> Tuple[torch.Tensor,
    ↪   torch.Tensor]:
        to_load, label, _ = self.all_files[index]
        x = load_single_exe(to_load, max_len=self.max_len,
        ↪   min_len=self.min_len, padding_idx=self.padding_idx)
        return x, torch.tensor(label)

def load_single_exe(path: Path, max_len: int = None, min_len: int
↪   = None, padding_idx: int = 256) -> torch.Tensor:
    """
    Create a torch.Tensor from the file pointed in the path
    :param path: a pathlib Path
    :return: torch.Tensor containing the bytes of the file as a
↪   tensor
    """
    with open(path, "rb") as h:
        if max_len is None:
            code = h.read()
        else:
            code = h.read(max_len)
    x = torch.frombuffer(bytearray(code), dtype=torch.uint8)
    x = x.to(torch.long)
    if min_len is not None: # Pad the tensor to the minimum length
    ↪   - required for some architectures
        if x.shape[0] < min_len:
            padding_idx = torch.tensor(padding_idx,
            ↪   dtype=torch.long)
            x = torch.nn.functional.pad(x, (0, min_len -
            ↪   x.shape[0]), mode='constant', value=padding_idx)
    return x
```

The maltorch library includes a Trainer that executes the full training loop and applies early stopping when the validation loss fails to improve. Its implementation, EarlyStoppingPyTorchTrainer, is initialized with an optimizer (e.g., Adam), the desired number of training epochs (e.g., 5), and the loss function to minimize (e.g., BCEWithLogitsLoss). This Trainer implements the `train` function that runs the full training/validation loop with early stopping, using your model, dataloaders, optimizer, and loss you passed when constructing EarlyStoppingTrainer.

```
from maltorch.zoo.malconv import MalConv
from maltorch.datasets.binary_dataset import BinaryDataset
from torch.utils.data import DataLoader
from maltorch.trainers.early_stopping_pytorch_trainer import
↪  EarlyStoppingPyTorchTrainer
import multiprocessing
import torch

malconv = MalConv()

training_dataset = BinaryDataset(
    csv_filepath="path/to/validation/csv
    padding_idx=256,
    max_len=2000000
)
validation_dataset = BinaryDataset(
    csv_filepath="path/to/validation/csv
    padding_idx=256,
    max_len=2000000
)
num_workers = max(multiprocessing.cpu_count() - 4,
↪  multiprocessing.cpu_count() // 2 + 1)
train_dataloader = DataLoader(
    training_dataset,
    batch_size=32,
    shuffle=True,
    num_workers=num_workers,
    collate_fn=training_dataset.pad_collate_func)
validation_dataloader = DataLoader(
    validation_dataset,
    batch_size=32,
    shuffle=True,
    num_workers=num_workers,
    collate_fn=training_dataset.pad_collate_func
)

criterion = torch.nn.BCEWithLogitsLoss()
optimizer = torch.optim.Adam(malconv.parameters())

trainer = EarlyStoppingPyTorchTrainer(
    optimizer=optimizer,
    epochs=5,
    loss=criterion
)
```

```
model = trainer.train(
    malconv,
    train_dataloader,
    validation_dataloader,
    patience=2
)
torch.save(model.state_dict(), "models/malconv/model.pth")
```

At inference time, you can easily load your saved model to predict the score of unknown samples as follows:

```
from maltorch.data_processing.sigmoid_postprocessor import
↪  SigmoidPostprocessor
from maltorch.zoo.malconv import MalConv

device = "cpu" # Specify the device to use (cpu, mps, cuda)
sigmoid_postprocessor = SigmoidPostprocessor()
malconv_model = MalConv.create_model(postprocessing=sigmoid_postpr⌋
↪  ocessor,device=device)

exe_folder =
↪  /path/to/where/you/have/the/executables/you/want/to/analyze
X = load_from_folder(exe_folder, "exe", device=device)
maliciousness_scores = malconv_model(X)
```

2.2.3 Image-based Representation

Malware detection based on the image representation of executables reframes the task of malware detection as a visual recognition task. Instead of operating directly on byte sequences, the raw bytes of a file are interpreted as pixel intensities and laid out in two dimensions to produce a bitmap representation of the file. Afterwards, a classifier is trained to decide whether the image corresponds to benign or malicious software (or to classify the malware into its corresponding family). This representation was first introduced by Nataraj *et al.* (2011), which observed that malware binaries belonging to the same family visualized as grayscale images are very similar in appearance with respect to layout and texture (see Figure 2.9). Leveraging this visual similarity, they classified malware into families using global texture descriptors (GIST) coupled with a k-nearest neighbors classifier. While later works explored alternative hand-crafted image features (Ahmadi *et al.*, 2016; Ahmed *et al.*, 2024; Liu *et al.*, 2019),

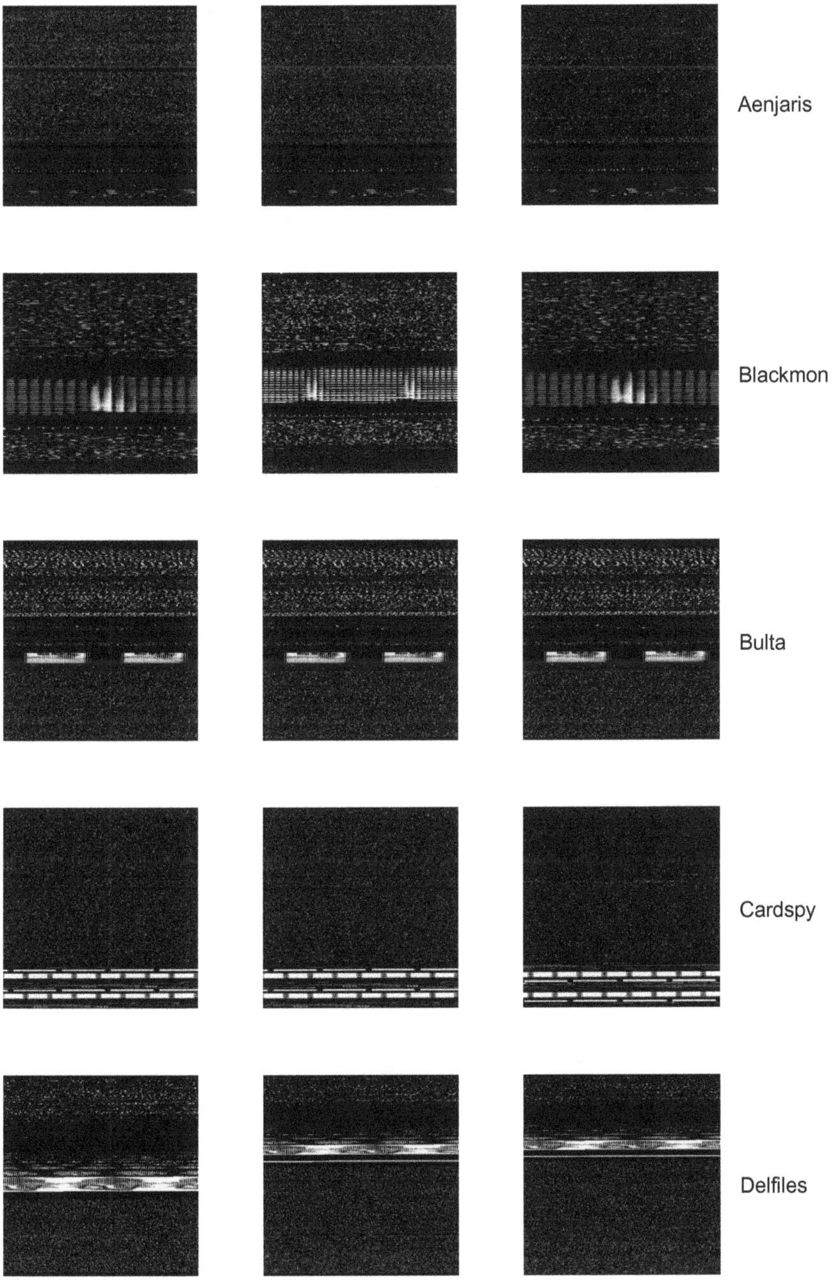

Fig. 2.9. Grayscale image representation of malware belonging to the Aenjaris, Blackmon, Bulta, Cardspy and Delfiles families.

the field has largely shifted to end-to-end models, first convolutional neural networks (Chaganti *et al.*, 2022; Gibert *et al.*, 2019; Vasan *et al.*, 2020) and more recently vision transformers (Gibert *et al.*, 2025; Wang *et al.*, 2024). This shift has been driven by the ability of these methods to learn discriminative features directly from images, eliminating the need for manual feature design.

A key design decision is how to map a one-dimensional byte sequence into a two-dimensional array. The most common scheme assigns each byte value (0-255) to a grayscale intensity and then folds the stream row by row into a fixed image width, with the height determined by file length. In the work of Nataraj *et al.* (2011) the width and height of the images is determined as follows:

```
def get_size(bytez_length: int) -> Tuple[int, int]:
    if (bytez_length < 10240):
        width = 32
    elif (10240 <= bytez_length <= 10240 * 3):
        width = 64
    elif (10240 * 3 <= bytez_length <= 10240 * 6):
        width = 128
    elif (10240 * 6 <= bytez_length <= 10240 * 10):
        width = 256
    elif (10240 * 10 <= bytez_length <= 10240 * 20):
        width = 384
    elif (10240 * 20 <= bytez_length <= 10240 * 50):
        width = 512
    elif (10240 * 50 <= bytez_length <= 10240 * 100):
        width = 768
    else:
        width = 1024
    height = int(bytez_length / width) + 1
    return width, height
```

The `get_size` function maps each file's byte length to a width "bin" and then computes the height as bytez_length/width + 1. Because both width and height depend on the file, two executables of different sizes produce images with different resolutions and aspect ratios. Vision classifiers and GPU batching, however, expect tensors of a single, fixed shape. To make the data compatible with a CNN or Vision Transformer, every image is therefore resampled to a common target resolution (e.g., 256×256: large binaries are down-scaled (many pixels collapsed into fewer), while small binaries are up-scaled (pixels are interpolated to compute more pixels). This normalization step standardizes input dimensions for training and inference, but it has consequences: down-scaling can discard fine, high-frequency cues (e.g., packer textures or section boundaries), and up-scaling may introduce interpolation artifacts.

This image-based pipeline has become popular largely because it lightens the computational burden relative to operating on byte sequences. By folding bytes into a 2-D grid and then resizing to a fixed resolution, security practitioners can efficiently train vision classifiers on commodity GPUs, as memory use depends on the chosen image size rather than on the raw file length. However, recent studies (Gibert *et al.*, 2025) have shown that image-based detectors tend to underperform byte-based models due to the loss of information that occurs when compressing the binary content into a 2-D representation. In addition, these vision classifiers are especially unreliable in the face of packing and encryption, which substantially alter the visual appearance of the binary.

2.2.3.1 *Training an Image-based Detector*

PyTorch's Torchvision library contains lots of implemented classification models such as AlexNet (Krizhevsky *et al.*, 2012), EfficientNet (Tan and Le, 2019), ResNet (He *et al.*, 2016), VGG (Simonyan and Zisserman, 2015), SwinTransformer (Liu *et al.*, 2021) and VisionTransformer (Dosovitskiy *et al.*, 2021). Now we will show you how you can train your own image-based malware detector from scratch. First, we need to implement a custom torch.utils.data.Dataset for generating the images from the executable files. This custom Dataset class will implement the functions `__init__`, `__len__`, and `__get_item__`.

(1) The `__init__` function initializes the dataset parameters (`width`, `height`) and builds the torchvision preprocessing pipeline:

```
PILToTensor ⇒ ConvertImageDtype(torch.float)
            ⇒ Resize(width, height)
            ⇒ Normalize(mean=0.5, std=0.5)
            ⇒ Grayscale(num_output_channels=3)
```

Then the detector reads the CSV file containing `path, label` pairs and stores them in `self.all_files`.

(2) The `__len__` function returns the number of samples in the dataset, i.e., `len(self.all_files)`.

(3) The `__get_item__` function retrieves the `(path, label)` at the given index, constructs a grayscale image from the file's raw bytes via `convert_to_grayscale_img` (which computes a size with `get_size`, creates a PIL `"L"` image, and applies the preprocessing), and returns the resulting normalized tensor together with the label as a tensor. Notice that we return a 3-D tensor (channels, height, width) instead of a 2-D tensor (height, width). This is because most of the classification models implemented by `torchvision` require an RGB image as input.

```
from typing import Tuple
from PIL import Image
from torch.utils.data import Dataset
from torchvision.transforms import Resize, Compose, Normalize,
↪  PILToTensor, ConvertImageDtype, Grayscale
import torch

class GrayscaleDataset(Dataset):
    def __init__(self, csv_filepath, width=256, height=256):
        self.all_files = []
        self.width = width
        self.height = height
        self.preprocess = Compose(
            [
                PILToTensor(),
                ConvertImageDtype(torch.float),
                Resize((self.width, self.height)),
                Normalize((0.5), (0.5)),
                Grayscale(num_output_channels=3)
            ]
        )

        with open(csv_filepath, "r") as input_file:
            lines = input_file.readlines()
            for line in lines:
                tokens = line.strip().split(",")
                self.all_files.append([tokens[0], int(tokens[1])])

    def __len__(self) -> int:
        return len(self.all_files)
```

```
    def __getitem__(self, index) -> Tuple[torch.Tensor,
    ↪  torch.Tensor]:
        to_load, label = self.all_files[index]
        img = self.convert_to_grayscale_img(to_load)
        return img, torch.tensor(label)

    def convert_to_grayscale_img(self, to_load) -> torch.Tensor:
        with open(to_load, "rb") as input_file:
            bytez = input_file.read()
        width, height = get_size(len(bytez))

        image = Image.new("L", (width,height))
        image.putdata(bytez)
        image = self.preprocess(image)

        return image
```

Now we can use the EarlyStoppingPyTorchTrainer implemented by maltorch to train our vision classifier (e.g., ResNet).

```
from maltorch.zoo.resnet18 import ResNet18
from maltorch.datasets.grayscale_dataset import GrayscaleDataset
from torch.utils.data import DataLoader
from maltorch.trainers.early_stopping_pytorch_trainer import
↪  EarlyStoppingPyTorchTrainer
import torch
import multiprocessing


resnet = ResNet18()
training_dataset = GrayscaleDataset(
    csv_filepath="path/to/training/csv",
    width=256,
    height=256
)

validation_dataset = GrayscaleDataset(
    csv_filepath="path/to/validation/csv",
    width=256,
    height=256
)

num_workers = max(multiprocessing.cpu_count() - 4,
↪  multiprocessing.cpu_count() // 2 + 1)
training_dataloader = DataLoader(
```

```
    training_dataset,
    batch_size=32,
    shuffle=True,
    num_workers=num_workers
)
validation_dataloader = DataLoader(
    training_dataset,
    batch_size=32,
    shuffle=True,
    num_workers=num_workers
)
criterion = torch.nn.BCEWithLogitsLoss()
optimizer = torch.optim.Adam(resnet.parameters())

trainer = EarlyStoppingPyTorchTrainer(
    optimizer=optimizer,
    epochs=5,
    loss=criterion
)
model = trainer.train(
    resnet,
    training_dataloader,
    validation_dataloader,
    patience=2
)
torch.save(model.state_dict(), "models/resnet18/model.pth")
```

At inference time, you can easily load your saved ResNet model to predict the scores for unknown samples as follows:

```
from maltorch.data_processing.grayscale_preprocessing import
↪ GrayscalePreprocessing
from maltorch.zoo.resnet18 import ResNet18
from maltorch.data_processing.sigmoid_postprocessor import
↪ SigmoidPostprocessor

device = "cpu" # Specify the device to use (cpu, mps, cuda)
grayscale_preprocessor = GrayscalePreprocessor(width=256,
↪ height=256, convert_to_3d_image=True)
sigmoid_postprocessor = SigmoidPostprocessor()

resnet_model =
↪ ResNet18.create_model(preprocessing=grayscale_preprocessor,
↪ postprocessing=sigmoid_postprocessor, device=device)
```

```
exe_folder =
↪   /path/to/where/you/have/the/executables/you/want/to/analyze
X = load_from_folder(exe_folder, "exe", device=device)
maliciousness_scores = resnet_model(X)
```

2.2.4 Structural Entropy

Malware authors employ a wide range of obfuscation techniques to evade detection, including packing and encryption, which alter the statistical distribution of bytes in an executable. To detect the presence of packed and encrypted code, security analysts have long relied on entropy analysis (Hamrock and Lyda, 2007).

Entropy, in the context of information theory, quantifies the unpredictability or randomness of data. Claude Shannon defined entropy mathematically as:

$$H(X) = -\sum_{i=1}^{n} p(x_i) \log_b p(x_i),$$

where X is a random variable with possible outcomes $\{x_1, x_2, ..., x_n\}$, n is the number of symbols, and $p(x_i)$ refers to the probability of outcome x_i, and b is the logarithm base (commonly 2).

For a byte sequence, entropy is calculated based on the frequency of bytes. Generally speaking, the entropy of a sequence of bytes refers to the amount of disorder (uncertainty) or statistical variation. If all byte values occur in equal numbers, the entropy will be at its maximum. On the other hand, if certain byte values occur with high probabilities, the entropy will be smaller. You can calculate the entropy of a byte sequence as follows:

```
import math
from collections import Counter

def entropy_bits_per_byte(byte_seq):
    n = len(byte_seq)
    if n == 0:
        return 0.0
    counts = Counter(byte_seq)
    H = 0.0
    for c in counts.values():
        p = c / n
```

```
        H -= p * math.log(p, 2)
    return H  # bits per byte (0..8 for bytes)

# Examples:
ex1 = bytes([0]*256)
ex2 = bytes(range(256))
print(entropy_bits_per_byte(ex1))  # 0.0
print(entropy_bits_per_byte(ex2))  # 8.0
```

Entropy analysis (Hamrock and Lyda, 2007) is therefore a useful method for detecting packed or encrypted code, as these obfuscation techniques tend to increase byte-level randomness, producing sections with unusually high entropy compared to ordinary executable code. In Table 2.1, you can observe the entropy variations between plain text, native executables, packed executables and encrypted executables processed by Bintropy.[16] Bintropy iterates through fixed-length data blocks in the binary (e.g., blocks of 256 bytes), summing the frequency of each block's observed byte values. From this, it calculates the block's entropy score.

However, the use of entropy statistics alone may not be enough to detect compressed executables as malware authors try to conceal encrypted or compressed code in a way that it evades high entropy filters. For instance, they may add additional padding to reduce the

Table 2.1. Computed statistical measures using the Bintropy tool (Hamrock and Lyda, 2007).

Data	Average Entropy	99.99% Confidence Intervals	Highest Entropy	99.99% Confidence Intervals
Plain text	4.347	4.066–4.629	4.715	4.401–5.030
Native executables	5.099	4.941–5.258	6.227	6.084–6.369
Packed executables	6.801	6.677–6.926	7.233	7.199–7.267
Encrypted executables	7.175	7.174–7.177	7.303	7.295–7.312

[16]https://github.com/packing-box/bintropy.

mean file entropy. Therefore, researchers started analyzing the structural entropy of executables Sorokin (2011). The structural entropy profile is generated by transforming an executable file into a one-dimensional time series that captures the variation in local entropy along the byte stream, as illustrated in Figure 2.10. This profile is generated by sliding a fixed-length window across the file and computing the Shannon entropy within each window. Two parameters govern this process:

- The window size defines the number of consecutive bytes considered when computing a single entropy value. Larger windows produce smoother entropy profiles but may obscure short, localized changes. Conversely, smaller windows produce more fine-grained signals at the cost of increased noise.
- The step size determines the stride between successive windows. A step equal to the window size produces non-overlapping windows, resulting in shorter structural entropy sequences and reduced computational cost. On the other hand, smaller steps introduce

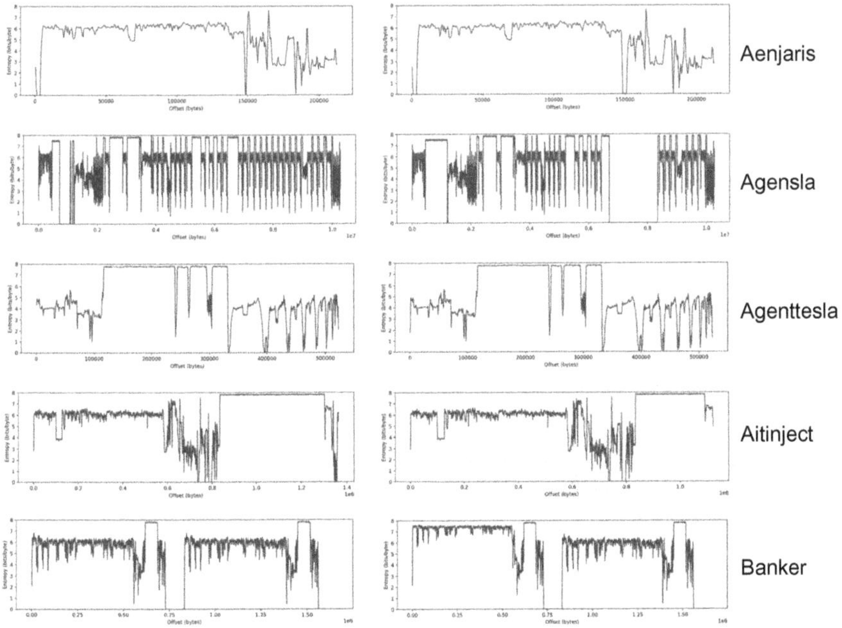

Fig. 2.10. Structural entropy representation of malware belonging to the Aenjaris, Agensla, Agenttesla, Aitinject, and Banker malware families.

overlap between adjacent windows, providing a more detailed representation of local entropy variations.

Formally, given a file of length N bytes, the number of entropy values extracted is

$$T = \left\lfloor \frac{N - \text{window\_size}}{\text{step}} + 1 \right\rfloor$$

with each value corresponding to the entropy of a segment of the file.

```
def structural_entropy_profile(
    bytes_tensor: torch.Tensor,
    window_size: int = 1024,
    step: int | None = None,
    normalized: bool = False,
    eps: float = 1e-12,
):
    """
    Compute the structural entropy (sliding-window Shannon
↪   entropy) of a byte tensor.

    Args:
        bytes_tensor: 1D tensor of dtype torch.uint8 containing
↪   file bytes.
        window_size:  window length in bytes (e.g., 1024).
        step:         slide/stride in bytes (default: window_size
↪   // 2).
        normalized:   if True, divides by 8 to return values in
↪   [0, 1].
        eps:          numerical floor to avoid log2(0).

    Returns:
        H:    1D float tensor of entropies per window (bits/byte
↪   or [0,1] if normalized).
        pos:  1D long tensor of window-center byte positions.
    """
    x = bytes_tensor.flatten().to(torch.uint8)
    n = x.numel()
    if n == 0:
        return torch.empty(0, dtype=torch.float32), torch.empty(0,
        ↪  dtype=torch.long)

    if step is None:
        step = max(1, window_size // 2)
```

```
# If file is shorter than window, compute a single global
↪  entropy
if n < window_size:
    counts = torch.bincount(x.long(),
    ↪  minlength=256).to(torch.float32)
    p = counts / float(n)
    p = p.clamp_min(eps)
    H = -(p * torch.log2(p)).sum()
    if normalized:
        H = H / 8.0
    return H.view(1), torch.tensor([n // 2], dtype=torch.long)

# Make overlapping windows as a view: shape (n_windows,
↪  window_size)
windows = x.unfold(0, window_size, step)
n_windows = windows.size(0)

# Histogram per window using scatter_add (vectorized, no
↪  Python loop)
counts = torch.zeros((n_windows, 256), dtype=torch.float32,
↪  device=windows.device)
ones = torch.ones_like(windows, dtype=torch.float32)
counts.scatter_add_(1, windows.long(), ones)  # add 1 at each
↪  byte value

# Probabilities and entropy
p = (counts / float(window_size)).clamp_min(eps)
H = -(p * torch.log2(p)).sum(dim=1)  # bits/byte in [0, 8]

if normalized:
    H = H / 8.0  # now in [0, 1]

# Window centers
starts = torch.arange(0, n_windows * step, step,
↪  device=windows.device, dtype=torch.long)
centers = starts + (window_size // 2)

return H, centers
```

Based on the assumption that different samples of the same malicious family have similar order of code and data areas, the structural entropy has been used for classifying malware into families. Similarly to the visualization of malware as grayscale images, the 1-D structural entropy profile can be used to produce family-specific, mutation-resilient fingerprints that can be compared with similarity metrics (e.g., Dynamic Time Warping (Berndt and Clifford, 1994)) or fed to convolutional neural networks (Gibert *et al.*, 2018) to cluster and classify malware samples into families.

2.2.4.1 *Training your own Structural Entropy-based Classifier*

To train our own malware classifier based on the structural entropy profile of the malicious executables we first need to implement a custom torch.utils.data.Dataset, named StructuralEntropyDataset. This Dataset implements the functions `__init__`, `__len__`, `__get_item__`:

(1) The `__init__` function initializes the dataset parameters (`window_size`, `step`) that define the byte window size and step used to compute the structural entropy profile, and reads the CSV file of `path,label` pairs.
(2) The `__len__` function returns the number of samples in the dataset, i.e., len(self.all_files).
(3) The `__get_item__` function retrieves the (`path,label`) at a given index, and produces a structural entropy profile from the file's raw bytes via `extract_structural_entropy`, and returns a normalized tensor and the label as a tensor. The function `extract_structural_entropy` reads the raw bytes of an executable, slides a window across the bytes (default 1024-byte window and step 512), and computes an entropy value per window.

In addition, StruturalEntropyDataset implements a custom `collate_fn`, named `pad_collate_func` to gather a list of structural entropy profiles and pad within the batch up to the longest sequence using zeros, with no truncation.

```
from torch.utils.data import Dataset
import torch
from typing import Tuple
from src.entropy_utils import structural_entropy_profile
from maltorch.datasets.binary_dataset import load_single_exe
from torch.nn.utils.rnn import pad_sequence

class StructuralEntropyDataset(Dataset):
    def __init__(self, csv_filepath: str, window_size: int = 1024,
    ↪  step: int = 512):
```

```
        self.all_files = []
        self.window_size = window_size
        self.step = step

        with open(csv_filepath, "r") as input_file:
            lines = input_file.readlines()
            for line in lines:
                tokens = line.strip().split(",")
                self.all_files.append([tokens[0], int(tokens[1])])

    def __len__(self) -> int:
        return len(self.all_files)

    def __getitem__(self, index) -> Tuple[torch.Tensor,
    ↪   torch.Tensor]:
        to_load, label = self.all_files[index]
        structural_entropy =
        ↪   self.extract_structural_entropy(to_load)
        return structural_entropy, torch.tensor(label)

    def extract_structural_entropy(self, to_load: str) ->
    ↪   torch.Tensor:
        x = load_single_exe(to_load)
        structural_entropy, _ = structural_entropy_profile(x,
        ↪   window_size=self.window_size, step=self.step,
        ↪   normalized=True)
        return structural_entropy

    def pad_collate_func(self, batch):
        """
        This should be used as the collate_fn=pad_collate_func for
↪   a pytorch DataLoader object in order to pad out files in a
↪   batch to the length of the longest item in the batch.
        """
        vecs = [x[0] for x in batch]
        labels = [x[1].unsqueeze(0) for x in batch]

        x = pad_sequence(
            vecs, batch_first=True, padding_value=0.0  # pad with
            ↪   float 0.0
        )
        y = torch.tensor(labels, dtype=torch.long)  # (B,)

        return x, y
```

The next step is to implement a malware classifier that classifies malware into families directly from the structural entropy profiles extracted from PE files. Each file is mapped to a 1-D real-valued sequence $x \in \mathbb{R}^T$ (entropy per sliding window along the byte stream). The following classifier is a compact 1-D convolutional neural network that learns local entropy motifs and aggregates them into a global representation. This CNN consists of three convolutional blocks (Conv1d-ReLU-MaxPool) with kernel sizes 7, 5, and 3, respectively, which progressively capture short-to medium-range patterns while downsampling the sequence. A global `AdaptiveMaxPool1d` layer then collapses the temporal dimension, producing a fixed-length 128-dimensional vector regardless of input length, which is passed through a fully-connected layer to generate logits over the malware families.

```
class TimeSeriesCNN(TimeSeriesModel):
    def __init__(self, num_classes: int, in_channels):
        super(TimeSeriesCNN, self).__init__(
            name="TimeSeriesCNN", gdrive_id=None
        )
        self.num_classes = num_classes
        self.in_channels = in_channels
        self.net = nn.Sequential(
            nn.Conv1d(in_channels, 32, kernel_size=7, padding=3),
            nn.ReLU(),
            nn.MaxPool1d(kernel_size=2),
            nn.Conv1d(32, 64, kernel_size=5, padding=2),
            nn.ReLU(),
            nn.MaxPool1d(kernel_size=2),
            nn.Conv1d(64, 128, kernel_size=3, padding=1),
            nn.ReLU(),
            nn.AdaptiveMaxPool1d(1),  # -> (N, 128, 1)
        )
        self.fc = nn.Linear(128, self.num_classes)

    def forward(self, x):        # x: (N, L)
        x = x.unsqueeze(dim=1)  # x: (N, C, L)
        x = self.net(x)                  # (N, 128, 1)
        x = x.squeeze(-1)                # (N, 128)
        return self.fc(x)                # logits (N, n_classes)
```

Lastly, we can use the EarlyStoppingPyTorchTrainer to train our time series classifier.

```
training_dataset = StructuralEntropyDataset(
    configuration["training_filepath"],
    window_size=configuration["window_size"],
    step=configuration["step"]
)
validation_dataset = StructuralEntropyDataset(
    configuration["validation_filepath"],
    window_size = configuration["window_size"],
    step = configuration["step"]
)
num_workers = max(multiprocessing.cpu_count() - 4,
↪  multiprocessing.cpu_count() // 2 + 1)
training_dataloader = DataLoader(
    training_dataset,
    batch_size=configuration["batch_size"],
    shuffle=True,
    num_workers=num_workers,
    collate_fn=training_dataset.pad_collate_func)
validation_dataloader = DataLoader(
    validation_dataset,
    batch_size=configuration["batch_size"],
    shuffle=True,
    num_workers=num_workers,
    collate_fn=validation_dataset.pad_collate_func
)

classifier = TimeSeriesCNN(
    num_classes=configuration["num_classes"],
    in_channels=1
)
classifier = classifier.to(device)

optimizer = torch.optim.Adam(classifier.parameters())

criterion = torch.nn.CrossEntropyLoss().to(device)
trainer = EarlyStoppingPyTorchTrainer(
    optimizer,
    configuration["num_epochs"],
    criterion
)
```

```
classifier = trainer.train(
    classifier,
    training_dataloader,
    validation_dataloader,
    configuration["patience"]
)
```

2.3 Assembly-based Malware Detectors

Assembly-based malware detectors are detection systems that operate directly on assembly-level representations of programs rather than relying solely on raw machine code or byte sequences. During compilation, a program's source code is translated into machine instructions, which can later be reversed into a human-readable form using disassemblers such as Ghidra,[17] Radare2,[18] Capstone,[19] or IDA Pro.[20] These tools reconstruct assembly code from executable binaries, providing analysts with a readable representation of the program's implementation. However, the resulting disassembly is a reconstruction, which is useful for analysis, but not an exact reproduction of the original assembly source, as symbolic information and structural annotations are typically lost during compilation.

Assembly-based malware detectors use this reconstructed assembly code as input, as shown in Figure 4.11 as an example, and extract:

- Statistical or structural patterns.
- Instruction sequences.
- Control flow graphs (CFGs) or Function call graphs (FCGs).

2.3.1 Assembly-based Feature Extraction

Ahmadi *et al.* (2016) defined a rich set of static features that can be extracted from a disassembled view (e.g. Listing 2.1) of a PE file:

Operation codes: Operation codes, also known as opcodes, are the mnemonic representation of machine instructions. This feature set

[17]https://github.com/NationalSecurityAgency/ghidra.
[18]https://github.com/radareorg/radare2.
[19]https://www.capstone-engine.org/.
[20]https://hex-rays.com/ida-pro.

```
undefined __cdecl FUN_004038cd(LPVOID param_1)
    004038cd 56             PUSH      ESI
    004038ce 8b 74 24 08    MOV       ESI,dword ptr [ESP +
    param_1]
    004038d2 85 f6          TEST      ESI,ESI
    004038d4 74 24          JZ        LAB_004038fa
    004038d6 56             PUSH      ESI
    004038d7 e8 13 0b 00    CALL      FUN_004043ef
                                   uint FUN_004043ef(int param_1)
            00
    004038dc 59             POP       ECX
    004038dd 85 c0          TEST      EAX,EAX
    004038df 56             PUSH      ESI
    004038e0 74 0a          JZ        LAB_004038ec
    004038e2 50             PUSH      EAX
    004038e3 e8 32 0b 00    CALL      FUN_0040441a
                                   undefined FUN_0040441a(uint *
    param_1,
            00
    004038e8 59             POP       ECX
    004038e9 59             POP       ECX
    004038ea 5e             POP       ESI
    004038eb c3             RET

                LAB_004038ec XREF[1]: 004038e0(j)
   004038ec 6a 00          PUSH      0x0
   004038ee ff 35 30 07    PUSH      dword ptr [DAT_00420730]
                                  = 00580000h
            42 00
   004038f4 ff 15 08 80    CALL      dword ptr [->KERNEL32.DLL
    ::HeapFree]                   = 7dd71499
            40 00
```

Listing 2.1. Disassembly excerpt.

forms a vector representing the frequency distribution of the selected opcodes. While the total number of opcodes varies depending on the architecture, the study focuses on a reduced subset of 93 opcodes that cover the most common and discriminative instructions.

Register: This set of features represents the frequency of register usage in the assembly code. The total number of registers in the x86/x86-64 architecture varies depending on the processor generation and supported extensions. In their work, the authors focused on a reduced subset of 24 registers (8 general-purpose 32-bit registers and 16 general-purpose 64-bit registers).

Symbols: This feature set represents the frequency of the symbols `-`, `+`, `*`, `]`, `[`, `?`, and `@`. A high occurrence of these symbols often indicates evasive code patterns, such as indirect calls or dynamic library loading used to avoid detection.

Application Programming Interface: This collection of features measures the frequency of use of Application Programming Interfaces. Unlike API-based features extracted directly from the binary, which only reveal imported libraries and functions, this approach also counts how many times each function has been invoked within the code. Since the total number of available APIs is large, their analysis was restricted to the 794 most frequently used APIs, identified from a dataset of nearly 500,000 malware samples.

Data Defines: Data defines, also known as data definition directives, are instructions to the assembler, not to the CPU, and are used to allocate and optionally initialize memory in the program. Unlike opcodes such as `MOV` or `JMP`, data defines do not generate executable instructions, but rather place data bytes in memory. Packed malware often contains large sequences of data defines instead of readable instructions. Therefore, the frequency of `db`, `dw`, and `dd` instructions are useful features for malware detection.

An example of source code for extracting the above features can be found at https://github.com/ManSoSec/Microsoft-Malware-Challenge.

2.3.2 Assembly N-Gram Features

While byte n-grams operate on the raw binary, opcode n-grams operate on the sequence of machine instructions (opcodes) that the binary represents. This requires a disassembly step: the binary file must be translated into assembly code, from which the sequence of opcodes (operation codes) can be extracted. An opcode is the part of an instruction that denotes the operation (e.g., `MOV`, `CALL`, `XOR`), as opposed to operands, which include register names, constants, and memory addresses. The idea is to capture the program's behavior in terms of what operations it performs, abstracting away memory addresses or data values that may vary between programs or between variants of malware. As noted by Shabtai *et al.* (2012), malware authors often insert junk data or varying operands to evade signature detection. Therefore, by disregarding operand values and focusing only on the operation codes, we achieve a more robust representation. For instance, the instructions `MOV EAX, 1234h` and `MOV EAX, 5678h` have different bytes (because the immediate constants differ), but both share the opcode `MOV`.

For each instruction, we extract the mnemonic code. For example, the sequence of x86 assembly instructions:

```
MOV EAX, [EBP-0x4]
XOR EAX, ESI
CALL DWORD PTR [0x4030f0]
ADD EAX, 1
```

yields the opcode sequence `[MOV, XOR, CALL, ADD,...]`. This sequence is analogous to a sentence of "words" (opcodes) from a limited vocabulary (the CPU's instruction set). The vocabulary size is the number of distinct opcodes in that architecture.

After obtaining the opcode sequence, feature extraction proceeds like the byte case: slide an n-length window over the opcode sequence to gather all opcode n-grams. For example, if we have the opcode sequence `[MOV, XOR, CALL, ADD,...]`, the 2-grams are `[MOV-XOR, XOR-CALL, CALL-ADD,...]`. Feature representation for opcode n-grams is analogous to byte n-grams, too. We can count the occurrences of each opcode n-gram in a program and use a BoW model. Many studies have represented opcode n-grams as binary features or as TF-normalized frequencies, similarly to byte n-grams (Santos *et al.*, 2013).

Implementation-wise, opcode n-gram extraction is more involved due to the disassembly step but it can be automated. For example, with the Capstone library in Python, one could write:

```python
from capstone import Cs, CS_ARCH_X86, CS_MODE_32

# Initialize Capstone disassembler (32-bit x86 example)
md = Cs(CS_ARCH_X86, CS_MODE_32)
md.detail = False # we only need mnemonic, not operand details
```

```
opcodes = []
for instr in md.disasm(file_bytes, 0x0): #Replace '0x0' for the
↪   entry point to the section you want to parse
    opcodes.append(instr.mnemonic.upper())

# Now opcodes list contains e.g. ["MOV", "XOR", "CALL", "ADD", ...]
n = 3
opcode_ngrams = Counter()
for i in range(len(opcodes) - n + 1):
    gram = tuple(opcodes[i:i+n])
    opcode_ngrams[gram] += 1
```

2.3.2.1 *Automatic Extraction of N-Gram Like Features with CNNs*

Recent advances in deep learning, and in particular the use of Convolutional Neural Networks (CNNs), provide a flexible way to automatically learn n-gram like features directly from opcode sequences. Instead of explicitly enumerating all n-grams, CNNs use convolutional filters/kernels that slide across the sequence and learn local patterns that are informative for the malware classification task.

Gibert *et al.* (2017, 2021) introduced a shallow CNN consisting of one convolutional layer with multiple filter sizes. This network takes as input a sequence of size up to L opcodes (e.g., $L = 2^{20}$), where each opcode is mapped to a unique token identifier. This sequence of token IDs is then passed through an embedding layer, which projects each token to a dense vector representation of dimension E (e.g., $E = 8$), resulting in an embedded sequence of shape $L \times E$. Following this step, a single one-dimensional convolutional layer with multiple filter widths (e.g., 3, 5, 7) is applied to the embedded input in order to capture local n-gram patterns of varying lengths. Because the filters are learned during training, the CNN automatically focus on the most discriminative local structures rather than depending on a manually selected set of n-grams. The resulting feature maps are then passed through a ReLU nonlinearity, followed by a global max-pooling operation, which extracts the most salient feature for each filter and produces a fixed-size representation independent of the input length. The pooled feature vectors from all features are then concatenated and fed into one fully-connected layer to obtain the class probabilities (Figure 2.11).

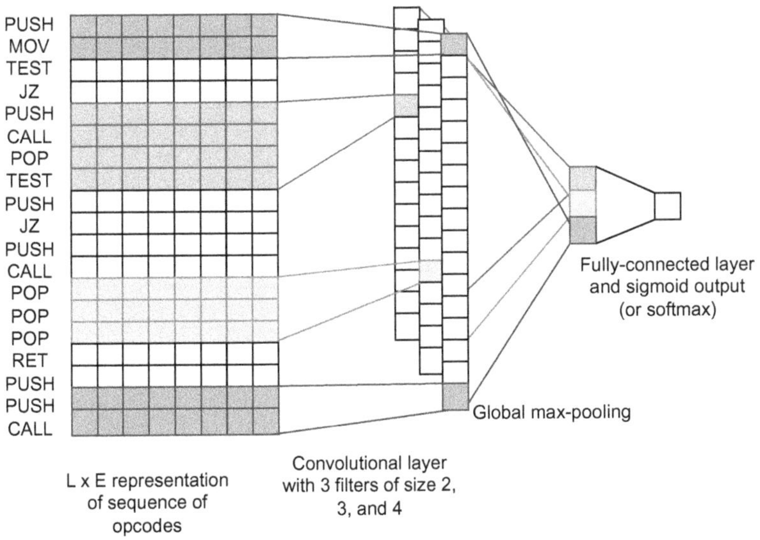

Fig. 2.11. Illustration of a toy CNN architecture with an embedding layer (size E), a convolutional layer with three filters of size 2, 3, and 4, respectively, a global max-pooling and a fully-connected layer.

2.3.2.2 *Train your own CNN based on opcode sequences*

In the following, we describe a shallow CNN for automatic N-gram extraction from opcode sequences. We will assume that each Windows Portable Executable file is first disassembled to obtain its assembly language source code using any of the tools mentioned in Section 2.3. From the assembly code, we extract only the opcode sequence by removing the operands and metadata. The resulting sequence is tokenized using a predefined vocabulary (augmented with a padding token assigned index 0) and subsequently truncated or padded to a fixed maximum length of 2^{20}.

The following is a simplified first pass for a shallow CNN with filter sizes $\mathcal{K} \in \{3, 5, 7\}$:

$$\mathbf{x} = [x_1, x_2, \ldots, x_L], \quad x_i \in \mathbb{N}$$

$$\mathbf{E} = \text{Embedding}(\mathbf{x}) \in \mathbb{R}^{L_{\max} \times d}$$

$$\mathbf{H}_k = \text{ReLU}(\text{Conv1D}_k(\mathbf{E})), \quad k \in \mathcal{K}$$

$$\mathbf{h}_k = \text{GlobalMaxPool}(\mathbf{H}_k) \in \mathbb{R}^{F_k}$$

$$\mathbf{h} = \text{Concat}(\{\mathbf{h}_k : k \in \mathcal{K}\})$$
$$\mathbf{o} = \mathbf{W}\mathbf{h} + \mathbf{b}$$
$$\hat{\mathbf{y}} = \text{Softmax}(\mathbf{o}) \textit{ or } \text{Sigmoid}(\mathbf{o})$$

The corresponding implementation is provided in Python through the maltorch library.

```
import torch
import torch.nn.functional as F
from torch import nn
from maltorch.zoo.model import EmbeddingModel


class ShallowConv(EmbeddingModel):
    def __init__(self,
                 embedding_size=8,
                 max_len=2 ** 20,
                 out_channels: int = 100,
                 threshold: float = 0.5,
                 padding_idx: int = 0):
        super(ShallowConv, self).__init__(
            name="ShallowConv", gdrive_id=None
        )
        self.embedding_1 = nn.Embedding(
            num_embeddings=257, embedding_dim=embedding_size,
            ↪ padding_idx=padding_idx
        )
        self.out_channels = out_channels
        self.conv1d_1 = nn.Conv1d(
            in_channels=embedding_size,
            out_channels=self.out_channels,
            kernel_size=(3,),
            stride=(1,),
            groups=1,
            bias=True,
        )

        self.conv1d_2 = nn.Conv1d(
            in_channels=embedding_size,
            out_channels=self.out_channels,
            kernel_size=(5,),
            stride=(1,),
            groups=1,
            bias=True,
        )
```

```
        self.conv1d_3 = nn.Conv1d(
            in_channels=embedding_size,
            out_channels=self.out_channels,
            kernel_size=(7,),
            stride=(1,),
            groups=1,
            bias=True,
        )

        self.dense_1 = nn.Linear(in_features=self.out_channels *
        ↪  3, out_features=1, bias=True)
        self.drop_1 = nn.Dropout1d()


        self.embedding_size = (embedding_size,)
        self.max_len = max_len
        self.threshold = threshold
        self.invalid_value = padding_idx
        self.padding_idx = padding_idx

    def embedding_layer(self):
        return self.embedding_1

    def embed(self, x):
        emb_x = self.embedding_1(x)
        emb_x = emb_x.transpose(1, 2)
        return emb_x

    def _forward_embed_x(self, x):
        conv1d_1 = self.conv1d_1(x)
        conv1d_2 = self.conv1d_2(x)
        conv1d_3 = self.conv1d_3(x)
        conv1d_1_activation = torch.relu(conv1d_1)
        conv1d_2_activation = torch.relu(conv1d_2)
        conv1d_3_activation = torch.relu(conv1d_3)

        global_max_pooling1d_1 = F.max_pool1d(
            input=conv1d_1_activation,
            ↪  kernel_size=conv1d_1_activation.size()[2:]
        )
        global_max_pooling1d_2 = F.max_pool1d(
            input=conv1d_2_activation,
            ↪  kernel_size=conv1d_2_activation.size()[2:]
        )
```

```
        global_max_pooling1d_3 = F.max_pool1d(
            input=conv1d_3_activation,
            ↪ kernel_size=conv1d_3_activation.size()[2:]
        )

        global_max_pooling1d_1_flatten =
        ↪ global_max_pooling1d_1.view(
            global_max_pooling1d_1.size(0), -1
        )
        global_max_pooling1d_2_flatten =
        ↪ global_max_pooling1d_2.view(
            global_max_pooling1d_2.size(0), -1
        )
        global_max_pooling1d_3_flatten =
        ↪ global_max_pooling1d_3.view(
            global_max_pooling1d_3.size(0), -1
        )

        concat_1 = torch.concat(
            [global_max_pooling1d_1_flatten,
            ↪ global_max_pooling1d_2_flatten,
            ↪ global_max_pooling1d_3_flatten], dim=1)
        drop_1 = self.drop_1(concat_1)
        dense_1 = self.dense_1(drop_1)
        return dense_1

    def embedding_matrix(self):
        return self.embedding_1.weight
```

2.3.3 Control Flow and Function Call Graph Representations

A computer program can be represented as either a Control Flow Graph (CFG) or as a Function Call Graph (FCG).

A CFG, illustrated in Figure 2.12, represents the control flow within a computer program at the level of basic blocks of instructions, defined as sequences of instructions with a single entry and single exit. In this type of graph, nodes are basic blocks of instructions and edges are directed control transfers (e.g., conditional jumps, unconditional jumps, fall-throughs, returns). CFGs capture the execution flows of a computer program and they have long been used by analysts to model, visualize, and analyze the internal logic of computer programs.

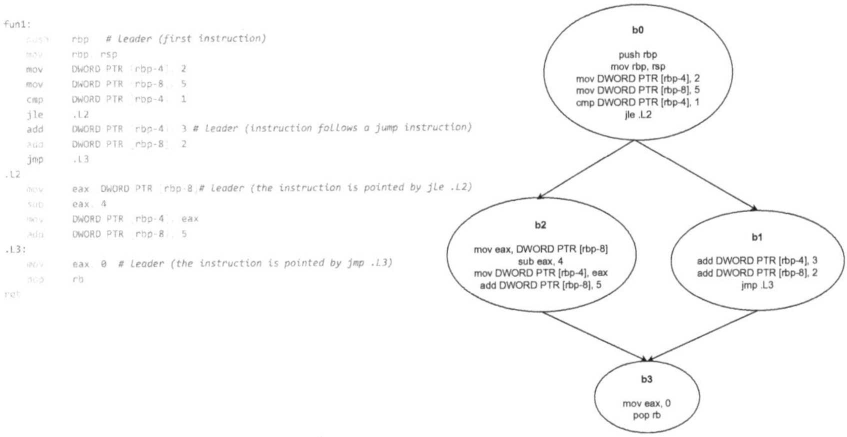

Fig. 2.12. Example of a small control flow graph.

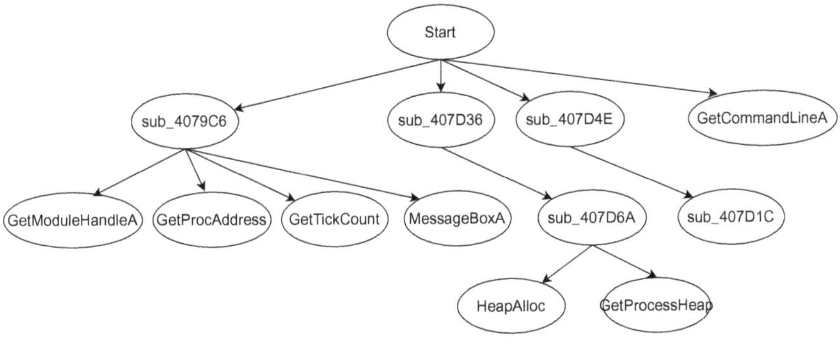

Fig. 2.13. Example of a small function call graph.

A FCG, illustrated in Figure 2.13, represents relationships between functions in a program. In this type of representation, nodes are functions identified by their entry addresses or names while edges are function calls (direct or indirect) between calling and called. FCGs describe the relationships between functions and provide a higher-level view of a program's structure and interactions.

To extract and visualize Control Flow Graphs (CFGs) and Function Call Graphs (FCGs), one can employ well-established binary analysis frameworks (e.g., IDA Pro, Ghidra, angr, and Radare2).

CFGs and FCGs have mainly been used for classifying malware into families. Most of the prior work in graphs for malware classification either (1) use graph matching, (2) transform the graphs into feature vectors, or (3) use graph neural networks.

In graph matching, given two graphs G_1 and G_2, the objective is to define a distance function that quantifies how similar G_2 is to G_1. This distance can then be used for nearest-neighbor classification over a large dataset; however, such approaches are often avoided due to their high computational cost (Hu *et al.*, 2009). A common approach is to create a graph edit distance (GED) matrix. GED measures the minimum cost of transforming one graph into another through a series of operations, such as inserting, deleting, or relabeling nodes and edges. However, computing the exact GED is computationally intractable for all but very small graphs. As a result, approaches such as those presented in Hu *et al.* (2009), Kinable and Kostakis (2011), and Elhadi *et al.* (2014) approximate this distance. For example, Kinable and Kostakis (2011) approximated the minimum GED between two graphs using Simulated Annealing. Then they applied clustering (K-medoids and DBSCAN) on these similarity scores to group malware by family.

Since many techniques for directly comparing graphs are computationally expensive and often rely on approximations, several studies have instead focused on transforming graph representations into fixed-length vectors (Hassen and Chan, 2017; Sun *et al.*, 2022; Zhang *et al.*, 2020; Zhao *et al.*, 2024). Once converted, traditional machine learning algorithms can then be applied for classification. For example, Sun *et al.* (2022) extract feature vector representations of CFGs using the graphs' spectral heat and wave signatures. Afterwards, they train and evaluate eight different machine learning classifiers, including Support Vector Machines and Decision Trees, among others.

Traditional graph-based methods relying on graph edit distance, graph kernels, or feature extraction to compare CFGs and FCGs require manual feature engineering or do not capture complex hierarchical relationships within program structures. Recently, graph neural networks (GNNs) have been proposed to address these limitations by learning node and graph representations automatically, allowing end-to-end malware classification directly from the graph representations (Bilot *et al.*, 2024; Chen *et al.*, 2023; Ling *et al.*, 2022; Malhotra *et al.*, 2024; Mohammadian *et al.*, 2025). For instance, Chen *et al.* (2023) construct function call graphs (FCGs) using Radare2, representing each node with a function embedding. This function embedding is either an ASM2Vec (Ding *et al.*, 2019) embedding or the Self-Attentive Function Embedding (SAFE) (Massarelli *et al.*, 2019). The resulting FCGs are then used to train a graph neural network (GNN) for malware detection. In a similar fashion, Mohammadian *et al.* (2025) proposes a malware detection framework that uses Control Flow Graphs (CFGs) and Function Call Graphs (FCGs) with two node embedding methods, namely Function Name Embedding (FNE) (Wang *et al.*, 2020) and Assembly Embedding (AE) (Peng *et al.*, 2024), and integrates graph reduction techniques such as Leaf Prune within a Graph Neural Network (GNN).

Despite their potential, the use of graph-based structures for malware classification face challenges related to their size and noise. The

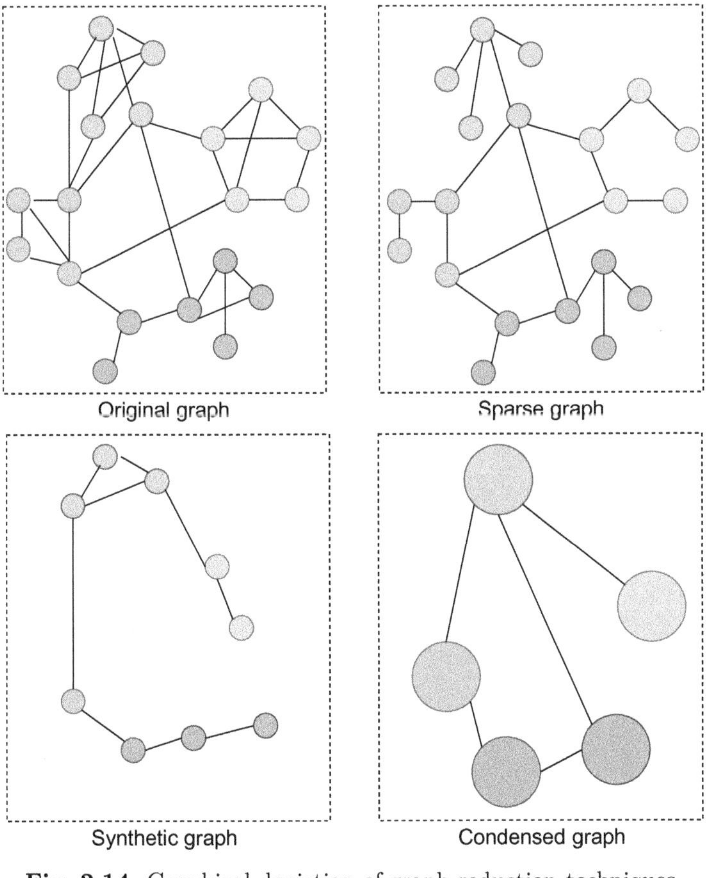

Fig. 2.14. Graphical depiction of graph reduction techniques.

generated graphs can be extremely large and complex, complicating the process of analyzing and understanding malware behavior and patterns because of the vast number of nodes and edges they contain. Moreover, these graphs frequently contain noisy or irrelevant information, such as redundant structures which obscure the graph structure. To address the issue of large graph sizes, several techniques, illustrated in Figure 2.14 haven been explored in the literature, including graph sparsification, condensation, and coarsening (Shokouhinejad *et al.*, 2025). Graph sparsification aims to create a sparse approximation by selecting essential edges or nodes based on some specific criteria. Graph condensation creates a much smaller graph by learning synthetic nodes and edges. Graph coarsening groups similar or closely connected nodes and aggregates their edges into super-edges.

2.4 Challenges and Open Problems

In this section, we discuss the key challenges and unresolved issues that limit the effectiveness and reproducibility of current machine learning-based approaches for malware detection and classification.

2.4.1 Limited Reproducibility and Comparability Across Studies

A persistent problem in Windows malware detection research is the absence of publicly available datasets. As a result, researchers typically rely on self-collected datasets. These self-collected datasets are rarely shared because most benign executables are proprietary software protected by copyright and restrictive licenses, making their redistribution, even for research purposes, illegal. To circumvent this limitation, researchers only publish the cryptographic hashes (e.g., SHA-256) of the files included in their datasets (Harang and Rudd, 2020; Joyce *et al.*, 2025). However, these hashes merely serve as identifiers and do not provide access to the actual executables. Therefore, retrieving the original binaries from the hashes is practically impossible unless one has access to an API-based repository such as VirusTotal Enterprise. This lack of data availability severely hinders reproducibility and comparability across studies because performance metrics are not directly comparable between works. For instance, a model that performs well on one dataset may exhibit significantly lower performance on another due to variations in malware families and benign software composition.

To make matters worse, most studies do not release the source code or implementation details of their methods. Without access to a functional codebase, reproducing experimental setups, such as feature extraction pipelines, model architectures, preprocessing steps, and hyperparameter configurations, becomes nearly impossible. Even when papers describe their methodologies in detail, subtle implementation choices can significantly influence the results. This issue is particularly acute for approaches that rely on graph-based representations, such as control flow graphs and function call graphs. These representations require more complex preprocessing pipelines that depend on the disassembly tool used (e.g., IDA Pro, Ghidra, Radare2, Capstone) and how functions and instruction blocks are preprocessed. Despite their popularity, virtually no study provides the code necessary to extract and preprocess these graphs from executable files. As a result, reproducing such methods require re-implementing intricate pipelines from scratch, often without sufficient methodological details, discouraging comparative analysis with prior work or extending existing approaches.

2.4.2 Concept Drift

Concept drift refers to the gradual or sudden changes in the statistical properties of data over time. In the context of malware detection, this phenomenon is especially critical because the characteristics of both malicious and benign software evolve continuously. Therefore, a robust malware detection system should not only perform well immediately after training but also maintain its effectiveness as new malware families emerge and existing ones adopt distinct obfuscation and evasion techniques. Yet, most existing studies rely on static datasets and single-time evaluations, overlooking the temporal dimension of malware evolution (Yang *et al.*, 2021). As a result, reported accuracies often overestimate long-term performance.

2.4.3 Vulnerability to Adversarial Attacks

While machine learning-based malware detectors have shown promise, they are vulnerable against adversarial examples, i.e., executables that have been deliberately manipulated by the attackers to evade detection while preserving their malicious functionality. Adversarial attacks exploit weaknesses in the model's feature space or learning process, enabling attackers to craft binaries that appear benign to the detector.

These attacks can be broadly categorized according to the representation targeted:

- Feature-based attacks modify discriminative characteristics used by static feature-based detectors (Cf. Section 2.2.1). Attackers may alter metadata fields, rename sections, inject benign strings, manipulate the Import and/or Export Address Tables, and so forth, to mislead the classifier. For example Gibert *et al.* (2025) demonstrated that cloning the code-signing certificate of known legitimate PE files can effectively evade detection by an EMBER LightGBM detector (Anderson and Roth, 2018).
- Byte-based attacks manipulate the structure of Portable Executable (PE) files to inject adversarial content that misleads byte-based detectors into misclassifying malware as benign. These attacks typically insert data at locations that do not affect the program's functionality, such as new sections (Demetrio *et al.*, 2021a), the overlay area (Suciu *et al.*, 2019), the gap between headers and sections (Demetrio *et al.*, 2021b), or the slack space between existing sections (Yuste *et al.*, 2022).
- Graph-based attacks obfuscate the control flow graph and function call graph representations using techniques like control-flow flattening, dummy node insertion, and basic block splitting.

Recently, several studies have attempted to address this vulnerability by developing defenses for byte-based malware detectors (Cf. Section 2.2.2) by adapting adversarial training (Lucas *et al.*, 2023), randomized smoothing (Gibert *et al.*, 2023b; Huang *et al.*, 2023), and (de)randomized smoothing (Gibert *et al.*, 2023a; Saha *et al.*, 2023) to the task of malware detection.

Adversarial training (Lucas *et al.*, 2023) aims to improve a model's robustness by exposing the model to adversarially modified samples during training. In each iteration, adversarial versions of malware binaries are generated and used alongside clean samples, encouraging the model to learn features that are invariant to such manipulations. Although this approach can improve the resistance of the models to simple perturbations, it is computationally expensive, as generating adversarial examples on-the-fly greatly increases the overall training time.

Randomized smoothing (Gibert *et al.*, 2023b; Huang *et al.*, 2023), on the other hand, seeks to improve the robustness of models by introducing controlled randomness. During inference, multiple noisy versions of the input are sampled and classified independently, and the final prediction is obtained by majority voting. This technique can also yield probabilistic robustness certifications, i.e., formal guarantees that small perturbations around an input will not alter the model's predictions. However, these robustness guarantees require a large number of noisy samples, which substantially increases the training time, and can only be established for small perturbation budgets. In real-world scenarios, attackers can perform much larger transformations, such as adding new sections, far beyond the range for which randomized smoothing provides certified protection.

Recent research has also explored (de)randomized smoothing variants (Gibert *et al.*, 2023a; Saha *et al.*, 2023) by splitting the byte sequence into fixed-size chunks of bytes, which are extracted sequentially, classified independently, and then aggregated via majority voting. This approach yields deterministic robustness certificates: given (i) the number of chunks predicted as benign and malicious, and (ii) a bounded perturbation budget (i.e., the size of the adversarial payload), it can certify whether any adversarial modification within that budget could flip the final classification. However, these guarantees are valid under small payload budgets (Gibert *et al.*, 2024). In practice, certification quickly breaks down as the perturbation budget increases. For instance, if an attacker appends or injects a payload comparable to the original binary size, the certified guarantees no longer hold as the payload would alter enough chunks to overturn the majority vote.

With the exception of the aforementioned defenses tailored specifically for byte-based detectors, defenses against adversarial attacks to bypass approaches based on feature engineering and graph representations remain largely unexplored and continues to be an open an pressing research problem.

2.4.4 Impact of Code Obfuscation and Packing

Several studies (Aghakhani *et al.*, 2020; Gibert *et al.*, 2025) have investigated the impact of packing on static, machine learning–based malware detectors, including feature-based, byte-based (end-to-end), and grayscale approaches. Both works concluded that biases in the distribution of packers between benign and malicious samples cause models to associate certain packers with "malicious" behavior and others with "benign" behavior. As a result, detectors tend to classify executables packed with "benign" packers as benign and those packed with "malicious" packers as malicious. This bias significantly increases the risk of false negatives, when malware is packed with a "benign" packer, and false positives, when legitimate software is packed with a "malicious" packer.

Furthermore, training the detectors to detect packers is trivial (99.9% accuracy), showing that packers leave very distinctive patterns or artifacts in the binary (e.g., byte distributions, section layouts), which ML models can recognize effortlessly. Consequently, when packers are unevenly distributed between benign and malicious samples, detectors tend to distinguish packers rather than malicious behavior, leading to misleadingly high accuracy and poor generalization to unseen packers.

Lastly, experiments demonstrate that industry-grade antivirus systems exhibit the same bias as machine learning-based detectors. Evaluations of several anti-malware engines have shown that many of them implicitly equate packing with maliciousness, flagging executables as malware solely based on the presence or type of packer used. For instance, Gibert *et al.* (2025) reported that nearly all benign samples packed with Hyperion[21] or Amber[22] were incorrectly classified as malicious by several well-known anti-virus engines.

---

[21]https://nullsecurity.net/tools/binary.html.
[22]https://github.com/EgeBalci/amber.

2.5 Conclusions

In recent years, machine learning–based malware detection has received significant attention, with research spanning feature-based, byte-based, opcode-based and graph-based approaches. These techniques have shown promise in automating malware classification and improving detection accuracy beyond traditional signature-based systems. However, despite considerable progress, several fundamental challenges continue to limit the reliability and scientific maturity of the field.

A major obstacle is the lack of publicly available and standardized datasets. Most studies rely on self-collected data that cannot be shared due to copyright or licensing restrictions, preventing direct comparison and independent validation of results. This issue is compounded by the frequent absence of released source code or preprocessing pipelines, making reproducibility difficult and slowing cumulative research progress. Without open datasets and reproducible experimental setups, it is nearly impossible to assess whether newly proposed models represent genuine advances or simply reflect dataset-specific biases.

Moreover, current detectors face serious robustness challenges. Machine learning models, especially those trained on static representations, remain vulnerable to adversarial attacks and to code obfuscation techniques, particularly packing, which can drastically alter the binary structure without changing the underlying behavior. These weaknesses highlight that existing models often rely on superficial statistical correlations rather than on deeper semantic understanding of program behavior.

In summary, ML-based malware detection has achieved meaningful progress but remains far from a solved problem. Future work must focus on reproducibility, robustness, and real-world generalization to ensure that machine learning models can evolve into trustworthy and practically deployable defenses against modern malware.

Bibliography

Abou-Assaleh, T., Cercone, N., Keselj, V., and Sweidan, R. (2004). N-gram-based detection of new malicious code, in *Proceedings of the 28th Annual International Computer Software and Applications*

Conference, 2004. COMPSAC 2004., Vol. 2, pp. 41–42 vol.2, doi: 10.1109/CMPSAC.2004.1342667.

Aghakhani, H., Gritti, F., Mecca, F., Lindorfer, M., Ortolani, S., Balzarotti, D., Vigna, G., and Kruegel, C. (2020). When malware is packin'heat; limits of machine learning classifiers based on static analysis features, in *Network and Distributed Systems Security (NDSS) Symposium 2020.*

Ahmadi, M., Ulyanov, D., Semenov, S., Trofimov, M., and Giacinto, G. (2016). Novel feature extraction, selection and fusion for effective malware family classification, in *Proceedings of the Sixth ACM Conference on Data and Application Security and Privacy*, CODASPY '16, ISBN 9781450339353, pp. 183–194, doi:10.1145/2857705.2857713.

Ahmed, I. T., Hammad, B. T., and Jamil, N. (2024). A comparative performance analysis of malware detection algorithms based on various texture features and classifiers, *IEEE Access* **12**, pp. 11500–11519, doi:10.1109/ACCESS.2024.3354959.

Anderson, H. S. and Roth, P. (2018). EMBER: An Open Dataset for Training Static PE Malware Machine Learning Models, *ArXiv e-prints* arXiv:1804.04637 [cs.CR].

Berndt, D. J. and Clifford, J. (1994). Using dynamic time warping to find patterns in time series, in *Proceedings of the 3rd International Conference on Knowledge Discovery and Data Mining*, pp. 359–370.

Bilot, T., El Madhoun, N., Al Agha, K., and Zouaoui, A. (2024). A survey on malware detection with graph representation learning, *ACM Computing Surveys* **56**, 11, doi:10.1145/3664649.

Chaganti, R., Ravi, V., and Pham, T. D. (2022). Image-based malware representation approach with efficientnet convolutional neural networks for effective malware classification, *Journal of Information Security and Applications* **69**, p. 103306, https://doi.org/10.1016/j.jisa.2022.103306.

Chen, Y.-H., Lin, S.-C., Huang, S.-C., Lei, C.-L., and Huang, C.-Y. (2023). Guided malware sample analysis based on graph neural networks, *IEEE Transactions on Information Forensics and Security* **18**, pp. 4128–4143, doi:10.1109/TIFS.2023.3283913.

Coull, S. E. and Gardner, C. (2019). Activation analysis of a byte-based deep neural network for malware classification, in *IEEE Security and Privacy Workshops (SPW).*

Demetrio, L., Biggio, B., Lagorio, G., Roli, F., and Armando, A. (2021a). Functionality-preserving black-box optimization of adversarial windows malware, *IEEE Transactions on Information Forensics and Security* **16**, pp. 3469–3478, doi:10.1109/TIFS.2021.3082330.

Demetrio, L., Coull, S. E., Biggio, B., Lagorio, G., Armando, A., and Roli, F. (2021b). Adversarial exemples: A survey and experimental evaluation of practical attacks on machine learning for windows malware detection, *ACM Transactions on Privacy and Security* **24**, 4, pp. 27:1–27:31, doi:10.1145/3473039.

Ding, S. H. H., Fung, B. C. M., and Charland, P. (2019). Asm2vec: Boosting static representation robustness for binary clone search against code obfuscation and compiler optimization, in *2019 IEEE Symposium on Security and Privacy (SP)*, pp. 472–489, doi:10.1109/SP.2019.00003.

Dosovitskiy, A., Beyer, L., Kolesnikov, A., Weissenborn, D., Zhai, X., Unterthiner, T., Dehghani, M., Minderer, M., Heigold, G., Gelly, S., Uszkoreit, J., and Houlsby, N. (2021). An image is worth 16x16 words: Transformers for image recognition at scale, in *9th International Conference on Learning Representations, ICLR 2021, Virtual Event, Austria, May 3–7, 2021.*

Elhadi, A. A. E., Maarof, M. A., Barry, B. I., and Hamza, H. (2014). Enhancing the detection of metamorphic malware using call graphs, *Computers & Security* **46**, pp. 62–78, https://doi.org/10.1016/j.cose.2014.07.004.

Gibert, D., Béjar, J., Mateu, C., Planes, J., Solis, D., and Vicens, R. (2017). Convolutional neural networks for classification of malware assembly code, in *Recent Advances in Artificial Intelligence Research and Development — Proceedings of the 20th International Conference of the Catalan Association for Artificial Intelligence, Deltebre, Terres de l'Ebre, Spain, October 25–27, 2017, Frontiers in Artificial Intelligence and Applications*, Vol. 300 (IOS Press), pp. 221–226, doi:10.3233/978-1-61499-806-8-221.

Gibert, D., Demetrio, L., Zizzo, G., Le, Q., Planes, J., and Biggio, B. (2024). Certified adversarial robustness of machine learning-based malware detectors via (de)randomized smoothing, ArXiv abs/2405.00392.

Gibert, D., Mateu, C., Planes, J., and Marques-Silva, J. (2021). Auditing static machine learning anti-malware tools against metamorphic attacks, *Computers & Security* **102**, p. 102159.

Gibert, D., Mateu, C., Planes, J., and Vicens, R. (2018). Classification of malware by using structural entropy on convolutional neural networks, in *Proceedings of the Thirty-Second AAAI Conference on Artificial Intelligence, (AAAI-18), the 30th innovative Applications of Artificial Intelligence (IAAI-18), and the 8th AAAI Symposium on Educational Advances in Artificial Intelligence (EAAI-18), New Orleans, Louisiana, USA, February 2–7, 2018* (AAAI Press), pp. 7759–7764.

Gibert, D., Mateu, C., Planes, J., and Vicens, R. (2019). Using convolutional neural networks for classification of malware represented as images, *J. Comput. Virol. Hacking Tech.* **15**, 1, pp. 15–28, doi: 10.1007/S11416-018-0323-0.

Gibert, D., Totosis, N., Patsakis, C., Le, Q., and Zizzo, G. (2025). Assessing the impact of packing on static machine learning-based malware detection and classification systems, *Computers & Security* **156**, p. 104495, https://doi.org/10.1016/j.cose.2025.104495.

Gibert, D., Zizzo, G., and Le, Q. (2023a). Certified robustness of static deep learning-based malware detectors against patch and append attacks, in *Proceedings of the 16th ACM Workshop on Artificial Intelligence and Security*, AISec '23 (Association for Computing Machinery), pp. 173–184, doi:10.1145/3605764.3623914.

Gibert, D., Zizzo, G., Le, Q. (2024). Towards a Practical Defense Against Adversarial Attacks on Deep Learning-Based Malware Detectors via Randomized Smoothing. In: Katsikas, S., *et al.* Computer Security. ESORICS 2023 International Workshops. ESORICS 2023. Lecture Notes in Computer Science, vol. 14399. Springer, Cham. https://doi.org/10.1007/978-3-031-54129-2_40

Goldberg, L. A., Goldberg, P. W., Phillips, C. A., and Sorkin, G. B. (1998). Constructing computer virus phylogenies, *Journal of Algorithms* **26**, 1, pp. 188–208, https://doi.org/10.1006/jagm.1997.0897.

Hamrock, J. and Lyda, R. (2007). Using entropy analysis to find encrypted and packed malware, *IEEE Security & Privacy* **5**, 02, pp. 40–45, doi: 10.1109/MSP.2007.48.

Harang, R. and Rudd, E. M. (2020). Sorel-20m: A large scale benchmark dataset for malicious pe detection, arXiv:2012.07634 [cs.CR].

Hassen, M. and Chan, P. K. (2017). Scalable function call graph-based malware classification, in *Proceedings of the Seventh ACM on Conference on Data and Application Security and Privacy*, pp. 239–248, doi:10.1145/3029806.3029824.

He, K., Zhang, X., Ren, S., and Sun, J. (2016). Deep residual learning for image recognition, in *2016 IEEE Conference on Computer Vision and Pattern Recognition (CVPR)*, pp. 770–778, doi:10.1109/CVPR.2016.90.

Hu, X., Chiueh, T.-c., and Shin, K. G. (2009). Large-scale malware indexing using function-call graphs, in *Proceedings of the 16th ACM Conference on Computer and Communications Security*, pp. 611–620, doi: 10.1145/1653662.1653736.

Huang, Z., Marchant, N., Lucas, K., Bauer, L., Ohrimenko, O., and Rubinstein, B. I. P. (2023). RS-Del: Edit distance robustness certificates for sequence classifiers via randomized deletion, in *Advances in Neural Information Processing Systems*, NeurIPS.

Jain, S. and Meena, Y. K. (2011). Byte level n-gram analysis for malware detection, in *Computer Networks and Intelligent Computing* (Springer, Berlin, Heidelberg), pp. 51–59.

Joyce, R. J., Miller, G., Roth, P., Zak, R., Zaresky-Williams, E., Anderson, H., Raff, E., and Holt, J. (2025). Ember2024 — a benchmark dataset for holistic evaluation of malware classifiers, in *Proceedings of the 31st ACM SIGKDD Conference on Knowledge Discovery and Data Mining*.

Kinable, J. and Kostakis, O. (2011). Malware classification based on call graph clustering, *Journal of Computer Virology* **7**, 4, pp. 233–245.

Kolter, J. Z. and Maloof, M. A. (2004). Learning to detect malicious executables in the wild, in *Proceedings of the Tenth ACM SIGKDD International Conference on Knowledge Discovery and Data Mining*, pp. 470–478, doi:10.1145/1014052.1014105.

Krcál, M., Svec, O., Bálek, M., and Jasek, O. (2018). Deep convolutional malware classifiers can learn from raw executables and labels only, in *6th International Conference on Learning Representations, ICLR*.

Krizhevsky, A., Sutskever, I., and Hinton, G. E. (2012). Imagenet classification with deep convolutional neural networks, in F. Pereira, C. Burges, L. Bottou, and K. Weinberger (eds.), *Advances in Neural Information Processing Systems*, Vol. 25 (Curran Associates, Inc.).

Li, B., Roundy, K., Gates, C., and Vorobeychik, Y. (2017). Large-scale identification of malicious singleton files, in *Proceedings of the Seventh ACM on Conference on Data and Application Security and Privacy*, pp. 227–238, doi:10.1145/3029806.3029815.

Ling, X., Wu, L., Deng, W., Qu, Z., Zhang, J., Zhang, S., Ma, T., Wang, B., Wu, C., and Ji, S. (2022). Malgraph: Hierarchical graph neural networks for robust windows malware detection, in *IEEE INFOCOM 2022 — IEEE Conference on Computer Communications*, pp. 1998–2007, doi:10.1109/INFOCOM48880.2022.9796786.

Liu, Y.-s., Lai, Y.-K., Wang, Z.-H., and Yan, H.-B. (2019). A new learning approach to malware classification using discriminative feature extraction, *IEEE Access* **7**, pp. 13015–13023, doi:10.1109/ACCESS.2019.2892500.

Liu, Z., Lin, Y., Cao, Y., Hu, H., Wei, Y., Zhang, Z., Lin, S., and Guo, B. (2021). Swin transformer: Hierarchical vision transformer using shifted windows, in *Proceedings of the IEEE/CVF International Conference on Computer Vision (ICCV)*.

Lucas, K., Pai, S., Lin, W., Bauer, L., Reiter, M. K., and Sharif, M. (2023). Adversarial training for Raw-Binary malware classifiers, in

32nd USENIX Security Symposium (USENIX Security 23) (USENIX Association, Anaheim, CA), ISBN 978-1-939133-37-3, pp. 1163–1180, https://www.usenix.org/conference/usenixsecurity23/presentation/lucas.

Malhotra, V., Potika, K., and Stamp, M. (2024). A comparison of graph neural networks for malware classification, *Journal of Computer Virology and Hacking Techniques* **20**, doi:10.1007/s11416-023-00493-y.

Massarelli, L., Di Luna, G. A., Petroni, F., Querzoni, L., and Baldoni, R. (2019). Safe: Self-attentive function embeddings for binary similarity, in *Proceedings of 16th Conference on Detection of Intrusions and Malware & Vulnerability Assessment (DIMVA)*.

Microsoft (2018). Microsoft portable executable and common object file format specification, Technical report, Microsoft Corporation, https://learn.microsoft.com/en-us/windows/win32/debug/pe-format.

Mohammadian, H., Higgins, G., Ansong, S., Razavi-Far, R., and Ghorbani, A. A. (2025). Explainable malware detection through integrated graph reduction and learning techniques, *Big Data Research* **41**, p. 100555, https://doi.org/10.1016/j.bdr.2025.100555.

Nataraj, L., Karthikeyan, S., Jacob, G., and Manjunath, B. S. (2011). Malware images: Visualization and automatic classification, in *Proceedings of the 8th International Symposium on Visualization for Cyber Security*, doi:10.1145/2016904.2016908.

Peng, H., Yang, J., Zhao, D., Xu, X., Pu, Y., Han, J., Yang, X., Zhong, M., and Ji, S. (2024). Malgne: Enhancing the performance and efficiency of cfg-based malware detector by graph node embedding in low dimension space, *IEEE Transactions on Information Forensics and Security* **19**, pp. 4881–4896, doi:10.1109/TIFS.2024.3389614.

Raff, E., Barker, J., Sylvester, J., Brandon, R., Catanzaro, B., and Nicholas, C. K. (2018a). Malware detection by eating a whole EXE, in *32nd AAAI Conference on Artificial Intelligence*, pp. 268–276.

Raff, E., Fleming, W., Zak, R., Anderson, H. S., Finlayson, B., Nicholas, C., and McLean, M. (2019). Kilograms: Very large n-grams for malware classification, *CoRR* abs/1908.00200.

Raff, E., Fleshman, W., Zak, R., Anderson, H. S., Filar, B., and McLean, M. (2021). Classifying sequences of extreme length with constant memory applied to malware detection, in *35th AAAI Conference on Artificial Intelligence*, pp. 9386–9394.

Raff, E. and Nicholas, C. (2018). Hash-grams: Faster n-gram features for classification and malware detection, in *Proceedings of the ACM Symposium on Document Engineering 2018*, doi:10.1145/3209280.3229085.

Raff, E., Sylvester, J., and Nicholas, C. (2017). Learning the pe header, malware detection with minimal domain knowledge, in *Proceedings of the 10th ACM Workshop on Artificial Intelligence and Security*, AISec '17 (Association for Computing Machinery), pp. 121–132, doi: 10.1145/3128572.3140442.

Raff, E., Zak, R., Cox, R., Sylvester, J., Yacci, P., Ward, R., Tracy, A., McLean, M., and Nicholas, C. (2018b). An investigation of byte n-gram features for malware classification, *Journal of Computer Virology and Hacking Techniques* **14**, 1, pp. 1–20, doi:10.1007/s11416-016-0283-1.

Reddy, D. K. S. and Pujari, A. K. (2006). N-gram analysis for computer virus detection, *Journal in Computer Virology* **2**, 3, pp. 231–239, doi:10.1007/s11416-006-0027-8, https://doi.org/10.1007/s11416-006-0027-8.

Saha, S., Wang, W., Kaya, Y., Feizi, S., and Dumitras, T. (2023). DRSM: De-randomized smoothing on malware classifier providing certified robustness, arXiv:2303.13372 [cs.CR], https://arxiv.org/abs/2303.13372.

Santos, I., Brezo, F., Ugarte-Pedrero, X., and Bringas, P. G. (2013). Opcode sequences as representation of executables for data-mining-based unknown malware detection, *Information Sciences* **231**, pp. 64–82, https://doi.org/10.1016/j.ins.2011.08.020, data Mining for Information Security.

Saxe, J. and Berlin, K. (2015). Deep neural network based malware detection using two dimensional binary program features, in *2015 10th International Conference on Malicious and Unwanted Software (MALWARE)*, pp. 11–20, doi:10.1109/MALWARE.2015.7413680.

Shabtai, A., Moskovitch, R., Feher, S., Clint ad Dolev, and Elovici, Y. (2012). Detecting unknown malicious code by applying classification techniques on opcode patterns, *Security Informatics* **1**, p. 1, https://doi.org/10.1186/2190-8532-1-1.

Shokouhinejad, H., Razavi-Far, R., Mohammadian, H., Rabbani, M., Ansong, S., Higgins, G., and Ghorbani, A. A. (2025). Recent advances in malware detection: Graph learning and explainability, arXiv:2502.10556 [cs.CR], https://arxiv.org/abs/2502.10556.

Simonyan, K. and Zisserman, A. (2015). Very deep convolutional networks for large-scale image recognition, in *3rd International Conference on Learning Representations, ICLR 2015, San Diego, CA, USA, May 7–9, 2015, Conference Track Proceedings*.

Sorokin, I. (2011). Comparing files using structural entropy, *Journal in Computer Virology* **7**, 4, pp. 259–265, doi:0.1007/s11416-011-0153-9.

Spafford, E. (2014). Is anti-virus really dead? *Computers & Security* **44**, p. iv, https://doi.org/10.1016/S0167-4048(14)00082-0.

Suciu, O., Coull, S. E., and Johns, J. (2019). Exploring adversarial examples in malware detection, in *2019 IEEE Security and Privacy Workshops (SPW)*, pp. 8–14, doi:10.1109/SPW.2019.00015.

Sun, Q., Abdukhamidov, E., Abuhmed, T., and Abuhamad, M. (2022). Leveraging spectral representations of control flow graphs for efficient analysis of windows malware, in *Proceedings of the 2022 ACM on Asia Conference on Computer and Communications Security*, pp. 1240–1242, doi:10.1145/3488932.3527294.

Tan, M. and Le, Q. V. (2019). Efficientnet: Rethinking model scaling for convolutional neural networks, in *Proceedings of the 36th International Conference on Machine Learning, ICML 2019, 9–15 June 2019, Long Beach, California, USA*, *Proceedings of Machine Learning Research*, Vol. 97 (PMLR), pp. 6105–6114, http://proceedings.mlr.press/v97/tan19a.html.

Tang, Y., Qi, X., Jing, J., Liu, C., and Dong, W. (2023). BHMDC: A byte and hex n-gram based malware detection and classification method, *Computers & Security* **128**, p. 103118, https://doi.org/10.1016/j.cose.2023.103118.

Vasan, D., Alazab, M., Wassan, S., Naeem, H., Safaei, B., and Zheng, Q. (2020). IMCFN: Image-based malware classification using fine-tuned convolutional neural network architecture, *Computer Networks* **171**, p. 107138, https://doi.org/10.1016/j.comnet.2020.107138.

Wang, F., Shi, X., Yang, F., Song, R., Li, Q., Tan, Z., and Wang, C. (2024). Malsort: Lightweight and efficient image-based malware classification using masked self-supervised framework with swin transformer, *Journal of Information Security and Applications* **83**, p. 103784, doi: https://doi.org/10.1016/j.jisa.2024.103784.

Wang, W., Wei, F., Dong, L., Bao, H., Yang, N., and Zhou, M. (2020). Minilm: Deep self-attention distillation for task-agnostic compression of pre-trained transformers, *Advances in Neural Information Processing Systems*, **33**, pp. 5776–5788.

Weinberger, K., Dasgupta, A., Langford, J., Smola, A., and Attenberg, J. (2009). Feature hashing for large scale multitask learning, in *Proceedings of the 26th Annual International Conference on Machine Learning*, pp. 1113–1120, doi:10.1145/1553374.1553516.

Yang, L., Ciptadi, A., Laziuk, I., Ahmadzadeh, A., and Wang, G. (2021). Bodmas: An open dataset for learning based temporal analysis of pe malware, in *4th Deep Learning and Security Workshop*.

Yuste, J., Pardo, E. G., and Tapiador, J. (2022). Optimization of code caves in malware binaries to evade machine learning detectors, *Computers & Security* **116**, p. 102643.

Zak, R., Raff, E., and Nicholas, C. (2017). What can *n*-grams learn for malware detection? in *2017 12th International Conference on Malicious and Unwanted Software (MALWARE)*, pp. 109–118, doi: 10.1109/MALWARE.2017.8323963.

Zhang, Y., Chang, X., Lin, Y., Mišić, J., and Mišić, V. B. (2020). Exploring function call graph vectorization and file statistical features in malicious pe file classification, *IEEE Access* **8**, pp. 44652–44660, doi: 10.1109/ACCESS.2020.2978335.

Zhao, H., Wu, Y., Zou, D., Liu, Y., and Jin, H. (2024). Malsensor: Fast and robust windows malware classification, *ACM Transactions on Software Engineering and Methodology* **34**, 1, doi:10.1145/3688833.

https://doi.org/10.1142/9789811262043_0003

Chapter 3

Dynamic Malware Analysis

Erick Galinkin
Drexel University, Philadelphia, PA, USA

3.1 Introduction

The use of artificial intelligence for malware analysis dates back quite far, as many early antivirus systems were, and some still are, *expert systems*. These expert systems consist of a series of `if-then` rules that by and large were written by human malware analysts and security professionals, and range from fairly primitive hash checks to sophisticated inspection of sequences of opcodes in a particular portable executable (PE) file. As malware has continued to grow in sophistication and become more diverse, these hand-crafted rules become increasingly difficult to generate and require instead the use of machine learning for development.

In the course of malware analysis, there are two overarching categories of techniques: *static analysis* and *dynamic analysis*. Static analysis concerns itself with inspection of a potentially malicious file without executing the file, via the use of a disassembler or some other analytic tool. In this chapter, we concern ourselves with dynamic analysis: the process of analyzing a file or files by executing the code and collecting runtime behaviors or post-run artifacts.

Dynamic analysis offers a number of benefits, but also has some important caveats associated with it. One key benefit of dynamic analysis is that it allows one to see exactly what a piece of malicious code does when executed, something that can be challenging when examining things like control flow graphs. On the other hand, dynamic analysis cannot in general explore all possible execution paths in a piece of code, a key benefit of static analysis. Dynamic analysis is also beneficial for dealing with samples at scale, since the execution and collection of artifacts can be automated in a sandbox or virtual machine. Furthermore, since much modern malicious code makes some use of network connectivity, dynamic analysis allows for the collection of network data, which static analysis will often be unable to do. On the other hand, dynamic analysis must grapple with anti-analysis techniques such as: anti-debugger protections; probing for CPU flags; checking for the presence of a virtual machine system; using non-OS APIs; and asynchronous execution (Afianian *et al.*, 2019; Olaimat *et al.*, 2021). In addition, in some cases, command and control servers may not be reachable or operational and must therefore be simulated.

One important note: while debugging is, strictly speaking, a dynamic analysis technique, we do not discuss interactive debugging here as it rarely lends itself well to the kind of scale necessary for machine learning techniques. There are, certainly, applications of machine learning and artificial intelligence within the space of debugging that could assist in the analysis of potentially malicious code; however, that sort of application is beyond the scope of this chapter. Furthermore, much of the malware analysis literature has focused on the Microsoft Windows operating system due to its prevalence in personal and professional computing settings. While the majority of techniques mentioned in this chapter are relevant to executable files across operating systems, some standard terminology is derived from its name in Windows.

3.2 Data Collection

In this section, we discuss how data for dynamic malware analysis can be collected. We begin by discussing setups for executing potentially malicious code and some potential steps for overcoming anti-analysis techniques. We then discuss the collection of system data and network data and how they differ.

3.2.1 Setups

In general, dynamic analysis is conducted in a *sandbox*: a virtual machine equipped with tooling to monitor system and API calls, collect network data, and snapshot changes in the environment. Data collection, whether at the network or system level, mandates a fully virtualized (Greamo and Ghosh, 2011) environment since we are, in general, executing code that is either known or suspected to be malicious. Consequently, sandboxing is crucial for preventing potentially damaging side effects to the host operating system, providing a layer of protection from malicious code. During execution, sandboxes will collect system and network data generated during execution of the submitted code. While much of malware analysis—and consequently, sandboxing—is focused on Microsoft Windows systems, sandboxes exist in browser environments, containers, and other systems. A number of commercial and non-commercial sandbox offerings exist, and are easily found via your preferred search engine.

3.2.2 Overcoming Anti-Analysis

Anti-emulation and anti-virtualization techniques (Chen *et al.*, 2008, 2016; Kang *et al.*, 2009) that may impact dynamic analysis tend to fall into three broad categories:

(1) **Interaction-based:** Checking for common human interactions, e.g., mouse movement during execution
(2) **Artifact-based:** Checking for the presence of processes, registry keys, virtual devices, or CPU instructions that indicate an emulated or virtualized environment
(3) **Timing-based:** Timing techniques check whether an operation takes longer than expected to execute or, alternatively, since many sandbox environments only permit fixed-length run times, the code may sleep for a period of time before beginning to execute.

Modern attacks, even those conducted by non-state actors, may be quite sophisticated compared to attacks in the past. Even so-called "commodity malware", widely available for purchase on hacking forums and chats, tend to incorporate anti-analysis mechanisms like anti-debugging and anti-reverse engineering; anti-emulation; anti-virtualization; and anti-sandbox (Sharma *et al.*, 2022).

When building a data collection system, it is important to ensure that your system is incorporating these sorts of anti-anti-analysis methods. Fortunately, many commercial and some non-commercial sandbox offerings have anti-anti-analysis methods built-in.

3.3 System Data

System data is collected from the code's interactions with the system itself and is divided into two broad categories: post-run comparative analysis and runtime behavior analysis. The data collected from these two approaches differ, though they can often be reconciled with ease. Comparative analysis offers the benefit of simplicity, as it simply takes a snapshot of the virtual machine image following a run and compares it with the "clean" virtual machine image, reporting all of the artifacts, e.g., registry keys, files, or permissions that were created, deleted, or modified between the two. Runtime behavior analysis, by contrast, offers a much more granular view of code execution including API calls, file accesses, and so on. While runtime behavior analysis does generate significantly more data, it can be challenging to make use of it all in machine learning applications, which we discuss in more depth in Sections 3.6 and 3.7.

3.3.1 Comparative Analysis

Comparative analysis follows a straightforward workflow:

(1) Begin with a "clean" virtual machine image upon which no malicious code has been executed
(2) Load and execute the potentially malicious file
(3) Take a snapshot of the post-execution environment
(4) Compare the pre-execution and post-execution environments

This exercise, assuming that the code executed properly, will often yield a number of artifacts:

File system artifacts consist of files (or directories) created, modified, or deleted by the code under analysis. In some cases, these artifacts include "dropped files" which are *second-stage payloads* that merit further analysis. In other cases, for example, ransomware, file system artifacts consist of the changes to, e.g., the encryption of, other files on disk. Some types of malware will also delete files in order to disable certain utilities, to create a denial of service condition, or to cover their tracks by deleting log files.

Registry artifacts are changes to the Windows Registry (a database of configurations and settings in Microsoft Windows) made by the executed code. In Linux systems, similar attributes are contained in a number of configuration files; and in MacOS, each application has a `.plist` file with the relevant attributes. Modifications to the registry or registry-equivalents are often excellent places to check for potential artifacts of maliciousness. For example, many malicious applications, e.g., backdoors, will modify a certain registry key[1] to cause their code to be launched when the user logs on, thus gaining persistence.

Mutex artifacts are primitive system objects that control simultaneous access to system resources. Malicious software will create named mutexes to detect if a system has already been infected. The creation of mutexes by malware may be specific to that malware or may be random (Kaur and Bindal, 2016) and so detection of known-bad or high-entropy mutexes provide another artifact for malware detection.

3.3.2 Runtime Behavior Analysis

Runtime behavior analysis, from the standpoint of the end-user, looks quite similar to comparative analysis. However, instead of generating artifacts from the comparison of snapshots, runtime behavior analysis traces user-level and kernel-level execution by monitoring instructions in the sandbox's memory (Mahmoud *et al.*, 2024). These execution events may include:

- Process creation and termination
- File creation, modification, and deletion
- Driver/image loading
- API calls
- Raw disk access

[1]`HKEY_CURRENT_USER\Software\Microsoft\Windows\CurrentVersion\Run`.

- Registry entry creation, modification, and deletion
- Named pipe creation, use, and deletion
- Network connections

On Windows machines, it is common to use the Sysmon[2] utility for host-level event collection. Each of these events will have an associated timestamp, event type and code, and a log of the system events associated with that event. It is also common for hashes, e.g., MD5, SHA256 of the file under analysis to be collected.

Each of the system event types listed above offer potential for detection of malware activity. For example, tracking process creation and termination provides a forensic accounting of the invocation and termination of particular processes and subprocesses. Some malicious code uses *process injection*, a technique to evade process-based defenses on victim systems where malicious code is injected into an otherwise benign process, often one created by the malicious code. Some methods of malware detection (Matsuda *et al.*, 2020) depend on dynamic linked libraries (DLLs) commonly loaded by malicious applications. Such behavior necessitates runtime behavior analysis and is not uncovered by comparative analysis. API calls offer particular insight into an executable's potential for malicious behavior, indicating system services used by the file under analysis such as networking or encryption. Named pipes can be used for inter-process communication, often with processes that have been launched by the malicious code using process injection.

While detailed network packet data is not itself always collected on the system, the importation of networking libraries, DNS lookups, and attempted network communications can all be captured on-system. These events provide useful artifacts for the detection of anti-analysis techniques and indications of potential command and control (C2) channels for the file under analysis. We discuss the collection of network data in more detail in Section 3.4.

3.4 Network Data

Network data collected from files under investigation generally comes in three forms: packet captures, HTTP archives, and NetFlow. Packet

[2]https://learn.microsoft.com/en-us/sysinternals/downloads/sysmon.

captures collect the totality of network traffic entering or generated from a sandbox. While this collection provides a complete view of network activity, network traffic can be quite complex, with potentially important correlations having no natural, direct relationships within network streams, e.g., a DNS request that resolves a command and control domain used in a subsequent HTTP stream. Although there are many types of malware command and control channels, HTTP remains a favorite among malware actors. HTTP archive files capture all HTTP sessions and streams, and are therefore artifacts that may contain potentially malicious network data. NetFlow collects network traffic as it enters or exits an interface, describing the overall direction and type of traffic, though it does not contain any information about what is contained within the flow.

3.4.1 Packet Capture

Packet capture files (pcaps) are a file type that stores data about network packets. The pcap Next Generation, pcapng, often still simply referred to as pcap, is a file format specification developed by the Internet Engineering Task Force (IETF) (Tüxen *et al.*, 2023). This pcapng format consists of an array of octets with a fixed length file header and one or more variable length packet records, and has been widely adopted. There are many other capture formats, but pcaps are most common and and enjoy the most support by commercial and open-source tools.

Network packets are a rich source of data, allowing for not only the recreation of network connections and streams, but also files sent over network streams. The field of network forensics engages in packet analysis and so-called "network carving" of files from these packet captures. While streams are timestamped, there can be numerous network requests generated by systems during analysis, including normal address resolution protocol (ARP) and server message block (SMB) requests generated by the operating system itself. Identifying potentially malicious traffic streams is critical for malicious software detection, and these analysis results can sometimes be frustrated by the "ambient noise" generated by the operating system.

Another potential source of trouble in packet analysis is encryption. There is a body of work on encrypted packet analysis (Kim *et al.*, 2020; Papadogiannaki and Ioannidis, 2021; Shen *et al.*, 2022) but that topic is beyond the scope of this chapter. To overcome the challenges posed by encrypted network traffic, many intrusion detection and intrusion prevention systems (IDS/IPS) implement full SSL inspection, where the IDS/IPS impersonates the recipient of the encrypted session, decrypts and inspects the packets, re-encrypts the content, and creates a new session between the IDS/IPS and the recipient, impersonating the sender. This is, in essence, a "man in the middle" (MITM) attack. By implementing full SSL inspection, we can collect the unencrypted network traffic of a system, something frequently seen in sandboxes, and as a result, we can take advantage of the information provided by deep packet inspection. For interested readers, Sikos (2020) offers a detailed survey of network packet analysis.

3.4.2 HTTP Archive

HTTP archive (HAR) files are JSON-formatted files for logging HTTP transactions. These archives are often used to troubleshoot web browsers and track website performance, but can also be used to capture HTTP sessions created by potentially malicious files. Since many malware families use HTTP for their command and control, HAR files often contain the majority of traffic that is likely to be of interest. In addition, since HAR files are JSON-formatted, they lend themselves well to common data storage, cleaning, and analysis practices.

3.4.3 NetFlow

NetFlow is a feature, initially introduced on Cisco routers, that now is supported by many brands of routers and network devices. The NetFlow specification, IETF RFC 3954 (Claise, 2004), is a template-based format that reports a "flow" as a unidirectional sequence of packets comprised of the number of packets in the flow, a timestamp, and seven values that uniquely identify the flow:

(1) Ingress interface
(2) Source IP address
(3) Destination IP address
(4) IP protocol number
(5) Source port for UDP or TCP (0 for non-UDP, non-TCP protocols)

(6) Destination port for UDP or TCP or type and code for ICMP (0 for other protocols)
(7) IP Type of Service

The two most widely used NetFlow versions are 5 and 9. When using NetFlow data, it is important to ensure that your records are all compatible. So version 9 is recommended, as version 9 is backwards-compatible and can include all of the version 5 fields, plus additional information such as IPv6 addresses and ports. In security applications, the source and destination IP addresses and ports are generally most important, as the overwhelming majority of malicious network traffic is conducted over TCP. Some malicious software is known for connecting to command and control, also known as "beaconing", on particular ports, providing a potential fingerprint of malicious activity.

3.5 Synthetic Data

While NetFlow and pcap data are widely used in cybersecurity, labeled datasets are quite rare due to a confluence of privacy concerns and the complexity of labeling real world network traffic data (Ring *et al.*, 2019). As a result, a number of approaches for generating synthetic network data have been proposed, with Generative Adversarial Networks (GANs) being one popular choice. In some applications, synthetically generated data seems to provide improved detection capabilities (Carter *et al.*, 2024b; Lu and Li, 2019). However, evaluating the quality of GAN-based data generators remains a significant problem, even in mature domains like image generation (Borji, 2019). (Wolf *et al.*, 2024) provide a standardized evaluation setup for NetFlow data, arguably the simplest network data format available. They conclude that NetFlow data generated by GANs and GPT-2 cannot be regarded as ideal proxy data for the original training data due to the data produced behaving substantially different from target data in domain-specific applications. Moreover, some work (Shumailov *et al.*, 2023) has shown that training on generated data can cause forgetting in models, analogously to the phenomenon of mode collapse in GANs (Thanh-Tung and Tran, 2020). Given these contradictory findings, a good rule of thumb with synthetic data is to use it sparingly if and when necessary.

3.6 Malware Detection

Malware detection is the task of determining whether a given file is malicious. Despite the fact that Fred Cohen (1987) demonstrated that this is, in a formal way, undecidable, the field of information security has dedicated a substantial amount of effort to the topic, from signature-based and heuristic detections to machine-learning systems. At the end of the day, malware detection is a familiar binary classification problem and as a consequence, many familiar algorithms, from the simplest statistical tests to large language models, have been used for this task to varying degrees of success. Though some efforts have been made to marry network and system data in making decisions about potentially malicious files, this approach remains largely open as it can be difficult to map network activity directly back to their spawned processes. Even so, in an analysis of the GandCrab malware (Usharani *et al.*, 2021) dynamic analysis features from on-system and network were combined to produce good ransomware detection rates on data sourced from real world exploit kits and ransomware samples. In the interest of clarity, we discuss malware detection with system data (Section 3.6.1) and network data (Section 3.6.2) independently.

3.6.1 Malware Detection with System Data

There are a number of ways to structure the data collected on-system, and the structure of that data informs what approaches will be most effective. The different approaches to collection and types of data are outlined in Section 3.3. Once collected, the data collected on system is often structured in one of three ways depending on the data collected:

(1) **Table:** General purpose
(2) **Graph:** Process call graphs, System call graphs
(3) **Sequence:** System calls, Registry operations, any temporal data

There is some overlap in how these data can be represented, as for example in Carter *et al.* (2024a), system call sequences are temporal data in a sequence. These sequences are subsequently converted to a vector using Sys2Vec embeddings that train a large language model-based classifier. However, one could instead place the sequence of system calls in a tabular data structure. In this case, one might want to use a different family of classifier, such as a decision tree, given the relatively weak performance of neural network architectures on tabular data (Borisov *et al.*, 2022).

We can compare an approach like this with that taken in Martignoni *et al.* (2008) where a hierarchical graph of behaviors is constructed from process execution logs and used to classify whether the target of analysis was malicious. The difference in data structure directly informed the detection algorithm even though the underlying problem is functionally identical and both studies had the opportunity to collect the same data.

3.6.2 Malware Detection with Network Data

As mentioned in Section 3.4, network data is often collected in the form of packet captures, but frequently, one will perform feature extraction on these to extract information like domain names, IP addresses, and other potential indicators of compromise. For example, in Nari and Ghorbani (2013), the unprocessed features consisted of behavior graphs for network flows. These network flow graphs were then processed into more useful features for the tree-based classifier. Similarly, in Alsabilah and Rawat (2023), Internet of Things (IoT) network flow data is processed with the use of rough set theory to extract features for an XGBoost classifier.

Aside from feature extraction techniques, many malware specimens use encrypted network traffic to communicate. If we cannot get unencrypted communications or we wish to detect on encrypted communication, approaches using TLS flows ala Anderson *et al.* (2018) are extremely promising. By using network flow data and cryptographic metadata like advertised and selected cipher suites, certificate validity, TLS extensions, subject alternative name (SAN) entries, and the client's public key length, we avoid the complications associated with deep packet analysis and instead categorize the difference between "typical" benign and malicious encrypted flows.

One place where artificial intelligence and machine learning techniques have been especially promising is in detecting malicious domains generated by domain generation algorithms. A variety of approaches to this task have been tried, with some of the successful approaches being as different as n-gram analysis (Mu, 2022) and convolutional neural networks (Wang *et al.*, 2021). Fortunately for researchers, this task lends itself well to the generation of synthetic data for training as seen in the DeepDGA paper (Anderson *et al.*, 2016) where autoencoders and GANs both prove effective at generating and detecting domains.

3.7 Malware Classification

While malware detection is concerned with the relatively simple task of binary classification, whether malware is present or not, malware classification concerns itself with the type or "family" of a piece of malicious code. With respect to type, there are a number of taxonomies in use (Grégio *et al.*, 2015; Maniriho *et al.*, 2022; Rutkowska, 2006), and malware families, e.g., Emotet, LockBit, and Jupyter Infostealer, are even more granular. Given the interest in categorizing and classifying malware, researchers have proposed to use machine learning models for the task.

A key difference between malware classification tasks and, for example, image classification tasks for which similar models may be used, is that in the real world, the approximate distribution of a class is fixed. That is, in image classification, a cat is a cat and will continue to be a cat. By contrast, in malware classification, there is an adversary who is constantly and deliberately working to evade our ability to classify their activities. Indeed, attacker knowledge that artificial intelligence and machine learning techniques are being used to detect malware has led to so-called adversarial examples and systems designed to defend against such examples (Demetrio *et al.*, 2021; Grosse *et al.*, 2017; Maniriho *et al.*, 2022; Park and Yener, 2020). Consequently, such systems have to be designed for *robustness* to these adversarial techniques and to account for similarities and potential overlap in malware taxonomies.

Malware families generally differ in terms of the objectives of the malicious code, e.g., backdoor, infostealer, cryptominer, ransomware; and the ways they seek to achieve these objectives. One approach to categorization is the use of API call analysis (Walker and Sengupta, 2020) which provides insight into what sorts of activities the malware is performing. As mentioned with the analysis of the GandCrab ransomware (Usharani *et al.*, 2021), this call analysis can be combined with network features to provide a richer picture and allow for malware to be classified into families. Ultimately, the techniques for detection described in Section 3.6 are all effective methods for malware family classification but the broader domain of the problem makes the problem more challenging. In particular, researchers must: choose the number of classes, perform feature extraction, and appropriately label samples with their classification—often using commercial antivirus engines.

Bibliography

Afianian, A., Niksefat, S., Sadeghiyan, B., and Baptiste, D. (2019). Malware dynamic analysis evasion techniques: A survey, *ACM Computing Surveys (CSUR)* **52**, 6, pp. 1–28.

Alsabilah, N. and Rawat, D. B. (2023). An adaptive flow-based NIDS for smart home networks against malware behavior using xgboost combined with rough set theory, in *2023 10th International Conference on Internet of Things: Systems, Management and Security (IOTSMS)* (IEEE), pp. 15–22.

Anderson, B., Paul, S., and McGrew, D. (2018). Deciphering malware's use of TLS (without decryption), *Journal of Computer Virology and Hacking Techniques* **14**, pp. 195–211.

Anderson, H. S., Woodbridge, J., and Filar, B. (2016). DeepDGA: Adversarially-tuned domain generation and detection, in *Proceedings of the 2016 ACM Workshop on Artificial Intelligence and Security*, pp. 13–21.

Borisov, V., Leemann, T., Seßler, K., Haug, J., Pawelczyk, M., and Kasneci, G. (2022). Deep neural networks and tabular data: A survey, *IEEE Transactions on Neural Networks and Learning Systems*.

Borji, A. (2019). Pros and cons of GAN evaluation measures, *Computer Vision and Image Understanding* **179**, pp. 41–65.

Carter, J., Mancoridis, S., Protopapas, P., and Galinkin, E. (2024a). Behavioral malware detection using a language model classifier trained on sys2vec embeddings. *HICSS*, pp. 7582–7591.

Carter, J., Mancoridis, S., Protopapas, P., and Galinkin, E. (2024b). IoT malware data augmentation using a generative adversarial network. *HICSS*, pp. 7572–7581.

Chen, X., Andersen, J., Mao, Z. M., Bailey, M., and Nazario, J. (2008). Towards an understanding of anti-virtualization and anti-debugging behavior in modern malware, in *2008 IEEE International Conference on Dependable Systems and Networks with FTCS and DCC (DSN)* (IEEE), pp. 177–186.

Chen, P., Huygens, C., Desmet, L., and Joosen, W. (2016). Advanced or not? A comparative study of the use of anti-debugging and anti-VM techniques in generic and targeted malware, in *ICT Systems Security and Privacy Protection: 31st IFIP TC 11 International Conference, SEC 2016, Ghent, Belgium, May 30–June 1, 2016, Proceedings 31* (Springer International Publishing, Switzerland), pp. 323–336.

Claise, B. (2004). Cisco Systems NetFlow Services Export Version 9, RFC 3954, doi:10.17487/RFC3954, https://www.rfc-editor.org/info/rfc3954.

Cohen, F. (1987). Computer viruses: Theory and experiments, *Computers & Security* **6**, 1, pp. 22–35.

Demetrio, L., Coull, S. E., Biggio, B., Lagorio, G., Armando, A., and Roli, F. (2021). Adversarial exemples: A survey and experimental evaluation of practical attacks on machine learning for Windows malware detection, *ACM Transactions on Privacy and Security (TOPS)* **24**, 4, pp. 1–31.

Greamo, C. and Ghosh, A. (2011). Sandboxing and virtualization: Modern tools for combating malware, *IEEE Security & Privacy* **9**, 2, pp. 79–82.

Grégio, A. R. A., Afonso, V. M., Filho, D. S. F., Geus, P. L. d., and Jino, M. (2015). Toward a taxonomy of malware behaviors, *The Computer Journal* **58**, 10, pp. 2758–2777.

Grosse, K., Papernot, N., Manoharan, P., Backes, M., and McDaniel, P. (2017). Adversarial examples for malware detection, in S. N. Foley, D. Gollmann, and E. Snekkenes (eds.), *Computer Security — ESORICS 2017* (Springer International Publishing, Cham), pp. 62–79.

Kang, M. G., Yin, H., Hanna, S., McCamant, S., and Song, D. (2009). Emulating emulation-resistant malware, in *Proceedings of the 1st ACM Workshop on Virtual Machine Security*, pp. 11–22.

Kaur, N. and Bindal, A. K. (2016). A complete dynamic malware analysis, *International Journal of Computer Applications* **135**, 4, pp. 20–25.

Kim, S.-Y., Yun, S.-W., Lee, E.-Y., Bae, S.-H., and Lee, I.-G. (2020). Fast packet inspection for end-to-end encryption, *Electronics* **9**, 11, p. 1937.

Lu, Y. and Li, J. (2019). Generative adversarial network for improving deep learning based malware classification, in *2019 Winter Simulation Conference (WSC)* (IEEE), pp. 584–593.

Mahmoud, R.-V., Anagnostopoulos, M., Pastrana, S., and Pedersen, J. M. (2024). Redefining malware sandboxing: Enhancing analysis through Sysmon and ELK integration, *IEEE Access* **12**.

Maniriho, P., Mahmood, A. N., and Chowdhury, M. J. M. (2022). A study on malicious software behaviour analysis and detection techniques: Taxonomy, current trends and challenges, *Future Generation Computer Systems* **130**, pp. 1–18.

Martignoni, L., Stinson, E., Fredrikson, M., Jha, S., and Mitchell, J. C. (2008). A layered architecture for detecting malicious behaviors, in *Recent Advances in Intrusion Detection: 11th International Symposium, RAID 2008* (Springer, Berlin, Heidelberg), pp. 78–97.

Matsuda, W., Fujimoto, M., and Mitsunaga, T. (2020). Detection of malicious tools by monitoring DLL using deep learning, *Journal of Information Processing* **28**, pp. 1052–1064.

Mu, Z. (2022). Predicting domain generation algorithms with n-gram models, in *2022 International Conference on Big Data, Information and Computer Network (BDICN)* (IEEE), pp. 31–38.

Nari, S. and Ghorbani, A. A. (2013). Automated malware classification based on network behavior, in *2013 International Conference on Computing, Networking and Communications (ICNC)* (IEEE), pp. 642–647.

Olaimat, M. N., Maarof, M. A., and Al-rimy, B. A. S. (2021). Ransomware anti-analysis and evasion techniques: A survey and research directions, in *2021 3rd International Cyber Resilience Conference (CRC)* (IEEE), pp. 1–6.

Papadogiannaki, E. and Ioannidis, S. (2021). A survey on encrypted network traffic analysis applications, techniques, and countermeasures, *ACM Computing Surveys (CSUR)* **54**, 6, pp. 1–35.

Park, D. and Yener, B. (2020). A survey on practical adversarial examples for malware classifiers, in *Reversing and Offensive-oriented Trends Symposium*, pp. 23–35.

Ring, M., Wunderlich, S., Scheuring, D., Landes, D., and Hotho, A. (2019). A survey of network-based intrusion detection data sets, *Computers & Security* **86**, pp. 147–167, https://doi.org/10.1016/j.cose.2019.06.005, https://www.sciencedirect.com/science/article/pii/S016740481930118X.

Rutkowska, J. (2006). Introducing stealth malware taxonomy, Tech. rep., COSEINC Advanced Malware Labs.

Sharma, A., Gupta, B. B., Singh, A. K., and Saraswat, V. (2022). Orchestration of APT malware evasive manoeuvers employed for eluding anti-virus and sandbox defense, *Computers & Security* **115**, p. 102627.

Shen, M., Ye, K., Liu, X., Zhu, L., Kang, J., Yu, S., Li, Q., and Xu, K. (2022). Machine learning-powered encrypted network traffic analysis: A comprehensive survey, *IEEE Communications Surveys & Tutorials* **25**, 1, pp. 791–824.

Shumailov, I., Shumaylov, Z., Zhao, Y., Gal, Y., Papernot, N., and Anderson, R. (2023). The curse of recursion: Training on generated data makes models forget, *arXiv preprint arXiv:2305.17493*.

Sikos, L. F. (2020). Packet analysis for network forensics: A comprehensive survey, *Forensic Science International: Digital Investigation* **32**, p. 200892.

Thanh-Tung, H. and Tran, T. (2020). Catastrophic forgetting and mode collapse in GANs, in *2020 International Joint Conference on Neural Networks (ijcnn)* (IEEE), pp. 1–10.

Tüxen, M., Risso, F., Bongertz, J., Combs, G., Harris, G., Chaudron, E., and Richardson, M. (2026). PCAP Now Generic (pcapng) Capture File Format, Internet-Draft draft-ietf-opsawg-pcapng-05, Internet Engineering Task Force, https://datatracker.ietf.org/doc/draft-ietf-opsawg-pcapng/05/, work in Progress.

Usharani, S., Bala, P. M., and Mary, M. M. J. (2021). Dynamic analysis on crypto-ransomware by using machine learning: Gandcrab ransomware, in *Journal of Physics: Conference Series*, Vol. 1717 (IOP Publishing, Bristol, UK), p. 012024.

Walker, A. and Sengupta, S. (2020). Malware family fingerprinting through behavioral analysis, in *2020 IEEE International Conference on Intelligence and Security Informatics (ISI)* (IEEE), pp. 1–5.

Wang, Z., Ren, X., Li, S., Wang, B., Zhang, J., and Yang, T. (2021). A malicious URL detection model based on convolutional neural network, *Security and Communication Networks* **2021**, 1, p. 5518528.

Wolf, M., Tritscher, J., Landes, D., Hotho, A., and Schlör, D. (2024). Benchmarking of synthetic network data: Reviewing challenges and approaches, *Computers & Security*, p. 103993.

https://doi.org/10.1142/9789811262043_0004

Chapter 4

Multimodal Techniques for Malware Classification

Jonathan Jiang and Mark Stamp
San Jose State University, USA

The threat of malware is a serious concern for computer networks and systems, highlighting the need for accurate classification techniques. In this research, we experiment with multimodal machine learning approaches for malware classification, based on the structured nature of the Windows Portable Executable (PE) file format. Specifically, we train Support Vector Machine (SVM), Long Short-Term Memory (LSTM), and Convolutional Neural Network (CNN) models on features extracted from PE headers. Next, we train these same models on features extracted from the other sections of PE files, and train each model on features extracted from the entire PE file. We then train SVM models on each of the nine header-section combinations of these baseline models, using the output layer probabilities of the component models as feature vectors. We compare the baseline cases to these multimodal combinations. In our experiments, we find that the best of the multimodal models outperforms the best of the baseline cases, indicating that it can be advantageous to train separate models on distinct parts of Windows PE files.

4.1 Introduction

Rapid development in technology has changed the way humans use and acquire knowledge and interact with society, leading to an increased reliance on personal computers and smart devices. In recent decades, valuable information has become available on the Internet and on personal computers, and such data is a natural target for cybercriminals (Alenezi *et al.*, 2020). Cybercrime and malware go hand-in-hand, and hence malware detection and classification are vital concerns in cybersecurity.

Windows Portable Executable (PE) files are among the most common victims of malware attacks. Due to their popularity, malware creators often choose to attack PE file formats (Katkar, 2006).

Traditional signature-based detection methods are fast, efficient, and accurate for known threats. However, due to their dependency on predefined patterns or signatures of known malware, they lack adaptability and are vulnerable to evasion techniques. Malware that can change its code structure while maintaining malicious functionality can easily escape from the signature-based antivirus scanning (Gibert, 2025). As a result, machine learning and deep learning techniques have become mainstays in the malware detection field.

In this research, we apply machine learning techniques to the problem of Windows PE malware classification using a multimodal approach. In this context, multimodal means that we apply machine learning techniques that combine multiple types of data, with the goal of improving the accuracy of the system. Specifically, in this work, we train learning models on different parts of PE files, then train another machine learning model with the probability vectors of the component models serving as features. While copious previous research has trained a wide variety learning models on a wide range of features, such as byte sequences, opcode sequences, API calls, various graph structures, features derived from code analysis, metadata, and so on, there is relatively little research that attempts to directly utilize the structure inherent in PE files (Lee *et al.*, 2023; Wang, 2022; Yuan *et al.*, 2020).

This research expands upon traditional methods by focusing on the structural characteristics of PE files, which are composed of headers and various additional sections, hereafter referred to as simply as sections. We extract features from PE headers and from the

PE sections. Then we train models just using the header-based features, we train models just using the sections-based features, and we train models using features from both the header and sections, i.e., the entire PE file. We then train multimodal learning models using the output of the header and section models as the feature vectors. In this context, the output of a model refers to the probability vector generated by the output layer of the model. We then compare the results of these different cases, namely header-based models, section-based models, models trained on the entire PE file, and multimodal models trained on the output of header and sections-based models. Note that in the multimodal cases, the training of the header-based model and the sections-based model can be viewed as a feature engineering step, with the output of these models yielding additional features that may be more informative, as compared to the original features used to train the component models.

For the header-based, sections-based models, and the models trained on the entire PE file, we experiment with Support Vector Machines (SVM), Long Short-Term Memory (LSTM) models, and Convolutional Neural Networks (CNN). For the multimodal models, we use SVMs to combine the output of the header-based and sections-based models.

The remainder of this chapter is organized as follows. Section 4.2 introduces relevant background topics, including an overview of the PE file format and the learning models employed in our experiments. In Section 4.3, we discuss representative examples of relevant related work. Section 4.4 presents our experiment, including dataset preparation, feature extraction, model design, hyperparameter tuning, and so on. In this section, we also compare and analyze our results. Section 4.5 summarizes the key findings of this research and provides some suggestions for further work.

4.2 Background

The Portable Executable (PE) file format is the standard for Windows executables. Due to their ubiquity, PE files are the predominant target for malware creators. According to a 2020 report from Kaspersky, nearly 90% of all malware detected daily occurred in

PE files.[1] Given the frequency of this format in malware attacks, understanding the structure and functionality of PE files may be advantageous for malware analysis. Furthermore, a deep understanding of PE file structure facilitates the extraction of useful features for machine learning-based malware detection. Next, we provide an overview of the PE file format, which is followed by an introduction to the three types of machine learning models considered in this research.

4.2.1 Overview of the PE File Format

The PE file format is derived from the Microsoft Common Object File Format (COFF). It is a highly modular and structured file format that ensures portability and compatibility on various Windows platforms (Bridge *et al.*, 2025). Compared to a single contiguous memory-mapped file, PE files utilize header information that provides detailed instructions to the Windows dynamic linker, enabling it to load code, including required libraries, into designated memory locations with the appropriate permissions. This approach is designed to ensure performance and safety during execution. Common PE format executable extensions include `.exe`, `.dll`, `.scr`, and `.sys`. While all of these file types adhere to the PE structure, each type includes unique metadata or characteristics to support their specific use cases (Daulaguphu, 2022).

An example layout of the Windows PE file is shown in Figure 4.1. Note that the PE file includes the DOS Header, DOS Stub, PE File Header (aka NT header), Section Table, and Sections. Next, we briefly discuss each of these components of a PE file.

DOS Header: The DOS Header is the first data structure in a PE file. It provides backward compatibility with MS-DOS applications, which were applications designed to run in the Microsoft Disk Operating System (MS-DOS) environment introduced in the early 1980s. The DOS Header occupies the first 64 bytes of the file, followed by a DOS stub program that outputs a message `"This program cannot be run in`

[1] https://www.kaspersky.com/about/press-releases/the-number-of-new-malicious-files-detected-every-day-increases-by-52-to-360000-in-2020.

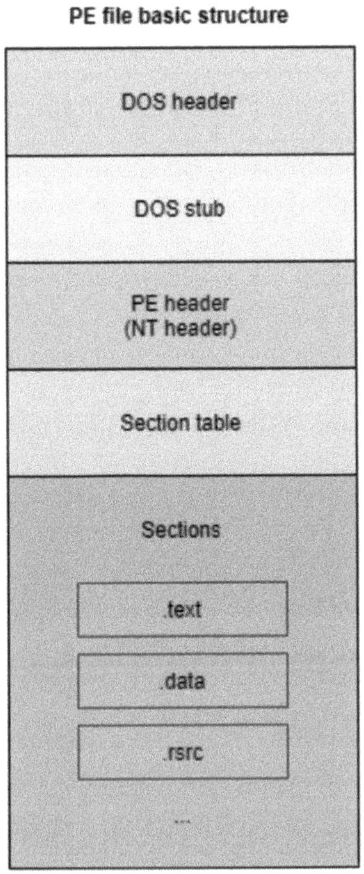

Fig. 4.1. Structure of a Portable Executable (PE) file (Reverse Engineering Portable Executables PE).

`DOS mode"`. This message is used to notify users that the file was intended to run under Windows, as opposed to the old DOS environment. The first and last elements of the DOS Header are `e_magic` and `e_lfanew`, respectively. This first element, `e_magic`, is the two-byte "magic number" `0x5A4D` (or `MZ` in ASCII), which is used to simply denote the file as an MS-DOS executable. The last member of the DOS Header structure, `e_lfanew`, is the offset to the NT headers. This field is crucial for the PE loader on Windows systems to determine where to locate the NT headers to begin loading the

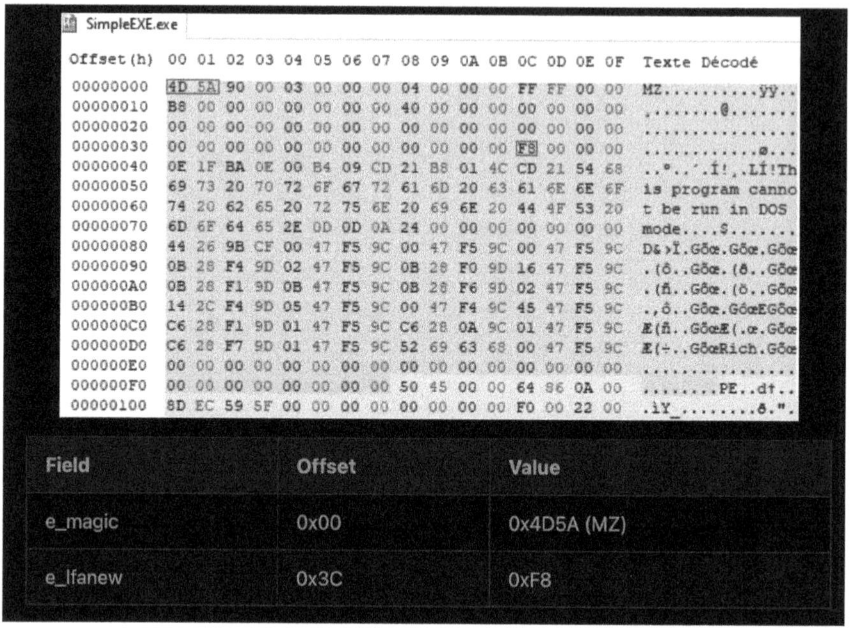

Fig. 4.2. DOS header (Skr1x, 2020).

executable. An example of a DOS header is illustrated in Figure 4.2.

PE Header: The PE Header (or NT header) begins with the PE signature (PE\0\0), which is a marker that identifies the file as a PE. It is followed by the COFF file header that provides metadata about the file, such as the target machine architecture, the number of sections, the file creation timestamp, and attributes that describe the file's characteristics (Bridge *et al.*, 2025).

Optional Header: Contrary to its name, the Optional Header is not optional, as it is required for all PE image files. The Optional Header provides necessary information like the entry point address, the preferred memory location for loading, the size of the image in memory, and various attributes like subsystem type and security features. This header helps to guide the Windows loader in correctly loading and executing the program. However, it is optional for files like object files, which do not require runtime information (Bridge *et al.*, 2025).

Section Table: The Section Table is a series of section headers. Each entry in the table provides information for a specific section of the file, including the section name, virtual size, virtual address, raw data size, and assigned permissions. These headers contain the crucial information required by the loader to correctly map each section into memory with appropriate attributes, such as read, write, or execute permissions. Both the Section Table and the Optional Header play important roles in the loading and execution of a PE file, but address different levels of detail: the Section Table focuses on sections, while the Optional Header provides a high-level view of the entire file and execution requirements.

Sections: The Sections represent the actual contents of the PE file, including executable code, initialized and uninitialized data, and various embedded resources. Common sections typically found in most PE files include the following:

`.text`: The .text section contains the executable instructions for the application. Within this section, the entry point can be found. In this research, it served as the starting point for section-based feature extraction. Note that an application may include multiple sections containing executable instructions.

`.data`: The .data section holds initialized data, such as global and static variables. It often includes constants and strings defined in the source code.

`.rdata` or **`.idata`**: The .radata or .idata sections generally store read-only data and the import table. The import table lists the Windows API functions used by the executable file, along with the names of their associated dynamic link libraries. This information allows the Windows loader to locate and link the required API functions from the appropriate system dynamic link libraries.

`.reloc`: The .reloc section contains the relocation table, which provides information needed when the executable is loaded at a base address different from the one initially specified. It helps adjust the addresses of code and data references accordingly. By default, most executable files assume a preferred base address. It will be the starting address in memory where they expect to be loaded. If the program is loaded at the preferred base address, then all its hard-coded addresses will be correct, and the program can run without modification. However, if the executable is loaded to a different base address, this section would provide the necessary information.

`.rsrc`: The .rsrc section contains various embedded resources used by the executable, such as icons, dialogues, images, menus, and version information. These resources are typically part of the application's user interface.

`.debug`: This .debug section stores debugging information, including symbols and source line references. It is used by debuggers to provide meaningful diagnostics during development.

4.2.2 Machine Learning Methods

This section introduces the machine learning methods that are used in the experiments considered in this chapter. Specifically, we discuss Support Vector Machines (SVM), Long Short-Term Memory (LSTM) models, and Convolutional Neural Networks (CNN).

4.2.2.1 *Support Vector Machines*

The main ideas behind SVMs are the following.

- **Separating hyperplane:** The goal is to separate labeled training data into two classes based on a hyperplane.
- **Maximize the margin:** When constructing the separating hyperplane, we maximize the margin, which is defined as the minimum separation between the two classes in the training set.
- **Work in a higher-dimensional space:** By moving the problem to a higher dimension, there is a better chance of finding a separating hyperplane.
- **Kernel trick:** A kernel function can be used to transform the data to a higher-dimensional space, with the goal of obtaining better

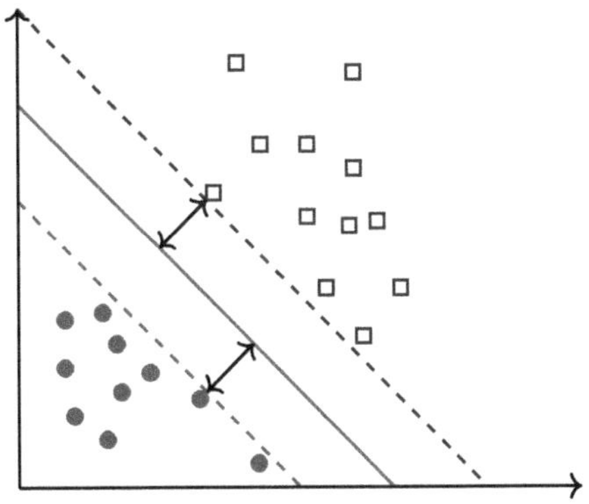

Fig. 4.3. The separating hyperplane of an SVM.

separation. The reason that this is considered a "trick" is because we are able to work in a higher-dimensional space while paying a minimal performance penalty.

Figure 4.3 provides a generic view of linearly separable data, along with the separating hyperplane of an SVM, which maximizes the margin.

According to Bennett and Campbell (2000, p. 9), "SVMs are a rare example of a methodology where geometric intuition, elegant mathematics, theoretical guarantees, and practical algorithms meet". We note in passing that the SVM technique easily generalizes to multiclass data, in which case the technique is sometimes referred to as Support Vector Classifier (SVC).

4.2.2.2 *Long Short-Term Memory*

In this section, we present long short-term memory (LSTM) networks in some detail. A vast number of variants of the LSTM architecture have been developed. However, according to an extensive empirical study (Greff *et al.*, 2017), "none of the variants can improve upon the standard LSTM architecture significantly".

In addition to being a tongue twister, LSTM networks are a class of Recurrent Neural Network (RNN) architectures that are designed to deal with long-range dependencies. That is, LSTMs can deal with "gaps" between the appearance of a feature and the point at which it is used by the model (Greff *et al.*, 2017). LSTM's claim to fame is that it can mitigate the effect of vanishing gradients, which is what enables

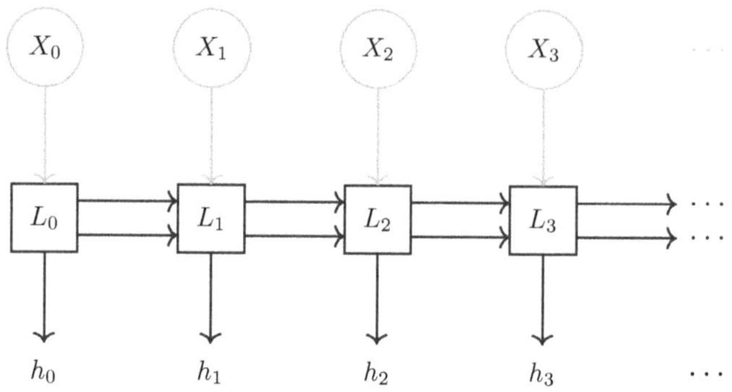

Fig. 4.4. A generic LSTM, showing the connections between states.

such models to account for longer-range dependencies (Hochreiter and Schmidhuber, 1997).

Before outlining the ideas behind LSTM, we note that the LSTM architecture has been one of the most commercially successful learning techniques ever developed. Among many other applications, LSTMs have been used in Google Allo (Khaitan, 2016), Google Translate (Wu *et al.*, 2016), Apple's Siri (Levy, 2016), and Amazon Alexa (Gupta, 2018). However, the commercial dominance of LSTM may be waning (Philipp *et al.*, 2018).

Figure 4.4 illustrates a generic LSTM. From this high-level perspective, an obvious difference from a plain vanilla RNN is that an LSTM has two "lines" entering and exiting each state. As in a standard RNN, one of these lines represents the hidden state, while the second line is designed to serve as a gradient "highway" during back-propagation. In this way, the gradient can "flow" much further back with less chance that it will vanish along the way.

In Figure 4.5, we expand one LSTM cell L_t that appears in Figure 4.4. Here, σ is the sigmoid function, τ is the hyperbolic tangent (i.e., tanh) function, the operators "$\otimes$" and "$\oplus$" are point-wise multiplication and addition, respectively, while "$\mathbin{\bigcirc\!\!\!\!|}$" indicates concatenation of vectors. The vector i_t is the "input gate", f_t is the "forget gate", and o_t is the "output gate". The vector g_t is an intermediate gate and is sometimes (awkwardly) referred to as the "gate gate" (Li *et al.*, 2017). We have much more to say about these gates below.

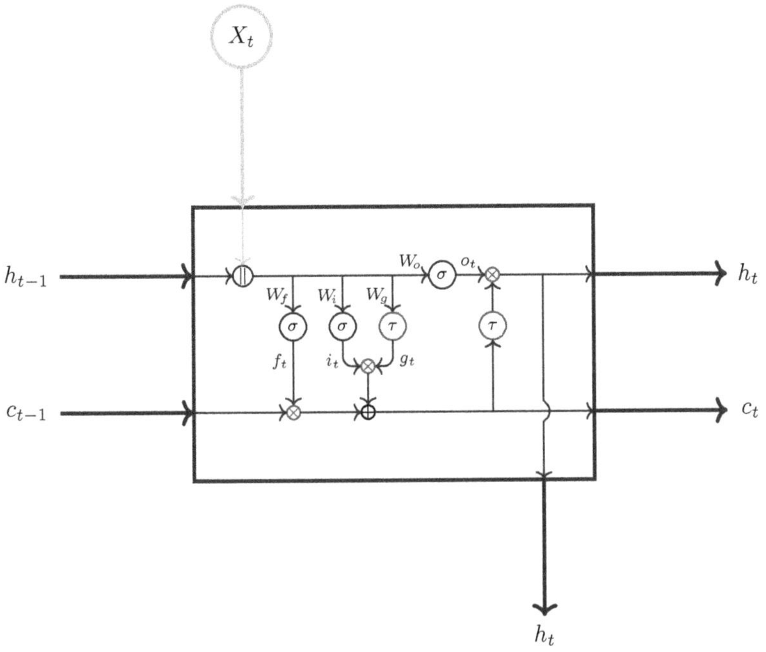

Fig. 4.5. One timestep of an LSTM.

The gate vectors that appear in Figure 4.5 are computed as

$$f_t = \sigma\left(W_f\begin{pmatrix}h_{t-1}\\X_t\end{pmatrix} + b_f\right) g_t = \tau\left(W_g\begin{pmatrix}h_{t-1}\\X_t\end{pmatrix} + b_g\right),$$
$$i_t = \sigma\left(W_i\begin{pmatrix}h_{t-1}\\X_t\end{pmatrix} + b_i\right) o_t = \sigma\left(W_o\begin{pmatrix}h_{t-1}\\X_t\end{pmatrix} + b_o\right),$$

where the b terms are biases. The outputs are given by

$$c_t = f_t \otimes c_{t-1} \oplus i_t \otimes g_t,$$
$$h_t = o_t \otimes \tau(c_t),$$

where, as mentioned above, "$\otimes$" is point-wise multiplication and "$\oplus$" is the usual point-wise addition. Note that each of the weight matrices is of size $n \times 2n$.

In matrix form, ignoring the bias terms, we have

$$\begin{pmatrix} i_t \\ f_t \\ o_t \\ g_t \end{pmatrix} = \begin{pmatrix} \sigma \\ \sigma \\ \sigma \\ \tau \end{pmatrix} W \begin{pmatrix} h_{t-1} \\ X_t \end{pmatrix},$$

where X_t and h_{t-1} are column vectors of length n, and W is a $4n \times 2n$ weight matrix of the form

$$W = \begin{pmatrix} W_i \\ W_f \\ W_o \\ W_g \end{pmatrix}.$$

Each of the gates i_t, f_t, o_t, and g_t is a column vector of length n. Recall that the sigmoid σ squashes its input to be within the range of 0 to 1, whereas the tanh function τ produces output within the range of -1 to $+1$.

To highlight the intuition behind LSTM, we follow a similar approach as that given in the excellent presentation in Li *et al.* (2017). Specifically, we focus on the extreme cases, that is, we pretend that the output of each sigmoid σ is either 0 or 1, and each hyperbolic tangent τ is either -1 or $+1$. Under this assumption, the forget gate f_t is a vector of 0s and 1s, where the 0s tell us the elements of c_{t-1} that the model will forget (i.e., set to 0) and the 1s indicate the elements that the model will remember (i.e., retain).

Again, assuming we only have the extreme cases, the input gate i_t and gate gate g_t together determine which elements of c_{t-1} to increment or decrement. Specifically, when element j of i_t is 1 and element j of g_t is $+1$, we increment element j of c_{t-1}. On the other hand, if element j of i_t is 1 and element j of g_t is -1, then we decrement element j of c_{t-1}. This serves to emphasize or de-emphasize particular elements in the new-and-improved cell state c_t.

Finally, the output gate o_t determines which elements of the cell state will become part of the hidden state h_t. Note that the hidden state h_t is fed into the output layer of the LSTM. Also note that before the cell states are operated on by the output gate, the values are first squeezed down to be within the range of -1 to $+1$ by the τ function.

Of course, in general, the LSTM gates are not simply counters that increment or decrement. But the intuition holds, that is, the gates keep track of incremental changes, thus allowing relevant information to "flow" over long distances via the cell state. In this way, an LSTM can mitigate the gradient issues that arise in other RNNs.

4.2.2.3 *Convolution Neural Network*

Artificial Neural Networks typically use fully connected layers, where a neuron at one layer is connected to all neurons at the layers above and below. A fully connected layer can deal effectively with correlations between any elements within the training vectors. However, due to these fully connected layers, the number of weights that must be determined via training can be vast. In contrast, a CNN is designed to deal with local structure, which results in a dramatic reduction in the number of weights that must be learned during training. Thus, a key benefit of CNNs is that convolutional layers can be trained far more efficiently than fully connected layers.

For images, most of the relevant structure (edges and gradients, for example) is local. Hence, CNNs would seem to be an ideal tool for image analysis. However, CNNs have performed well in a wide variety of other problem domains. In general, any problem for which there exists a data representation where local structure predominates is a candidate for a CNN. In addition to images, local structure is of primary importance in fields such as text analysis and speech recognition, to give two examples.

A convolutional layer is illustrated in Figure 4.6. In this case, five filters are trained on an RGB color image. By initializing the filters with different values, they can potentially learn different features.

CNNs typically employ multiple convolutional layers. The first convolutional layer learns intuitive features, such as edges and gradients, while higher convolutional layers learn progressively more abstract features, which ultimately allows for discrimination between complex classes, such as "cat" and "dog". Pooling layers are frequently employed between convolutional layers, which serve to reduce the dimensionality, while also playing a role in translation invariance. Various regularization techniques are used when training CNNs so as to mitigate issues related to overfitting. For example, cutout regularization forces the model to consider different parts of an image when training.

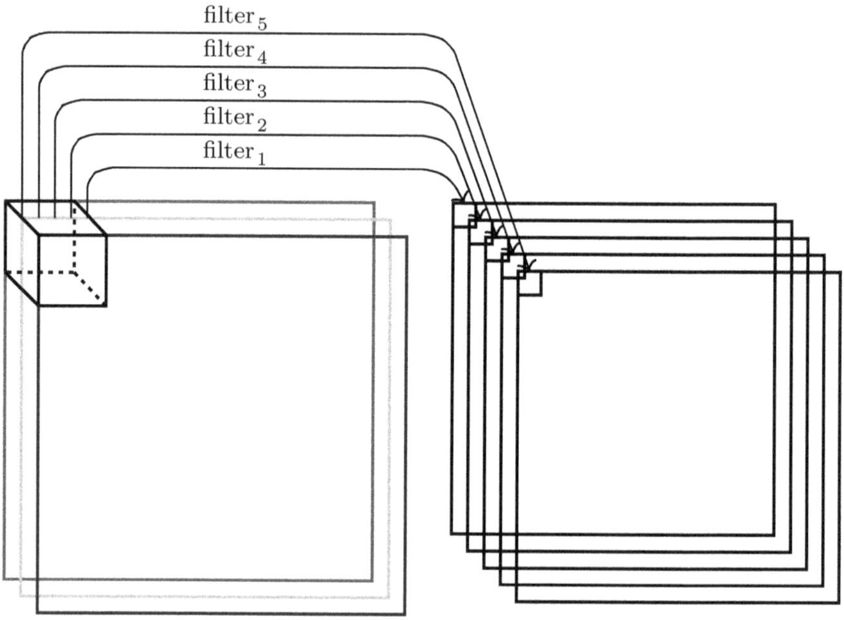

Fig. 4.6. A convolutional layer.

A detailed discussion of CNNs can be found at Karpathy (2018), while Cornelisse[2] provides some interesting insights. Kalfas presents a more intuitive discussion of CNNs,[3] and visual representations can be found at Deshpande (2018). For our purposes, it is important to note that image-based analysis has recently proven highly effective for malware classification and analysis (Jain *et al.*, 2020; Prajapati and Stamp, 2021; Yajamanam *et al.*, 2018).

4.3 Related Work

In this section, we review examples of related work where PE file features have been used for malware classification. But first, we mention that, in general, features used for malware analysis can be considered

[2]https://medium.freecodecamp.org/an-intuitive-guide-to-convolutional-neural-networks-260c2de0a050.

[3]https://medium.com/data-science/modeling-visual-neurons-with-convolutional-neural-networks-e9c01ddfdfa7.

static or dynamic (Damodaran *et al.*, 2015). Static features are those that can be obtained directly from the malware file, whereas dynamic features require code execution or emulation. Examples of static features include byte histograms and opcode sequences, whereas API calls and various graph-based features typically must be collected in a dynamic mode. Dynamic features are generally more robust with respect to obfuscation techniques, while it is typically far more efficient to collect static features. In the experiments reported in this paper, we only consider static features.

In Anderson and Roth (2018), the first EMBER dataset was introduced and analyzed. This dataset consists of a large set of static features extracted from 1.1 million PE files. The features include byte histograms, metadata in the header, and import table characteristics. The result from this study shows that machine learning techniques applied to these static features can distinguish between malware and benign with good accuracy.

Rezaei *et al.* (2021) proposed a method focusing on using features from the PE header. They combined deep learning techniques and clustering techniques with 324 bytes of the header to train a malware classification model. The result of this model shows good accuracy in malware classification, even when faced with obfuscation techniques. Similarly, Kattamuri *et al.* (2023) developed the SOMLAP dataset, which includes 51,409 samples, and from each sample, they extract 108 PE header attributes. They first apply feature reduction techniques using swarm optimization algorithms, including Ant Colony Optimization (ACO), Cuckoo Search Optimization (CSO), and Grey Wolf Optimization (GWO), which is followed by traditional machine-learning techniques. This research claimed to achieve a high malware detection accuracy. The two papers discussed in this paragraph illustrate the potential effectiveness of using header-based features.

Raff *et al.* (2018) proposed an end-to-end deep learning approach that avoids the need for manual feature selection. This approach feeds the entire byte sequence of PE files directly into a neural network, skipping typical feature engineering steps. This allows the network to independently learn meaningful feature patterns. This approach showed high accuracy on large-scale datasets with one downside being heavy computational time. In addition, the technique struggled with obfuscated malware.

Damodaran *et al.* (2015) evaluated static, dynamic, and hybrid feature sets using Hidden Markov Models (HMMs). This paper highlights the trade-offs between different feature selection strategies and serves as a useful reference for optimizing feature selection methods. Static features like opcode sequences were found to be almost as effective as dynamic features in most cases. Hybrid approaches, which combine static and dynamic features, introduced additional complexity and failed to outperform standard approaches.

Finally, Wen and Chow (2021) proposed a malware detection model based on CNNs. In this research, variable-size binary fragments obtained from PE files are considered. The research simulated real-world scenarios where network packet size limitations result in incomplete file captures, aiming to demonstrate the ability to deal with such fragmented input. The dataset was derived from antivirus tools and included examples of zero-day malware. Even with these challenges, the model still performed relatively well.

In the list below, we summarize the related work discussed in this section. Taken as a whole, these studies demonstrate that a wide variety of PE-based feature selection and extraction methods have been used to build high-performing malware detection systems. Typical features include header fields, byte sequences, specific sections of the file, and even the full binary content analyzed using learning techniques. Together, these features enhance the performance of both traditional machine learning and modern deep learning models in malware classification.

Anderson and Roth (2018). Combining static features improved malware detection

Rezaei *et al.* (2021). Header-based features are more robust against obfuscation

Kattamuri *et al.* (2023). High accuracy with swarm optimization on header features

Raff *et al.* (2018). Achieved high accuracy using PE file byte sequences, but struggled with obfuscation

Damodaran *et al.* (2015). Static features are nearly as effective as dynamic features; hybrid approaches add complexity without consistent gain

Wen and Chow (2021). Good accuracy using CNN models on fragmented inputs, and effective for zero-day malware scenario.

Multimodal Machine Learning (MML) has developed as an innovative approach, utilizing diverse data modalities to enhance the performance of models. Barua *et al.* (2023) review key advancements and challenges in MML, including the current state of the field, and they provide insights into challenges and potential solutions, while also discussing several frameworks and trends. One significant finding in their paper is the growing trend toward deep learning approaches. These approaches have gained attention due to their ability to effectively process complex multimodal data, particularly in areas such as representation learning, fusion techniques, and alignment strategies. Several deep learning architectures are mentioned for their contributions to MML applications, including CNNs, Recurrent Neural Networks (RNN), and transformer-based architectures.

In another paper, Zhai *et al.* (2023) proposed an online classification model for darknet traffic classification that integrates a CNN and a Bidirectional Gated Recurrent Unit (BiGRU) to extract spatial and temporal features from packet payloads. To enhance the overall representation of network traffic, the model incorporates flow-level abstract features processed by a Multilayer Perceptron (MLP). The authors state that this multimodal approach improves accuracy across multiple categories while reducing time and memory consumption by approximately 50%. The authors claim that compared to state-of-the-art traffic classification models, the proposed method demonstrates superior classification performance.

Further, in Shobhit and Bera (2021), Shobhit and Bera proposed a deep learning-based malware detection system with a unique architecture that combines image representations, text representations, and Generative Adversarial Networks (GANs). This so-called ModCGAN system architecture comprises several key components, including an Image Autoencoder, a Text Autoencoder, and a GAN. They utilized log files containing API call sequences to generate both image and text representations. These representations are fed into the respective autoencoders and combined into a single feature vector. This feature vector is then used for malware classification purposes. The results demonstrated that this multi-modal approach effectively captures the dynamic behavior of malware, resulting in improved malware detection accuracy compared to traditional single-modality methods.

Lastly, in Guo *et al.* (2023), Guo *et al.* propose another innovative approach called Multimodal Dual-Embedding Networks (MDENet), which they use to detect malware with highly similar features. MDENet leverages malware features from different modalities, such as malware images (generated from numeric features of malware samples) and malware "sentences" (created by organizing tokenized malware features into sentence-like structures). MDENet achieves good accuracy in both classifying known malware and detecting new, unknown families. Its effectiveness is validated through experiments on the popular Mailing dataset and the MAL-100+ dataset. This study provides further evidence of the value of a multimodal approach in addressing challenging malware problems.

4.4 Experiments and Results

In this section, we present experimental results comparing the performance of various multimodal approaches to typical machine learning models. We train models using histograms, byte sequences, and bytes interpreted as 2-dimensional images, depending on the model under consideration. For each of the three model types discussed in Section 4.2.2, namely, SVM, LSTM, and CNN, we train a model on the header, we train another model on the sections, and we train a third model on the entire file. Then we consider multimodal experiments, where we train an SVM on the output of each of the nine combinations of header and section models. We evaluate all of our models based on accuracy, which is computed as

$$\text{accuracy} = \frac{\text{TP} + \text{TN}}{\text{TP} + \text{TN} + \text{FP} + \text{FN}},$$

where we have TP = True Positives, TN = True Negatives, FP = False Positives, and FN = False Negatives.

However, before we discuss our experimental results, we provide details on the dataset and features utilized in the experiments.

4.4.1 Dataset

All the experiments presented in this study are based on malware samples from the Malicia dataset—specifically, `vesion release_malicia_1.0` dataset—which consists of 11,371 malicious files in raw PE file format, along with metadata that includes a class label for each sample (Nappa *et al.*, 2015). The dataset contains a large number of families, many of which have only a few samples, so we restrict our attention to the following five malware families.

Cridex is designed to steal banking credentials. In addition, after infecting a system, Cridex may integrate the compromised device into a botnet and exploit it for malicious activities, such as generating spam or executing Distributed Denial of Service (DDoS) attacks (Cridex malware).

Harebot is classified as both a backdoor and a rootkit. It installs itself on Windows systems without the user's consent, enabling attackers to gain unauthorized access to devices, networks, applications, and sensitive user information (ZulaZuza, n.d.).

SecurityShield is malware disguised as antivirus software. It secretly monitors and collects information about a user's activity while falsely reporting virus detections to coerce users into purchasing unnecessary software (SecurityShield).

Zbot, also known as Zeus, is a Trojan that commonly spreads through spam emails, social media links, or drive-by downloads. It monitors infected systems to steal sensitive information such as banking credentials and passwords (Win32/Zbot).

ZeroAccess is a Trojan horse equipped with an advanced rootkit, allowing it to conceal its presence, create hidden files, install backdoors, and download additional malware for various malicious purposes.

Figure 4.7 lists the number of samples that we consider from each of these malware families. In total, the dataset for our experiments consists of 2114 samples and five classes, with a large imbalance between classes.

4.4.2 SVM Results

For the SVM model, we use byte histogram features. The raw byte sequences are extracted and interpreted as integer values ranging from 0 to 255. These integer values are then gathered into relative histograms, which yields a feature vector of length 256, where each element is between 0 and 1, and the sum of all 256 elements is 1, i.e., the vector satisfies the requirements of a discrete probability

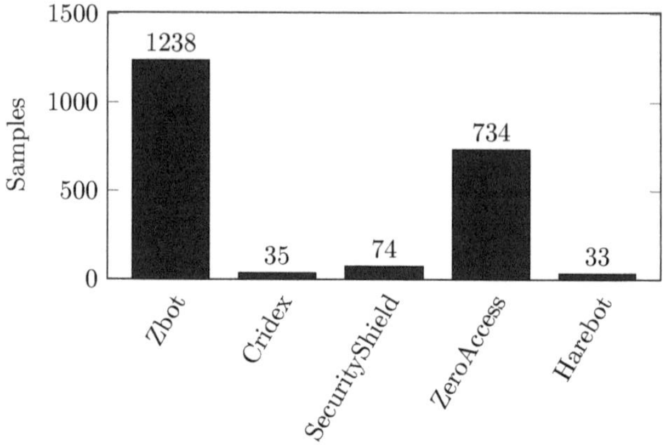

Fig. 4.7. Number of samples for each malware family.

Table 4.1. SVM hyper-parameters tested.

Hyperparameter	**Values Tested**	**Description**
C	{0.001, 0.01, 0.1, 1, **10**}	Regularization parameter
γ	{0.001, **0.01**, 0.1, 1}	Kernel coefficient
kernel	{poly, linear, **rbf**}	Kernel type

Note: Selected values in boldface.

distribution. These histograms then serve as the feature sets for our SVM classification models.

We use an 80-20 stratified split for training and testing, and 5-fold cross-validation. To determine the hyperparameters, we perform a grid search on the values listed in Table 4.1, using the header features. Note that the values selected are in boldface in Table 4.1.

In Figure 4.8, we observe that the SVM performs well when applied to histogram features. The best results are for a model that is trained on only the sections, while the header model performs slightly worse, and the entire file gives marginally worse results than the sections model.

4.4.3 LSTM Results

Our LSTM models are trained on byte sequences. Since the PE header is typically 324 bytes, this is the sequence length used for

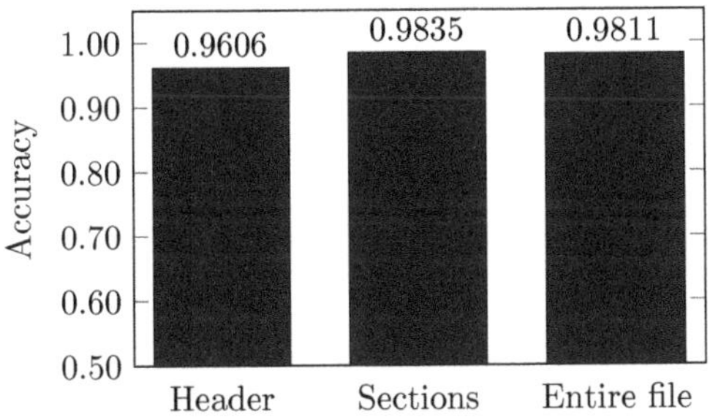

Fig. 4.8. SVM: accuracy comparison across experiments.

Table 4.2. Hyperparameters and architecture for LSTM.

Hyperparameter	**Value**
Batch size	30
Epochs	10
Data used for validation	20%
Input sequence length (bytes)	324
Number of LSTM units	64
Activation function (hidden layer)	Sigmoid
Number of dense units (output layer)	5
Activation function (output layer)	Softmax
Loss function	Categorical cross-entropy
Optimizer	Adam

our header model. For efficiency, when training the sections model and the "entire" PE file model, we experiment with lengths of 1000 and 2000 bytes.

The structure of the LSTM models is detailed in Table 4.2. Note that the only variation between the models is the input sequence length.

From Figure 4.9, we observe that while the LSTM model performed reasonably well when trained in the PE header, the other models yielded very poor results. The malware files under consideration are typically much larger than 2000 bytes, and hence better results might be obtainable using longer sequence lengths. However, LSTM models are computationally expensive to train for large sequence lengths, and we have already obtained strong results for the sections and entire file cases using SVM models.

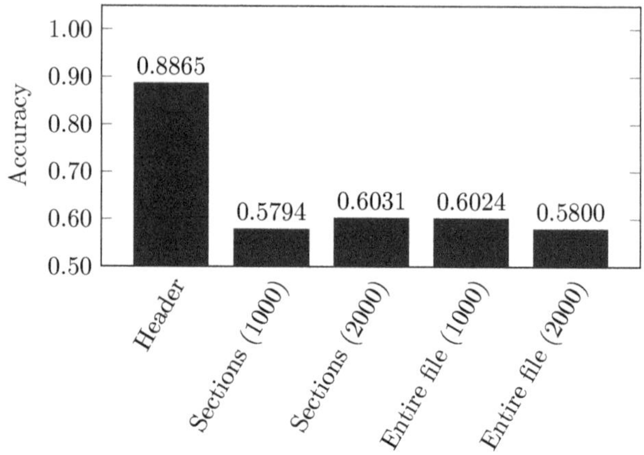

Fig. 4.9. LSTM: accuracy comparison across experiments.

4.4.4 CNN Results

For our CNN models, we convert the raw bytes into simple images as follows. For the header model, we generate a 16×16 "byte image" from the first 256 bytes of the PE header as

$$\text{header image} = \begin{bmatrix} b_0 & b_1 & b_2 & \cdots & b_{15} \\ b_{16} & b_{17} & b_{18} & \cdots & b_{31} \\ b_{32} & b_{33} & b_{34} & \cdots & b_{47} \\ \vdots & \vdots & \vdots & \ddots & \vdots \\ b_{240} & b_{241} & b_{242} & \cdots & b_{255} \end{bmatrix},$$

where b_k is the kth byte of the PE file. In an analogous manner we construct byte images of size 32×32 for both the sections and entire file features, beginning at byte b_{324} in the sections case, and beginning at byte b_0 for the entire file case. Note that in both of these latter two cases, we are considering precisely 1024 bytes. These byte images are then converted into grayscale images using the Python library Pillow (Pillow). The conversion process involves interpreting the binary data as a sequence of unsigned 8-bit integers, and each value corresponds to the intensity of the corresponding grayscale pixel, and the pixel intensity values are then assigned to the image using the `putdata` method.

Table 4.3. CNN model details.

Layer (Type)	Output Shape	Number of Parameters
`conv2d (Conv2D)`	(None, 30, 30, 32)	320
`max_pooling2d (MaxPooling2D)`	(None, 15, 15, 32)	0
`flatten (Flatten)`	(None, 7200)	0
`dense_1 (Dense)`	(None, 128)	921,728
`dense_2 (Dense)`	(None, 5)	645

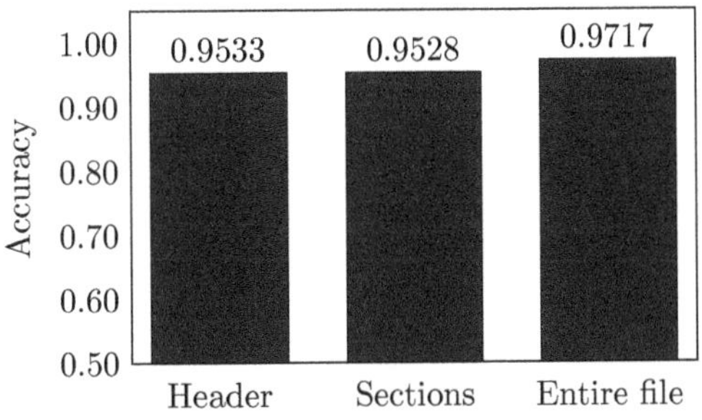

Fig. 4.10. CNN: accuracy comparison across experiments.

We experimented with various CNN architectures. Details on the selected architecture are given in Table 4.3.

Figure 4.10 shows that our CNN models perform well in all three cases, with images based on the first 1024 bytes of the entire file yielding the best accuracy. These results demonstrates the efficacy of image-based techniques in general—and CNNs in particular—in the realm of malware classification.

4.4.5 Multimodal Models

For our multimodal experiments, we test all combinations of one of our header-based models with one of our sections-based models. Since we trained models with header features and models with sections features for each of three distinct cases (SVM, LSTM, and CNN), we have a total of nine multimodal combinations.

To combine our models in a multimodal fashion, the output layer probabilities of the header-based model and the sections-based model are concatenated, and the resulting vector serves as the feature vector for an SVM classifier. Since each model is trained to distinguish between five classes, the feature vectors for the final SVM classifier are all of length 10.

We note in passing that for this multimodal approach, training the header-based model and the sections-based model can be viewed as feature engineering steps, since these component models take the raw features as input and produce new features for the final SVM classifier. We also note that this feature engineering step is straightforward for LSTM and CNN models, but an SVM does not directly generate probabilities. Therefore, for our header-based and sections-based SVM models, we set `svm.SVC(probability=True)` in `scikit-learn`, which introduces a post-training probability calculation step.

The results for all of our multimodal models are summarized in Figure 4.11. In these results, multimodal models are specified in the form

$$(M_h, M_s) \to M_m,$$

where M_h is the model trained using header-based features, M_s is the model trained using section-based features, and M_m is the multimodal model that acts as the classifier, based on the output—in the form of vectors of probabilities—of the models M_h and M_s. Each subfigure represents the accuracy achieved by different combinations of models. Note that Figures 4.11(a) through (c) are sorted by the header model, while Figures 4.11(d) through (f) give the same results, but sorted by the sections model. As mentioned above, in all cases, SVM is used as the multimodal M_m classifier.

Figure 4.12 provides a comparison of the best multimodal model result to the best results obtained with each of the individual models, namely, SVM, LSTM, and CNN. The best of the multimodal models are

$$(\text{LSTM}, \text{CNN}) \to \text{SVM} \quad \text{and} \quad (\text{CNN}, \text{CNN}) \to \text{SVM},$$

which achieve accuracies of 0.9929 and 0.9930, respectively. We observe that these best multimodal accuracies are about 1% better than the best of the individual models.

While a 1% improvement may not seem that impressive at first glance, it is important to note that the second-best model had already

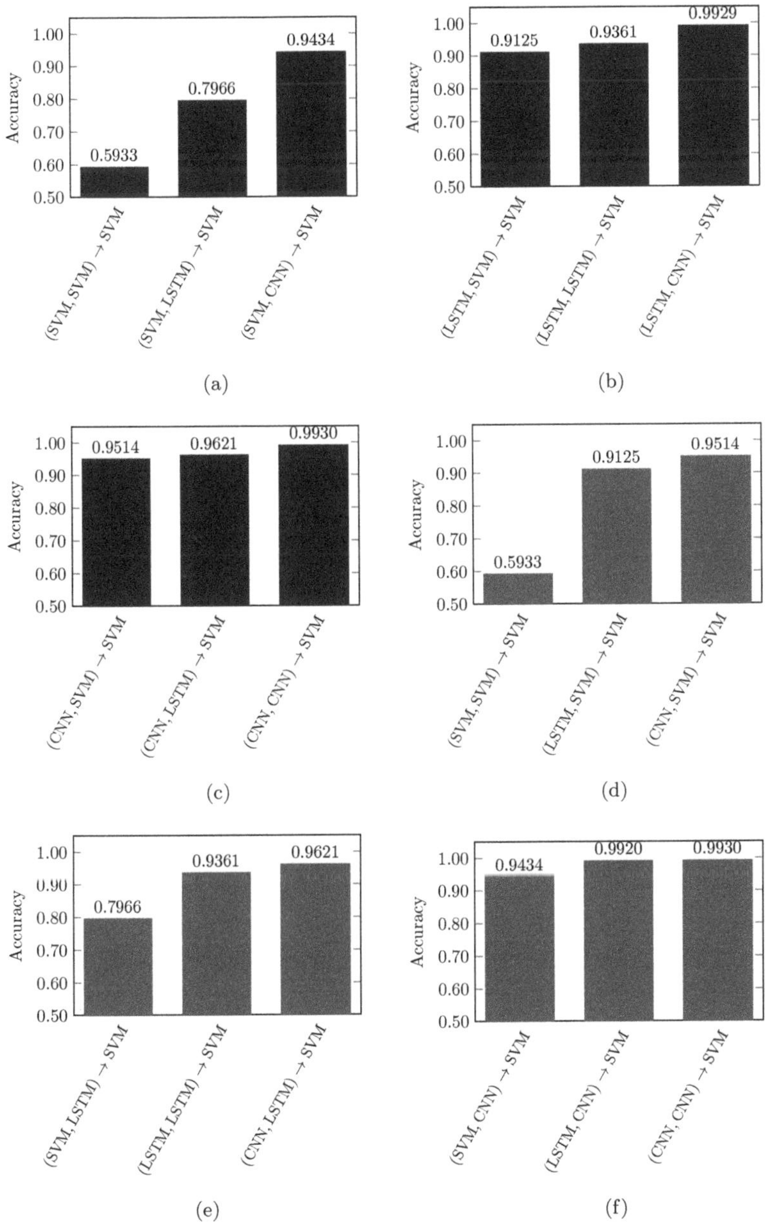

Fig. 4.11. Accuracy of multimodal combinations. (a) SVM header models, (b) LSTM header models, (c) CNN header models, (d) SVM sections models, (e) LSTM sections models, and (f) CNN sections models.

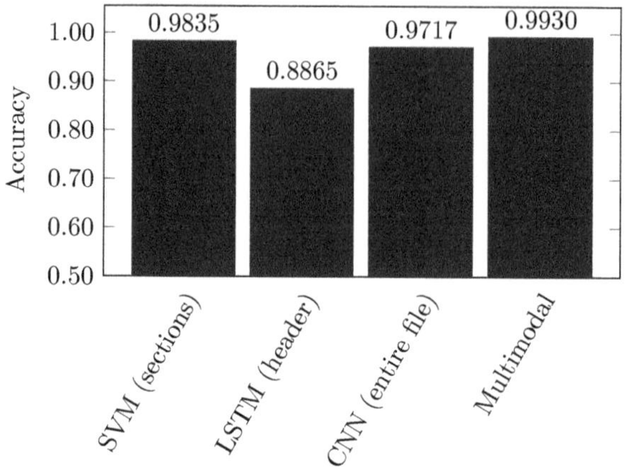

Fig. 4.12. Accuracy comparison across all experiments.

attained more than 98% accuracy. Therefore, the results show that the number of samples misclassified by our best multimodal model is about half the number that were misclassified by the best of the individual models. Thus, we conclude that the multimodal approach to PE malware classification we have considered appears to have genuine merit. The results of all multimodal combinations tested are summarized in Figure 4.11.

4.5 Conclusion and Future Work

In this chapter, we demonstrated the effectiveness of combining multiple machine-learning models in a multimodal sense, and how this approach can enhance malware classification accuracy. For our baseline cases, we trained SVM, LSTM, and CNN models on features extracted from the PE header, and on features extracted from the other sections of the PE file, and we also trained these same models on the overall PE file. We then generated multimodal models, where the output layer probabilities of a PE-header model and a PE-sections model were combined and used as feature vectors to train an SVM classifier. In this multimodal approach, we were able to take advantage of the unique strengths of specific learning techniques on different parts of the Windows PE file, which improved classification accuracy, as compared to the baseline cases.

There are many potential directions for improvements and extensions of the research presented here. Testing the techniques considered in this work on a larger, more diverse, and more challenging dataset would aid in more accurately quantifying the effectiveness of such a multimodal approach. We could also consider additional features, such as opcode sequences, API calls, and various graph structures, and we could employ advanced feature engineering techniques, such as Word2Vec (Chandak *et al.*, 2021). In a similar vein, it has been demonstrated that the method used to generate images from raw data can affect the accuracy of CNN classifiers (Rust-Nguyen *et al.*, 2023), and hence, more sophisticated image-generation techniques should be considered. Experiments involving additional learning techniques would also be interesting—in particular, Graph Neural Networks have shown considerable promise in the malware domain (Malhotra *et al.*, 2024), and such techniques are likely to provide unique strengths in a multimodal setting.

Bibliography

Alenezi, M. N., Alabdulrazzaq, H. K., Alshaher, A. A., and Alkharang, M. M. (2020). Evolution of malware threats and techniques: A review, *International Journal of Communication Networks and Information Security* **12**, 3, pp. 326–337.

Anderson, H. S. and Roth, P. (2018). EMBER: An open dataset for training static PE malware machine learning models, https://arxiv.org/abs/1804.04637.

Barua, A., Ahmed, M. U., and Begum, S. (2023). A systematic literature review on multimodal machine learning: Applications, challenges, gaps and future directions, *IEEE Access* **11**, pp. 14804–14831.

Bennett, K. P. and Campbell, C. (2000). Support vector machines: Hype or hallelujah? *SIGKDD Explorations* **2**, 2, pp. 1–13.

Bridge, K. *et al.* (2025). PE format, https://learn.microsoft.com/en-us/windows/win32/debug/pe-format.

Chandak, A., Lee, W., and Stamp, M. (2021). A comparison of word2vec, hmm2vec, and pca2vec for malware classification, in M. Stamp, M. Alazab, and A. Shalaginov (eds.), *Malware Analysis Using Artificial Intelligence and Deep Learning* (Springer, Cham), pp. 287–320.

Cridex malware (2017). Cridex malware. Computer Hope, https://www.computerhope.com/jargon/c/cridex-malware.htm.

Damodaran, A., Troia, F. D., Visaggio, C. A., Austin, T. H., and Stamp, M. (2015). A comparison of static, dynamic, and hybrid analysis for malware detection, *Journal of Computer Virology and Hacking Techniques* **13**, 1, pp. 1–12.

Daulaguphu, S. (2022). A comprehensive guide to PE structure, the layman's way, https://tech-zealots.com/malware-analysis/pe-portable-executable-structure-malware-analysis-part-2/#:~:text=And%20PE%20file%20format%20is,scr%2C%20and%20.

Deshpande, A. (2018). A beginner's guide to understanding convolutional neural networks, https://adeshpande3.github.io/A-Beginner%27s-Guide-To-Understanding-Convolutional-Neural-Networks/.

Gibert, D. (2025). Machine learning for windows malware detection and classification: Methods, challenges, and ongoing research, in D. Gritzalis, K.-K. R. Choo, and C. Patsakis (eds.), *Malware: Handbook of Prevention and Detection* (Springer, Cham), pp. 143–173.

Greff, K., Srivastava, R. K., Koutník, J., Steunebrink, B. R., and Schmidhuber, J. (2017). LSTM: A search space odyssey, *IEEE Transactions on Neural Networks and Learning Systems* **28**, 10, pp. 2222–2232, https://arxiv.org/pdf/1503.04069.pdf.

Guo, J., Xu, Y., Xu, W., Zhan, Y., Sun, Y., and Guo, S. (2023). MDENet: Multi-modal dual-embedding networks for malware open-set recognition, https://arxiv.org/abs/2305.01245.

Gupta, A. (2018). Alexa blogs: How Alexa is learning to converse more naturally, https://www.amazon.science/blog/how-alexa-is-learning-to-converse-more-naturally.

Hochreiter, S. and Schmidhuber, J. (1997). Long short-term memory, *Neural Computation* **9**, 8, pp. 1735–1780, https://doi.org/10.1162/neco.1997.9.8.1735.

Jain, M., Andreopoulos, W., and Stamp, M. (2020). Convolutional neural networks and extreme learning machines for malware classification, *Journal of Computer Virology and Hacking Techniques* **16**, 3, pp. 229–244.

Karpathy, A. (2018). Convolutional neural networks for visual recognition, http://cs231n.github.io/convolutional-networks/.

Katkar, S. (2006). Virus Bulletin: Inside the PE file format, https://www.virusbulletin.com/virusbulletin/2006/06/inside-pe-file-format/.

Kattamuri, S. J., Penmatsa, R. K. V., Chakravarty, S., and Madabathula, V. S. P. (2023). Swarm optimization and machine learning applied to pe malware detection towards cyber threat intelligence, *Electronics* **12**, 2.

Khaitan, P. (2016). Google AI blog: Chat smarter with Allo, https://ai.googleblog.com/2016/05/chat-smarter-with-allo.html.

Lee, H., Kim, S., Baek, D., Kim, D., and Hwang, D. (2023). Robust IoT malware detection and classification using opcode category features on machine learning, *IEEE Access* **11**, pp. 18855–18867.

Levy, S. (2016). The iBrain is here—and it's already inside your phone. *Wired*, https://www.wired.com/2016/08/an-exclusive-look-at-how-ai-and-machine-learning-work-at-apple/.

Li, F.-F., Johnson, J., and Yeung, S. (2017). Lecture 10: Recurrent neural networks, http://cs231n.stanford.edu/slides/2017/cs231n_2017_lecture10.pdf.

Malhotra, V., Potika, K., and Stamp, M. (2024). A comparison of graph neural networks for malware classification, *Journal of Computer Virology and Hacking Techniques* **20**, pp. 53–69.

Nappa, A., Rafique, M. Z., and Caballero, J. (2015). The MALICIA dataset: Identification and analysis of drive-by download operations, *International Journal of Information Security* **14**, 1, pp. 15–33.

Philipp, G., Song, D., and Carbonell, J. G. (2018). The exploding gradient problem demystified—Definition, prevalence, impact, origin, tradeoffs, and solutions, https://arxiv.org/pdf/1712.05577.pdf.

Pillow (2011). Pillow, https://pillow.readthedocs.io/en/stable/.

Prajapati, P. and Stamp, M. (2021). An empirical analysis of image-based learning techniques for malware classification, in M. Stamp, M. Alazab, and A. Shalaginov (eds.), *Malware Analysis Using Artificial Intelligence and Deep Learning* (Springer, Cham), pp. 411–435.

Raff, E., Barker, J., Sylvester, J., Brandon, R., Catanzaro, B., and Nicholas, C. K. (2018). Malware detection by eating a whole EXE, in *The Workshops of the The Thirty-Second AAAI Conference on Artificial Intelligence, AAAI Technical Report*, Vol. WS-18, pp. 268–276.

Reverse Engineering Portable Executables PE (2022). Reverse engineering portable executables PE—part 2. Mossé Cyber Security Institute, https://library.mosse-institute.com/articles/2022/05/reverse-engineering-portable-executables-pe-part-2/reverse-engineering-portable-executables-pe-part-2.html.

Rezaei, T., Manavi, F., and Hamzeh, A. (2021). A PE header-based method for malware detection using clustering and deep embedding techniques, *Journal of Information Security and Applications* **60**, p. 102876.

Rust-Nguyen, N., Sharma, S., and Stamp, M. (2023). Darknet traffic classification and adversarial attacks using machine learning, *Computers & Security* **127**, p. 103098, https://www.sciencedirect.com/science/article/pii/S0167404823000081.

SecurityShield (2019). SecurityShield. Microsoft Security Intelligence, https://www.microsoft.com/en-us/wdsi/threats/malware-encyclopedia-description?Name=SecurityShield.

Shobhit and Bera, P. (2021). ModCGAN: A multimodal approach to detect new malware, in *2021 International Conference on Cyber Situational Awareness, Data Analytics and Assessment*, CyberSA, pp. 1–2.

Skr1x (2020). Introduction to the PE file format, https://skr1x.github.io/portable-executable-format/.

Wang, Q. (2022). Support vector machine algorithm in machine learning, in *2022 IEEE International Conference on Artificial Intelligence and Computer Applications*, ICAICA, pp. 750–756.

Wen, Q. and Chow, K. (2021). CNN based zero-day malware detection using small binary segments, *Forensic Science International: Digital Investigation* **38**, p. 301128.

Win32/Zbot (2017). Win32/Zbot. Microsoft Security Intelligence, https://www.microsoft.com/en-us/wdsi/threats/malware-encyclopedia-description?Name=Win32/Zbot.

Wu, Y. *et al.* (2016). Google's neural machine translation system: Bridging the gap between human and machine translation, https://arxiv.org/abs/1609.08144.

Yajamanam, S., Selvin, V. R. S., Troia, F. D., and Stamp, M. (2018). Deep learning versus gist descriptors for image-based malware classification, in P. Mori, S. Furnell, and O. Camp (eds.), *Proceedings of the 4th International Conference on Information Systems Security and Privacy*, ICISSP, pp. 553–561.

Yuan, B., Wang, J., Liu, D., Guo, W., Wu, P., and Bao, X. (2020). Byte-level malware classification based on Markov images and deep learning, *Computers & Security* **92**, p. 101740.

Zhai, J., Sun, H., Xu, C., and Sun, W. (2023). ODTC: An online darknet traffic classification model based on multimodal self-attention chaotic mapping features, *Electronic Research Archive* **31**, 8, pp. 5056–5082.

ZulaZuza (n.d.). EnigmaSoft: Rootkit.HareBot, https://www.enigmasoftware.com/rootkitharebot-removal/.

https://doi.org/10.1142/9789811262043_0005

Chapter 5

Opportunities and Challenges of Explainable Artificial Intelligence in Cybersecurity

Giuseppina Andresini, Annalisa Appice, and Donato Malerba
University of Bari Aldo Moro, Bari, Italy

In the last decade, the amazing achievements of research in Artificial Intelligence (AI), in particular in Machine Learning (ML) and Deep Learning (DL), have significantly changed how cybersecurity analysts analyze cyber-data (e.g., software applications, network traffic data) to identify signs of malicious behaviors. However, even though ML and DL techniques have been proven accurate in several problems, in general, it is still too difficult to interpret and explain their decisions. In recent years, this lack of interpretability and explainability has become a major drawback of several ML and DL techniques, even in cybersecurity applications (e.g., malware detection and network intrusion detection). With the aim of filling this gap, in this chapter we review the main opportunities and challenges for the use of eXplainable AI (XAI) techniques in cybersecurity. In particular, we overview the recent advances to equip ML- and DL-driven decisions of modern cyber-threat detection systems with explainability facilities, to allow cybersecurity professionals to understand, validate, and effectively respond to cyber-alerts. In addition, we illustrate the recent advancements regarding the extraction of explainable smart data from raw cyber-data, to gain accuracy, and possibly robustness, when learning decision models for cyber-threat detection problems. Finally, as XAI techniques have recently proved able to identify vulnerabilities of ML- and DL-based decision processes, we illustrate a few pioneering recent studies that have contributed to using XAI to secure ML and DL decision-making processes. On the other hand, recent research trends in Adversarial Learning have shown that adversarial attacks may be tailored to attack explanations (in addition to decision models), requiring us to identify emerging directions for designing more secure explanation techniques.

5.1 Introduction

Over the past decade, the emergence of Machine Learning and Deep Learning in decision modeling has spurred the evolution of a new generation of cybersecurity systems. These systems widely use ML and DL intelligence to enhance the accuracy of the security defenses of several private and public organizations. While the primary focus of cybersecurity systems remains on accurate detection and classification of cyber-threats, there has been a growing emphasis on the explainability of decision models in recent years. Explainability in decision models refers, in part, to the ease with which humans can comprehend the underlying assumptions and reasoning of these models. In particular, DL decision models, which have achieved amazing accuracy in several cybersecurity problems, are represented implicitly through a multitude of numerical weights. Hence, their decisions are often perceived as opaque. To handle this issue, recent research in the field of eXplainable Artificial Intelligence (XAI) has significantly contributed to elucidating the impact of specific input features on cyber-threat alerts, paving the way to building trust among cybersecurity stakeholders.

This chapter is organized into three main parts. First, we review the general background in XAI by providing a contemporary taxonomy of XAI techniques (Section 5.2). Then, we delve into recent studies that incorporate XAI, in conjunction with both ML and DL, within the realm of cybersecurity. In this regard, we survey recent research studies utilizing both post-hoc and intrinsic XAI techniques to elucidate cyber-threat alerts made by DL-based decision models. This elucidation aids cybersecurity analysts in identifying and recognizing interpretable cyber-threat signatures (Section 5.3.1). Furthermore, we explore studies leveraging XAI-extracted knowledge to enhance the accuracy, simplicity, and/or robustness of decision models trained for cyber-threat detection problems (Section 5.3.2). In addition, we illustrate recent research studies that have used XAI techniques to identify vulnerabilities in AI-powered cyber-threat detection systems, and how these vulnerability explanations may guide the creation of realistic cyber-objects (e.g., executable malware) which are able to deceive target decision models (Section 5.3.3). Finally, we address the safety concerns inherent in current ML and DL explanations (Section 5.4). In particular, adversarial examples, data poisoning, model manipulation, and backdoor attacks pose significant challenges. Hence, we explore recent developments in adversarial attacks on explanations of decision models and identify emerging directions for designing more secure explanation models, with an emphasis on cybersecurity problems. Finally, we draw conclusions, summarize lessons learned, and illustrate open challenges inspiring future research directions (Section 5.5).

5.2 Background

During the past decade, the cybersecurity literature has placed increasing emphasis on the significant role of AI, particularly its rapidly advancing DL subfield, as a powerful learning paradigm for bolstering the resilience of digital security in private and public organizations, as well as in private citizen digital devices. However, a notable challenge arises from the fact that many AI and DL techniques develop decision models that are essentially black-boxes. These decision models are implicitly represented as numerical synaptic weights within the network, and their interpretation is often hindered by the intricacy and complexity of the deep neural network structure. At one time, the opacity of these black-boxes was deemed acceptable as long as the primary criterion for evaluating the quality of cybersecurity systems was their accuracy, typically measured using standard evaluation metrics such as F1-score, AUC, and predictive accuracy. In certain classification scenarios, accurate black-box models may suffice. However, in today's cybersecurity landscape, while the primary goal remains to provide accurate classifications of cyberdata, there is a growing preference in cybersecurity applications for decision models that are easier to interpret and explain (Andresini *et al.*, 2022).

Regarding the right to explanation, the seminal paper by van Lent *et al.* (2004) introduced the concept of XAI to describe the ability of AI systems to elucidate the actions of AI-controlled units in simulation gaming applications. As the importance of XAI in enhancing trust in AI models has grown in the last decade, both academics and practitioners have increasingly focused their research efforts on this topic. Significant attention has been directed towards the concept of explainability in AI decision-making processes, which refers to how easily humans can comprehend the underlying assumptions and reasoning. The more explainable a certain decision is, the easier it is for a human to understand or explain the underlying reasoning (Lakkaraju *et al.*, 2019). It is worth noting that the terms "explainability" and "interpretability" are often used interchangeably in the literature. However, Ali *et al.* (2023) have recently clarified the distinction between these two terms as follows:

> Explainability is the process of revealing the decision-making mechanisms of models, elucidating how inputs and outputs are mathematically interlinked. It relates to the ability to understand why decision models make their decisions. So, an explainable technique summarizes the reasons for a decision of a decision model... Interpretability is the process of understanding the underlying workings of the decision model by disclosing their intrinsic properties. It relates to the ability to understand how decision models make their decisions. AI systems that explain the internals of an AI model in a manner that humans can comprehend are known as model intrinsic techniques.

Several recent surveys (Ali *et al.*, 2023; Guidotti *et al.*, 2019; Nauta *et al.*, 2023) have addressed the concept of XAI by examining techniques, available tools, and evaluation metrics. Ali *et al.* (2023) present one of the latest XAI taxonomies, which revolves around the notion that explanations should be formulated with consideration to four dimensions inherent in a typical decision model development process: data explainability, post-hoc explainability, model explainability, and explainability assessment. This taxonomy entails categorizing XAI techniques based on:

- **Scope:** Input feature importance is commonly measured to explain the relationships between decision model inputs and corresponding outputs. This is typically done either at a global level, to illustrate the overall behavior of the decision model, or at a local level, to depict the behavior in a single decision. In particular, local explainers like LIME (Ribeiro *et al.*, 2016), SHAP (Lundberg and Lee, 2017), GradCAM (Selvaraju *et al.*, 2020), and Counterfactual (Mittelstadt *et al.*, 2019) elucidate specific decisions. Instead, global explainers like DALEX (Baniecki *et al.*, 2021) explain the behavior of a decision model across the entire dataset. For example, SHAP can provide both local and global explanations.
- **Complexity:** In general, the more complex the decision model, the more intricate the understanding of its decisions. XAI techniques can be categorized as either intrinsic or post-hoc depending on when explanations are generated. Intrinsic techniques enable the development of decision models that should be self-explanatory, with interpretability inherently built in. The Attention mechanism (Bahdanau *et al.*, 2015), which causes a machine learning algorithm to focus on the most useful of its input data, is an example of an intrinsic technique. Some ML algorithms like Decision Trees, Linear Regression, and Logistic Regression learn a decision model that is intrinsically interpretable. On the other hand, post-hoc XAI techniques elucidate existing decision models. They typically do not delve into the inner workings of the model being explained, often creating a surrogate of the original decision model to generate explanations. Examples of post-hoc techniques are LIME, SHAP, DALEX, GradCAM, and Counterfactual.
- **Model:** Explanations may be generated through a model-agnostic or model-specific pipeline. Model-agnostic techniques like LIME, SHAP, and DALEX are independent of the type of model being explained. Some model-agnostic techniques are often employed to offer post-hoc explanations at both global and local levels. Model-specific techniques can be used in combination with specific models. GradCAM is an example of a model-specific XAI technique used to explain the decisions made by a Convolution Neural Network (CNN).

- **Methodology:** Explanations are primarily generated using backpropagation and perturbation techniques. Backpropagation techniques (also known as Gradient techniques) back-propagate the signal from the output to the input of a neural model. A gradient function is used to compute derivatives of the outputs with respect to the parameters of each layer, update the weights of the neural model, and minimize the difference between the outputs and the ground truth labels. Both GradCAM and Attention are examples of this category of XAI techniques. On the other hand, the perturbation techniques replace input features by resorting to filling operations or generative algorithms, and use masking, conditional sampling, and other methods to change the feature set of the input space of a given sample. These techniques examine the impact of these changes on the decision model output. LIME, SHAP, and DALEX are examples of Perturbation techniques.

Recent studies have achieved relevant milestones in XAI research by quantifying the level of explainability for AI-based systems (Sovrano and Vitali, 2023). This topic has recently garnered considerable attention in the XAI community following proposals for EU laws that regulate AI and establish obligations for explainability based on the user and the degree of automation in decision-making processes. In fact, the EU is indirectly advocating for more transparent, user-centered, and accountable decision models to ensure the explainability of how work is performed in AI-based automated decision-making systems. In this regard, seminal work by Bibal *et al.* (2021) define the primary explainability requirements for Business-to-Consumer and Business-to-Business activity, stipulating that automated decision making systems should, at minimum, provide information about: the main input features used in a decision taken by the AI, all features processed by the AI, the specific decision made by the AI, and the underlying logical model followed by the AI. Sovrano and Vitali (2023) have recently extended the work of Bibal *et al.* (2021) by defining a model-agnostic approach and metric to objectively quantify how much of the information required by law is explained by an AI system.

Finally, Ali *et al.* (2023) summarize the desirable qualities of explanation techniques (i.e., translucency, portability, explanatory power, algorithmic complexity, and generalizability), individual explanations (i.e., fidelity, consistency, accuracy, stability, comprehensibility, certainty, interpretability, and representativeness), and human-friendly explanations (i.e., explanation by contrast, specificity, sociological context, abnormality, factuality, privacy, reliability, and causality) by surveying the recent state-of-the-art studies on these qualities.

5.3 XAI in Cybersecurity

Several recent studies in cybersecurity have observed that explaining classifications of cyber-data can help turn predictions into actions. Explanations may disclose measurable factors on which features of cyber-data influence the prediction of a future state of a sample and to what extent (Rjoub *et al.*, 2023). These factors can provide cybersecurity analysts with a deeper understanding of why an alert is triggered. Moreover, explaining the effect of certain input features of processed cyber-data on cyber-threat predictions can facilitate the translation of predictions into domain knowledge, enabling decision-making systems to better leverage the trust of process stakeholders (Andresini *et al.*, 2022). It should be noted that the demand for explainable security alerts, like any other AI-based decisions, aligns with the emerging EU vision, which extends the right to explanation outlined by the GDPR to AI and particularly DL-based solutions (Sartor and Lagioia, 2020), including in cybersecurity. At present, several XAI techniques have been explored in cybersecurity as part of the effort to explain decisions and improve accuracy. In addition, a few recent studies have investigated XAI advancements in the realm of Adversarial Learning. Several recent surveys have also covered research in XAI for cybersecurity (Capuano *et al.*, 2022; Reynaud and Roxin, 2025; Rjoub *et al.*, 2023; Zhang *et al.*, 2022).

5.3.1 XAI to Explain Cyber-Alerts

Much XAI research in cybersecurity has been devoted to using XAI techniques to explain AI decisions regarding cyber-alerts. These studies identify signatures of input features that are important in guiding AI decision-making processes for cyber-threat detection in various cybersecurity problems. In this regard, Warnecke *et al.* (2020)

describe the pioneering investigation of how post-hoc XAI techniques can be applied to generate explanations for the predictions of DL decision models trained for both malware detection and vulnerability discovery applications. Their study compares several post-hoc XAI techniques in terms of the accuracy of explanations, as well as security-focused aspects such as completeness, efficiency, and robustness. This study has inspired several subsequent investigations of the performance of post-hoc XAI techniques in several applications of DL in cybersecurity. For example, Andresini *et al.* (2021) use DALEX to explain how the decision process of a deep neural net model must change over time to fit possible concept drifts emerging in the distribution of network traffic data.

At present, the majority of cybersecurity researchers who use SHAP do so to explain decisions made by cyber-threat detection models trained primarily for network intrusion detection or malware detection. For example, Wang *et al.* (2020) use SHAP to identify the most relevant input features to recognize network traffic intrusions through a DL model. Keshk *et al.* (2023) use SHAP to explain the effect of input features on individual predictions made by a DL model trained for monitoring security in an IoT network. This study also examines global explanations of model decisions to give insights into the complex functioning of the intrusion detection system, providing the experts with deep knowledge about cyber-attacks. Piras *et al.* (2022) use SHAP, coupled with a statistical analysis of input features, to interpret the decisions yielded by several decision models trained with ML techniques for the detection of domain generation algorithms. In particular, this study highlights that different decision models may use input features in different ways. Hence, analysts should adapt to these different explanations and debug accordingly. Al-Essa *et al.* (2024) use SHAP to compare the effect of input features on the assignment of a network traffic trace to a class with both a simple DL model and an ensemble DL model. Their XAI analysis identifies the input features that are less important in the decisions yielded by the single model, but which gain importance in the decisions yielded by the ensemble model for some "R2L" intrusions that are wrongly classified by the single model as benign, but correctly recognized as "R2L" attacks by the ensemble. This allows the authors to explain how the ensemble can outperform the single model. Al-Essa *et al.* (2022a) also use SHAP to analyze how adversarial training and fine-tuning may change decisions of DL models trained for malware and network intrusion detection problems. In this regard, Figure 5.1 shows the global and local explanation analyses performed with SHAP to explain the decisions of the DL model trained with both adversarial training and fine-tuning. In particular, the explained decision model was developed for the task of Android malware classification, performed with data feature vectors included in the CICMalDroid20 dataset (Mahdavifar *et al.*, 2022). The global explanation map shown in Figure 5.1(a) ranks input features of CICMalDroid20 samples according to their effect on the decisions regarding each class recorded in the CICMalDroid20 dataset. The higher the explanation score, the greater the effect of the considered input feature on the decision assigning the sample to a selected class. For instance, this global explanation map shows that both *stat64* and *pipe* have greater effect than the other input features to recognize, in general, a malware specimen belonging to the class "Banking". These global insights are in line with local explanation scores plotted in Figure 5.1(b) for a specific sample which was recorded in the CICMalDroid20 dataset as belonging to class "Banking". Specifically, the local explanation map of the decision process on this sample shows how each input feature has an effect on the decision regarding each class. Notably, *pipe* and *stat64* have a great effect on deciding the local classification of the sample in class "Banking". In addition, the SHAP score line measured for this sample with respect to class "Banking" (that is, the ground truth class of the explained sample) is clearly separated from the score lines of the remaining classes, and shows how several input features combine to place the sample in the correct class "Banking".

Further studies experiment with the consideration of a surrogate model that was trained to produce explanations of binary decisions produced in network intrusion detection applications (Sy, 2009). The surrogate model is a decision tree, trained from network flow traces sampled around a counterfactual-based local decision boundary. Marino *et al.* (2018), on the other hand, describe an Adversarial Learning approach to understand why some of the network flow traces are misclassified by a DL model. In their study, the explanations are formulated in terms of the minimal modifications required to change the output of the black-box for any misclassified network traffic trace.

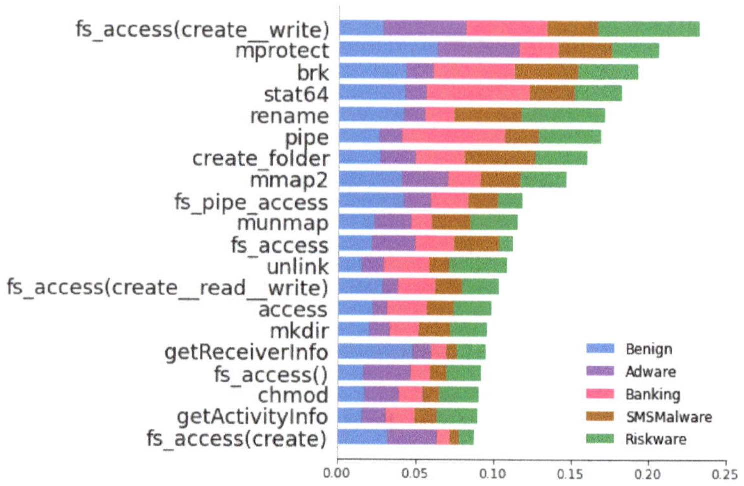

(a)

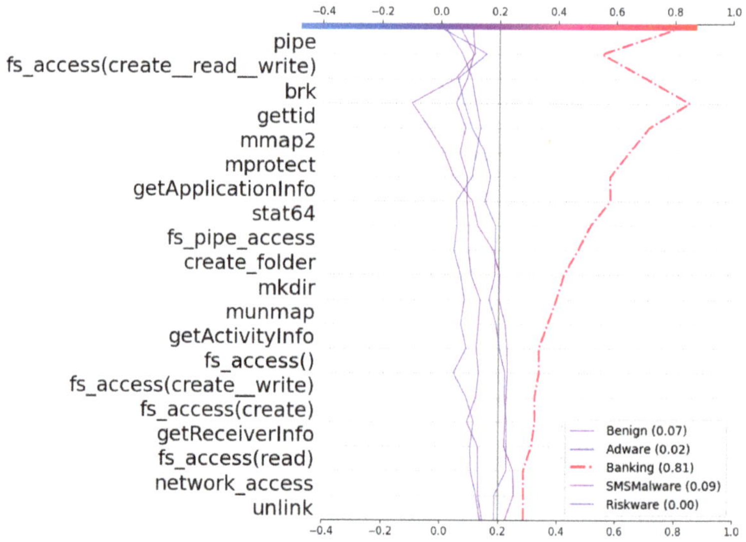

(b)

Fig. 5.1. (a) Global and (b) local explanations obtained with SHAP for decisions produced with a deep neural model trained for malware classification in CICMalDroid20 in Al-Essa *et al.* (2022a). The local explanation regards an Android application originally labeled in class "Banking".

Fan *et al.* (2021) define quantitative metrics to measure stability, robustness, and effectiveness of explanations, and they have performed a sanity check study of several XAI techniques in terms of these three metrics. Their study is performed considering the two problems of malware detection and familial identification, respectively. This study shows that the use of XAI can help the security analyst obtain knowledge of the most typical malicious behavior(s) during the malware analysis process.

Finally, Andresini *et al.* (2022) explore the effect of several properties (i.e., compactness, robustness, and separability) of explanations produced through the attention mechanism in a DL model trained for network intrusion detection. Their analysis reveals important relationships between the input features of the analyzed traces of the processed network traffic and the observed categories of intrusions. For example, the explanation of the decisions reported in Andresini *et al.* (2022) recognizes *service_ecr_i* as a relevant network traffic flow characteristic for the detection of "Smurf" attacks, a subcategory of denial-of-service (DoS) intrusions, since in these Smurf attacks, the targets are flooded with ECHO REPLAY packets from each host on the broadcast address. Following this research direction, Rose *et al.* (2024) have continued to use attention for explanation in cybersecurity. In particular, the authors adopt an imagery representation of a feature-vector description of cyber-data. In addition, they consider attention information synthesized through a Vision Transformer (ViT) model trained for cyber-threat detection problems, to explain malicious signatures driving the ViT decisions. The authors perform analysis on the inertia of the visual explanations derived for samples belonging to the same class, as well as analysis of the feature-level distances computed among the attention signatures associated with the different classes. Figure 5.2 shows the attention-based visual signatures extracted from the five classes recorded in CICMalDroid20, while Figure 5.3 shows the maps of the average Euclidean distance, computed pixel-wise, between the attention-based visual signature of each class type and the attention-based visual signatures of the remaining class types in CICMalDroid20. For example, the distance results show that system call *statfs64*, which is used to obtain information on the mounted file system, takes on distinct values in all five classes. This system call assumes, in fact, a different value in the visual signatures of the five classes. On the other hand,

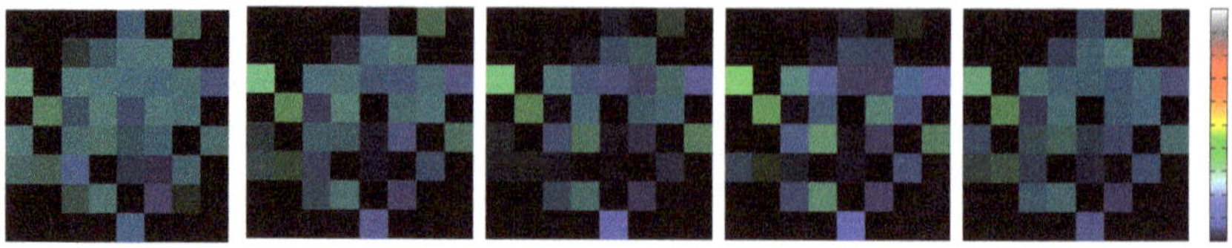

(a) (b) (c) (d) (e)

Fig. 5.2. Attention-based visual signatures extracted from the training set of CICMalDroid20 in Rose *et al.* (2024). (a) Benign, (b) Adware, (c) Banking, (d) SMS and (e) Riskware.

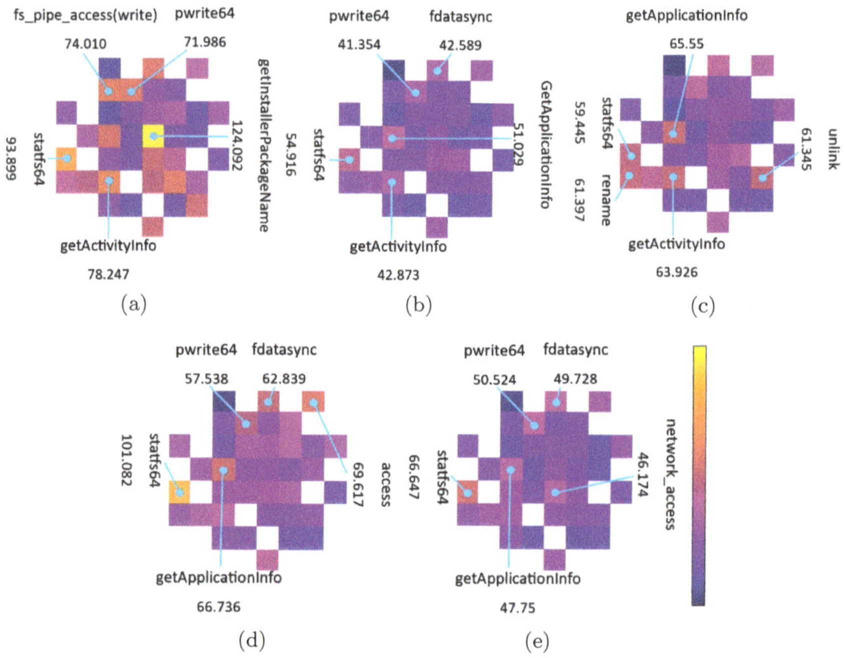

Fig. 5.3. Average Euclidean distance computed pixel-wise in Rose *et al.* (2024) between the attention-based visual signature of a class type and the attention-based visual signatures of the remaining class types in CICMalDroid20. For each class type, the pixels associated with the top-five features that measure the greatest distance are highlighted. (a) Benign, (b) Adware, (c) Banking, (d) SMS and (e) Riskware.

system call *pwrite64*, which writes bytes from buf to a file at an offset, takes on distinct values for four of the classes: "Benign", "Adware", "SMS" and "Riskware", while the *fdatasync* call, which is used for selective synchronization, discriminates between the classes: "Adware", "SMS" and "Riskware". This information is consistent with the study of Ham *et al.* (2013) that already identified the joint presence of system calls like *statfs64*, *pwrite* and *fdatasync* as a sign of malicious Android apps. More recently, the study of Chew *et al.* (2020) has also suggested monitoring *pwrite64* to identify signs of malicious behaviors.

5.3.2 XAI to Gain Accuracy and Simplicity

Some recent cybersecurity studies have delved into how XAI techniques can reveal valuable insights to enhance the accuracy of training a decision model for cyber-threat detection. For instance, Caforio *et al.* (2021) convert network traffic features into imagery pixels to train a CNN for classifying network traffic traces. Their study describes the use of the GradCAM technique to generate coarse localization maps that highlight the most important regions (features) of the network traffic data for predicting network intrusions. Since decisions made on samples belonging to the same class are expected to be explained with similar localization maps, the final classification of any new network trace is based on the class of the nearest-neighbor's historical localization map. This study demonstrates that cyber-threat detection models can leverage explanation information to enhance accuracy, in addition to decision explainability.

Al-Essa *et al.* (2022a) employ the adversarial training strategy to mitigate overfitting in training a DL model for both network intrusion detection and malware detection. In addition, they use SHAP to generate local explanations of decisions made during the adversarial training stage. These local explanations are then used to create a new feature set that describes the effect of the original cyber-data characteristics on the classifications of the examples processed during the adversarial training stage. Finally, a transfer learning strategy, namely fine-tuning, is used to improve the accuracy performance of the DL model via the explanation of knowledge.

Both Ho *et al.* (2022) and Seneviratne *et al.* (2022) use a ViT in problems of network intrusion detection and malware classification, respectively. Both these studies take advantage of the attention mechanism to gain accuracy without paying specific attention to the possibility of using attention information to explain decisions. Similarly, Andresini *et al.* (2022) show that the attention mechanism may be used to improve the accuracy of a DL model trained for network intrusion detection, by focusing the attention of the deep neural network on factors that are more relevant for recognizing attacks in network traffic data. Wu *et al.* (2021) explore the performance of a DL model enriched with an attention mechanism to detect Android malware. In particular, their study describes an interpretation step to automatically produce natural language descriptions of output to interpret key malicious behaviors. Finally, Rose *et al.* (2024) have recently evaluated the performance of a ViT-based classification model trained for both malware detection and network intrusion detection problems. Specifically, they introduce an XAI-based revision of the Knowledge Distillation strategy, which uses explainable knowledge synthesized through the attention layers of a ViT teacher to distill information to guide the training of a CNN student. Notably, the results of the extensive experimentation described in Rose *et al.* (2024) show that the distilled attention information contributes to gaining accuracy in various malware detection and network intrusion detection problems.

Adversarial training, ensemble learning, and XAI have been recently investigated in Al-Essa *et al.* (2024). In this study, both adversarial training and XAI information are used to enhance diversity among DL models selected to populate the ensemble model. Extensive experiments illustrated in Al-Essa *et al.* (2024) show that the proposed XAI-based ensemble algorithm outperforms several recent state-of-the-art cyber-threat detection methods in various problems of network intrusion detection and malware detection.

Al-Essa *et al.* (2022b, 2023) investigate how an XAI technique can disclose useful information concerning the robustness of the input characteristics in DL models and how this knowledge can be used in malware detection problems, both to pursue simpler DL models that are still accurate, and to fool DL models. In particular, the authors explore how global XAI knowledge (extracted with DALEX) can be used to identify the minimum amount of input characteristics to train a simple DL model by preserving high accuracy. In addition, in Al-Essa *et al.* (2023), DALEX is used to identify the minimum number of input features to perturb in order to evade DL models trained for malware detection.

Finally, a few recent studies have started the investigation of the accuracy performance of Graph Neural Networks (GNNs) in several domains, including network traffic data analysis, where data have a natural graph structure. GNNs are powerful graph-based DL models, which have recently gained significant attention and demonstrated remarkable accuracy performance due to their ability to capture relationships between data. Various explainability techniques have been proposed to shed light on the inner mechanisms of GNNs. The pioneering study exploring the use of GNNs in network intrusion detection was described in Lo *et al.* (2022), where a GraphSAGE-based model is used to address a network intrusion detection problem. Baahmed *et al.* (2023) extend the study of Lo *et al.* (2022) by comparing the performance of GraphSAGE with that of other well-established ML models. In addition, the authors explore how to explain intrusions detected with a GNN approach. To this aim, they adapt GNNExplainer (Ying *et al.*, 2019), which is the pioneer XAI technique for explaining GNN decisions, to the edge-level classification model. In particular, GNNExplainer is used in Baahmed *et al.* (2023) to examine the effect of input features on intrusion decisions and analyze the most influential sub-graphs, to explain some intrusion edges (e.g., "Bot" attacks) or benign edges.

5.3.3 XAI to Disclose Vulnerabilities

Pintor *et al.* (2022) describe *secml*, an open-source Python library for secure and explainable AI. The *secml* library implements the most popular attacks against ML and DL decision models, including test-time evasion attacks, to generate adversarial examples against deep neural networks and training-time poisoning attacks against Support Vector Machines and many other ML algorithms. In addition, it integrates some XAI techniques (e.g., feature- and prototype-based explanation techniques) to help security analysts understand why and how these attacks are successful. Staying within the realm of offensive Adversarial Learning in cybersecurity problems, Demetrio *et al.* (2019) use an XAI technique, known as feature attribution, to identify the most influential input features that contribute to decisions made by MalConv (Raff *et al.*, 2018), which is a CNN model trained directly from raw input bytes of Windows Portable Executable (PE) files to recognize malicious executables without any complex feature extraction step beforehand. The XAI analysis described in Demetrio *et al.* (2019) shows that MalConv does not learn any meaningful knowledge for malware detection from the data and text sections of executable files, but rather tends to learn to discriminate between benign and malware samples based on information found in the file header. Based on this finding, the authors of the study propose a realistic attack algorithm that generates adversarial malware binaries by only changing a few tens of bytes in the file header of Windows PE malware files.

Following this offensive research direction, Rosenberg *et al.* (2020) show that information provided by XAI can actually be leveraged by motivated adversaries to fool a target decision model. Hence, it is mandatory to account for the higher vulnerability of explainable decision models to adversarial attacks. In addition, this study presents an approach that uses XAI to generate adversarial examples for malware classifications. This approach finds the importance of all input features for a specific sample using explainability techniques, and then conducts a feature-specific modification, feature-by-feature. The study also introduces the concept of transferability of explainability to transfer attacks to black-box decision models. A remarkable conclusion drawn in Rosenberg *et al.* (2020) is that XAI techniques can be leveraged by adversaries, and this argues for training more interpretable decision models that account for the higher vulnerability of those models to adversarial attacks.

Kuppa and Le-Khac (2021) present a black-box attack that leverages XAI techniques to compromise the confidentiality and privacy properties of target decision models. Their study tests the proposed approach with datasets and models used in cybersecurity domains, showing that the proposed approach can achieve offensive goals of attackers, also under black-box threat models, which reflect the real-world setting.

Melis *et al.* (2022) investigate whether gradient-based attribution techniques, commonly adopted to explain model decisions by identifying the most relevant input features, can be used to help identify and select more robust algorithms in problems of Android malware detection. They also examine the performance of two different metrics to represent what we are calling the base-breadth of explanations, and a security measure called Adversarial Robustness Metric, by showing that a strong connection exists between the breadth of the base of features that contribute to explanations, and the adversarial robustness of those explanations. This study highlights that popular techniques like Gradient*Input and Integrated Gradients are strongly correlated to security when applied to both linear and non-linear detectors, while more elementary explanation techniques like the simple Gradient do not provide reliable information about the robustness of such classifiers. This study does assume that attackers know the parameters of a differentiable decision model.

Severi *et al.* (2021) describe the use of XAI techniques to guide the selection of relevant input features and values to create effective backdoor triggers in a model-agnostic fashion. Their study considers multiple benchmark datasets for malware classification, including Windows PE files, PDFs, and Android applications, to show the effectiveness of the produced attacks against a diverse set of decision models and evaluate the effect of various constraints imposed on the attacker. In addition, the study experiments with some potential defensive strategies, showing the difficulties of completely defending against these attacks, especially when the attacks blend in with the legitimate sample distribution.

Imran *et al.* (2024) have recently used SHAP to identify input features that allow adversarial Windows PE malware created with several evasion attack methods to be correctly classified by a target malware detection classifier trained with LGBM, while Lobascio *et al.* (2025) conduct the same analysis of feature robustness by considering a target DL model trained with the adversarial training strategy.

Finally, Rose *et al.* (2025) have recently explored the use of Counterfactuals (Guidotti, 2024) to identify the vulnerabilities of a DL model trained with LIEF input features (Şandor *et al.*, 2023) for Windows PE malware detection. Counterfactuals are XAI techniques to provide "what-if" explanations of a decision model prediction. In particular, a counterfactual explains the minimal perturbation to an input sample that changes the original prediction. LIEF is a well-known open-source library to perform static analysis of a Windows PE file. LIEF allows us to parse the binary code of a Windows PE file into a vector of 2381 raw static features. In Rose *et al.*

(2025), counterfactual explanations are produced regarding the group of LIEF features that describe the byte distribution (namely byte histogram features) in the binary. These counterfactuals are used to cause appropriate changes in Windows PE codes through either padding or section injection manipulations. The applied changes aim to preserve the Windows PE-compatible format, obtain an executable file, and maintain the malicious nature of the executable file, evading a decision model. Both counterfactuals and manipulations are done in a black-box setting. Figure 5.4 gives a histogram of the number of Windows PE malware for which each LIEF-extracted byte histogram feature is selected to generate a counterfactual in the empirical study conducted in Rose *et al.* (2025). De Rose *et al.* used the PEMML dataset[1] for their evaluation. That dataset includes about 207k Windows binaries, comprising about 115k malware specimens and about 87k benign. The plot in Figure 5.4 shows that byte "0x7D" is one of the input features of the target decision model most often changed to create counterfactuals and, as a result, considered to drive the creation of an adversarial Windows PE malware. In addition, the byte histogram feature of byte "0x44" is the

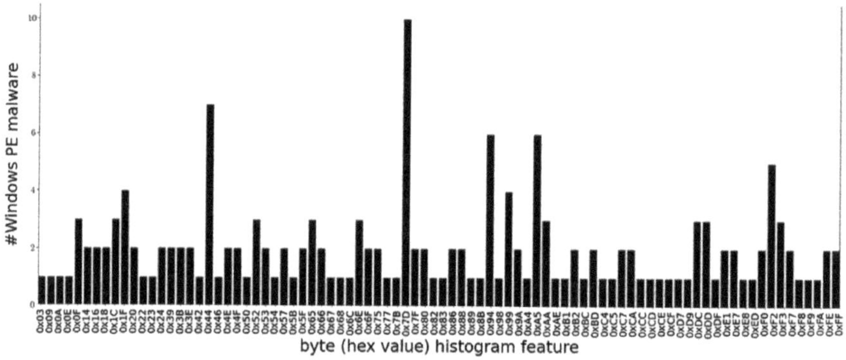

Fig. 5.4. Analysis of the byte histogram features selected in Rose *et al.* (2025) to create counterfactual (CF) explanations (X-axis) versus the number of Windows PE malware specimens from PEMML in which the input feature was changed with a counterfactual (Y-axis).

[1] https://practicalsecurityanalytics.com/pe-malware-machine-learning-dataset/.

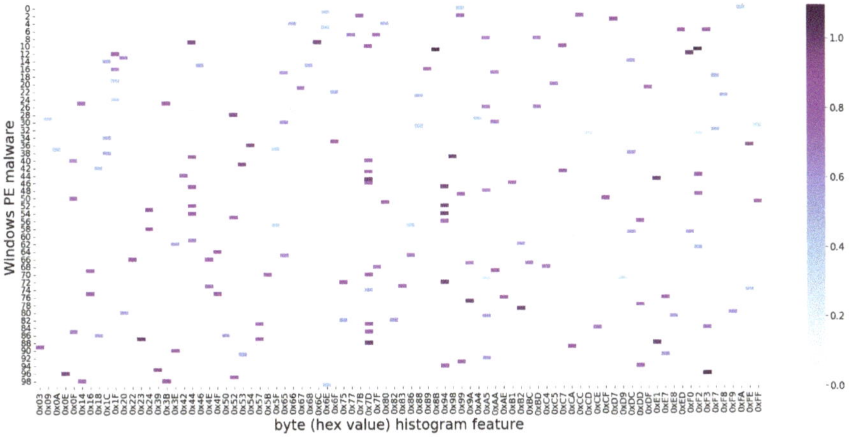

Fig. 5.5. Analysis of the byte histogram features selected in Rose *et al.* (2025) to create counterfactual (CF) explanations: difference between the values of the feature observed in both the original file and the generated counterfactual.

next most often changed, according to this histogram. Hence, these counterfactual insights reveal that the addition of adversarial payloads filled with these two bytes often provides the opportunity to evade the target model. Focusing the attention on the byte histogram features that are involved in the counterfactuals produced in Rose *et al.* (2025), Figure 5.5 shows the heatmap of the differences computed between the values observed for each selected byte histogram feature in both the original Windows PE malware (from PEMML) and the corresponding counterfactual generated. The heatmap of these counterfactual-guided changes explains that the byte histogram feature of byte "0x7D" should be significantly increased (with one exception) to achieve a change in the model decision, while the byte histogram feature of bytes "0x1F", "0x5F" and "0x68" need smaller changes with respect to the original values to evade the decision model.

Further comments can be made regarding the evasion ability of adversarial Windows PE malware produced in Rose *et al.* (2025) leveraging counterfactuals. In particular, the evaluation study conducted in Rose *et al.* (2025) compares the evasion ability of adversarial Windows PE malware generated with OLIVANDER (the counterfactual-based evasion method described in Rose *et al.* (2025) and run with padding or section injection), GAMMA (Demetrio *et al.*, 2021) (run with padding or section injection) and AMG (Kozák *et al.*, 2024) (run with all manipulations described in Kozák *et al.* (2024), padding or section injection). OLIVANDER, GAMMA and AMG are black-box evasion methods used to create adversarial Windows PE malware to fool the same target DL model trained in the LIEF feature space. Table 5.1 reports the *evasion rate* measured for AMG, AMG^{PAD}, AMG^{INJ}, $\text{GAMMA}^{\text{PAD}}$, $\text{GAMMA}^{\text{INJ}}$, $\text{OLIVANDER}^{\text{PAD}}$ and $\text{OLIVANDER}^{\text{INJ}}$. The *evasion rate* results show that $\text{OLIVANDER}^{\text{PAD}}$ produces the highest percentage of adversarial Windows PE malware that fool the target model in this comparative study, with $\text{OLIVANDER}^{\text{INJ}}$ as runner-up. Figure 5.6 shows the average number of anti-malware systems accessed via VirusTotal which are evaded by each Windows PE malware from the original PEMML malware dataset and the constructed adversarial malware dataset. This plot shows that $\text{OLIVANDER}^{\text{INJ}}$ achieves, on average, the higher evasion ability versus commercial anti-malware systems, with $\text{GAMMA}^{\text{INJ}}$ as runner-up. In general, this study confirms that XAI can be successfully used to identify the vulnerabilities of a competitive DL model trained for the Windows PE malware dataset, and to create a benchmark of adversarial Windows PE malware that researchers may leverage to test the robustness of Windows PE malware detectors.

Table 5.1. *evasion rate* of AMG, AMG^{PAD}, AMG^{INJ}, $\text{GAMMA}^{\text{PAD}}$, $\text{GAMMA}^{\text{INJ}}$, $\text{OLIVANDER}^{\text{PAD}}$ and $\text{OLIVANDER}^{\text{INJ}}$ as obtained in the evaluation study conducted in Rose *et al.* (2025).

Method	Evasion Rate (%)
AMG	35
AMG^{PAD}	32
AMG^{INJ}	6
$\text{GAMMA}^{\text{PAD}}$	10
$\text{GAMMA}^{\text{INJ}}$	58
$\text{OLIVANDER}^{\text{PAD}}$	79
$\text{OLIVANDER}^{\text{INJ}}$	75

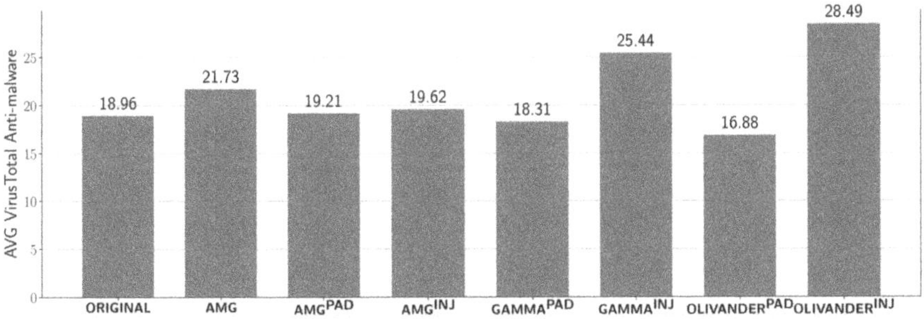

Fig. 5.6. Average (AVG) number of real-world anti-malware evaded in VirusTotal by the original malware set (ORIGINAL) and the malware set modified by replacing original malware with adversarial malware produced with AMG, AMG^{PAD}, AMG^{INJ}, $\text{GAMMA}^{\text{PAD}}$, $\text{GAMMA}^{\text{INJ}}$, $\text{OLIVANDER}^{\text{PAD}}$, $\text{OLIVANDER}^{\text{INJ}}$ according to the evaluation conducted in Rose *et al.* (2025).

5.4 Security of XAI

Recent advances in adversarial learning research have shown the vulnerabilities of several state-of-the-art XAI techniques, putting their security and trustworthiness into question. In the last few years, adversarial attacks and defenses against explainability of XAI models have attracted much attention in the AI and Security community. Alvarez-Melis and Jaakkola (2018) present the seminal study that analyses the notion of explanation robustness, while Ancona *et al.* (2018) describe the concept of explainability sensitivity. The pioneering study of Ghorbani *et al.* (2019) describes the first adversarial attack against explanations produced through gradient-based feature attributions. Subsequently, several attack methods against explanations have been formulated in recent years. In particular, Baniecki and Biecek (2024) have compiled a list of attacks on XAI techniques along with a categorization with respect to the change strategy:

- Attacks to change the data by producing adversarial samples to manipulate the explanation without impacting the prediction.
- Attacks to change the model by using fine-tuning or regularizing weights to manipulate explanations without impacting the predictive performance.
- Attacks to change both the data and the model.

Existing studies on security of XAI consider different XAI techniques (e.g., SHAP, LIME, GradCAM, CAM, Counterfactual) and different decision model algorithms (e.g., MLP, CNN, VGG, sent, Logistic Regression, XGBoost, Random Forest). Notably, the survey of Baniecki and Biecek (2024) shows that the most vulnerable explanation models are the first-introduced and most popular XAI techniques, e.g., SHAP and Grad-CAM. In addition, most studies on XAI security consider imagery datasets; one exception being Kuppa and Le-Khac (2020), which analyses the consistency, correctness, and confidence security properties of gradient-based XAI techniques for decision models trained in malicious PDF, Android malware, and network traffic intrusion detection problems.

Noppel *et al.* (2023) extend a fooling explanation mechanism through fine-tuning and backdoors to create a red-herring attack that manipulates the explanation to cover an adversarial change in the prediction of a target decision model. A few researchers have investigated how to obtain reliable explanations. Meyer *et al.* (2023) formalize theoretical and empirical characterizations of the factors influencing explanation stability under data shifts. Slack *et al.* (2020) describe a scaffolding technique that hides the biases of any given decision model by allowing an adversarial entity to craft an arbitrary desired explanation. This study shows that the proposed method can effectively manipulate explanations produced with LIME and SHAP for tabular data decisions. Slack *et al.* (2021) also describe a framework to obtain Bayesian versions of LIME and KernelSHAP, which output credible intervals for the levels of importance of features, by capturing the associated uncertainty. The resulting explanations allow users to make concrete inferences about their quality and are highly consistent and stable. Baniecki *et al.* (2022) describe a genetic algorithm to manipulate model explanations using a gradient algorithm to perform fooling via data poisoning efficiently for neural networks. Their study evaluates the robustness of the XAI method known as Partial Dependence (PD) and provides a sanity check for the future use of PD by responsible machine learning practitioners.

Finally, a few researchers have started the development of defense methods to fix vulnerabilities of some XAI techniques by using multiple approaches, such as regularizing a neural network, forcing the network to remain unchanged under perturbation, aggregating explanations produced by multiple methods, introducing a smooth surface regularization procedure to force robust attributions, or accounting for robustness in the search process. A recent list of defense methods against explanation attacks has been described in Baniecki and Biecek (2024). In any case, except for Kuppa and Le-Khac (2020), to the best of our knowledge, existing studies do not consider the peculiar characteristics of efforts to fool or otherwise tamper with explanations in cybersecurity problems of malware and intrusion detection.

5.5 Lessons Learned and Future Challenges

XAI plays a crucial role in the development of effective AI- and DL-based cybersecurity systems by contributing to building trust among security stakeholders in these systems. In addition, the recent literature has clearly shown that explanations may help us in:

- Making cyber-threat detection decisions understandable to humans.
- Revealing "new" cyber-attack signatures or showing that AI decisions are taken according to "known" signatures.
- Gaining accuracy in cyber-threat detection models, allowing us to strive for model simplicity and, in several cases, model robustness.

On the other hand, XAI techniques have an active role in the adversarial learning field as they may disclose knowledge needed to create new possibilities for fooling decision models used in several cybersecurity problems, paving the way for future investigations to secure AI decisions, and mitigating the detected vulnerabilities. Despite the widespread use of XAI in various domains, including cybersecurity, XAI techniques must demonstrate their robustness to adversarial actions in order to make the transition from academia to becoming a crucial component of the defense security line. Therefore, best practices include the development and evaluation of the robustness of explainability, in addition to the robustness of predictions, and the development of defensive strategies for both cyber-threat detection models and cyber-data explanations.

Furthermore, there is a need to consider the broader societal impact that the security of XAI may have. Ethical adversarial attacks could potentially be used by cybersecurity experts to thwart criminals using AI and tamper with their security systems. Ethical adversarial explanations may be employed to ensure that XAI techniques remain robust in real-world applications. Another issue is the necessity of involving humans in the loop, with human-machine interaction at the core of the explanation process. This is crucial for designing cybersecurity systems that humans can understand and use.

Acknowledgments

Giuseppina Andresini is partially supported by the project FAIR (Future AI Research) (PE00000013), Spoke 6 (Symbiotic AI), under the NRRP MUR program funded by the European Union (NextGenerationEU). Annalisa Appice and Donato Malerba are partially supported by project SERICS (PE00000014) under the NRRP MUR National Recovery and Resilience Plan funded by the European Union (NextGenerationEU).

Bibliography

Al-Essa, M., Andresini, G., Appice, A., and Malerba, D. (2022a). An XAI-based adversarial training approach for cyber-threat detection, in *IEEE International Conference on Dependable, Autonomic and Secure Computing, International Conference on Pervasive Intelligence and Computing, International Conference on Cloud and Big Data Computing, International Conference on Cyber Science and Technology Congress, DASC/PiCom/CBDCom/CyberSciTech 2022* (IEEE), pp. 1–8, doi:10.1109/DASC/PICOM/CBDCOM/CY55231.2022.9927842.

Al-Essa, M., Andresini, G., Appice, A., and Malerba, D. (2022b). XAI to explore robustness of features in adversarial training for cybersecurity, in M. Ceci, S. Flesca, E. Masciari, G. Manco, and Z. W. Ras (eds.), *Foundations of Intelligent Systems - 26th International Symposium, ISMIS 2022, Proceedings*, *Lecture Notes in Computer Science*, Vol. 13515 (Springer, Cham, Switzerland), pp. 117–126, doi:10.1007/978-3-031-16564-1_12.

Al-Essa, M., Andresini, G., Appice, A., and Malerba, D. (2023). Striving for simplicity in deep neural models trained for malware detection, in R. Meo and F. Silvestri (eds.), *Machine Learning and Principles and Practice of Knowledge Discovery in Databases — International*

Workshops of ECML PKDD 2023, Revised Selected Papers, Part III, Communications in Computer and Information Science, Vol. 2135 (Springer, Cham), pp. 529–540, doi:10.1007/978-3-031-74633-8_40.

Al-Essa, M., Andresini, G., Appice, A., and Malerba, D. (2024). PANACEA: A neural model ensemble for cyber-threat detection, *Machine Learning* **113**, 8, pp. 5379–5422, doi:10.1007/S10994-023-06470-2.

Ali, S., Abuhmed, T., El-Sappagh, S. H. A., Muhammad, K., Alonso-Moral, J. M., Confalonieri, R., Guidotti, R., Ser, J. D., Rodríguez, N. D., and Herrera, F. (2023). Explainable artificial intelligence (XAI): what we know and what is left to attain trustworthy artificial intelligence, *Information Fusion* **99**, p. 101805, doi:10.1016/J.INFFUS.2023.101805.

Alvarez-Melis, D. and Jaakkola, T. S. (2018). Towards robust interpretability with self-explaining neural networks, in S. Bengio, H. M. Wallach, H. Larochelle, K. Grauman, N. Cesa-Bianchi, and R. Garnett (eds.), *Advances in Neural Information Processing Systems 31: Annual Conference on Neural Information Processing Systems 2018, NeurIPS 2018*, pp. 7786–7795.

Ancona, M., Ceolini, E., Öztireli, C., and Gross, M. (2018). Towards better understanding of gradient-based attribution methods for deep neural networks, in *6th International Conference on Learning Representations, ICLR 2018, Conference Track Proceedings* (OpenReview.net).

Andresini, G., Appice, A., Caforio, F. P., Malerba, D., and Vessio, G. (2022). ROULETTE: A neural attention multi-output model for explainable network intrusion detection, *Expert Systems with Applications* **201**, p. 117144, doi:10.1016/J.ESWA.2022.117144.

Andresini, G., Pendlebury, F., Pierazzi, F., Loglisci, C., Appice, A., and Cavallaro, L. (2021). INSOMNIA: Towards concept-drift robustness in network intrusion detection, in N. Carlini, A. Demontis, and Y. Chen (eds.), *AISec@CCS 2021: Proceedings of the 14th ACM Workshop on Artificial Intelligence and Security, Virtual Event,* (ACM), New York, NY, pp. 111–122, doi:10.1145/3474369.3486864.

Baahmed, A. R. E., Andresini, G., Robardet, C., and Appice, A. (2023). Using graph neural networks for the detection and explanation of network intrusions, in R. Meo and F. Silvestri (eds.), *Machine Learning and Principles and Practice of Knowledge Discovery in Databases — International Workshops of ECML PKDD 2023, Revised Selected Papers, Part III, Communications in Computer and Information Science*, Vol. 2135 (Springer, Cham), pp. 201–216, doi:10.1007/978-3-031-74633-8_13.

Bahdanau, D., Cho, K., and Bengio, Y. (2015). Neural machine translation by jointly learning to align and translate, in Y. Bengio and Y. LeCun (eds.), *3rd International Conference on Learning Representations, ICLR 2015, Conference Track Proceedings*.

Baniecki, H. and Biecek, P. (2024). Adversarial attacks and defenses in explainable artificial intelligence: A survey, *Information Fusion* **107**, p. 102303, doi:10.1016/J.INFFUS.2024.102303.

Baniecki, H., Kretowicz, W., and Biecek, P. (2022). Fooling partial dependence via data poisoning, in M. Amini, S. Canu, A. Fischer, T. Guns, P. K. Novak, and G. Tsoumakas (eds.), *Machine Learning and Knowledge Discovery in Databases — European Conference, ECML PKDD 2022, Proceedings, Part III*, *Lecture Notes in Computer Science*, Vol. 13715 (Springer, Cham), pp. 121–136, doi: 10.1007/978-3-031-26409-2_8.

Baniecki, H., Kretowicz, W., Piatyszek, P., Wisniewski, J., and Biecek, P. (2021). Dalex: Responsible machine learning with interactive explainability and fairness in python, *Journal of Machine Learning Research* **22**, pp. 214:1–214:7.

Bibal, A., Lognoul, M., de Streel, A., and Frénay, B. (2021). Legal requirements on explainability in machine learning, *Artificial Intelligence and Law* **29**, 2, pp. 149–169, doi:10.1007/S10506-020-09270-4.

Caforio, F. P., Andresini, G., Vessio, G., Appice, A., and Malerba, D. (2021). Leveraging grad-cam to improve the accuracy of network intrusion detection systems, in C. Soares and L. Torgo (eds.), *Discovery Science — 24th International Conference, DS 2021, Proceedings*, *Lecture Notes in Computer Science*, Vol. 12986 (Springer, Cham), pp. 385–400, doi:10.1007/978-3-030-88942-5_30.

Capuano, N., Fenza, G., Loia, V., and Stanzione, C. (2022). Explainable artificial intelligence in cybersecurity: A survey, *IEEE Access* **10**, pp. 93575–93600, doi:10.1109/ACCESS.2022.3204171.

Chew, C., Kumar, V., Patros, P., and Malik, R. (2020). Escapade: Encryption-type-ransomeware: System call based pattern detection. in *Proceedings of 14th International Conference on Network and System Security (NSS 2020), LNCS 12570*, pp. 388–407, doi:10.1007/978-3-030-65745-1_23.

Demetrio, L., Biggio, B., Lagorio, G., Roli, F., and Armando, A. (2019). Explaining vulnerabilities of deep learning to adversarial malware binaries, in P. Degano and R. Zunino (eds.), *Proceedings of the Third Italian Conference on Cyber Security, Pisa, Italy, February 13–15, 2019*, *CEUR Workshop Proceedings*, Vol. 2315 (CEUR-WS.org).

Demetrio, L., Biggio, B., Lagorio, G., Roli, F., and Armando, A. (2021). Functionality-preserving black-box optimization of adversarial Windows malware, *IEEE Transactions on Information Forensics and Security* **16**, pp. 3469–3478, doi:10.1109/TIFS.2021.3082330.

Fan, M., Wei, W., Xie, X., Liu, Y., Guan, X., and Liu, T. (2021). Can we trust your explanations? Sanity checks for interpreters in Android malware analysis, *IEEE Transactions on Information Forensics and Security* **16**, pp. 838–853, doi:10.1109/TIFS.2020.3021924.

Ghorbani, A., Abid, A., and Zou, J. Y. (2019). Interpretation of neural networks is fragile, in *The Thirty-Third AAAI Conference on Artificial Intelligence, AAAI 2019, The Thirty-First Innovative Applications of Artificial Intelligence Conference, IAAI 2019, The Ninth AAAI Symposium on Educational Advances in Artificial Intelligence, EAAI 2019* (AAAI Press), pp. 3681–3688, doi:10.1609/AAAI.V33I01.33013681.

Guidotti, R. (2024). Counterfactual explanations and how to find them: literature review and benchmarking, *Data Mining and Knowledge Discovery* **38**, 5, pp. 2770–2824, doi:10.1007/S10618-022-00831-6.

Guidotti, R., Monreale, A., Ruggieri, S., Turini, F., Giannotti, F., and Pedreschi, D. (2019). A survey of methods for explaining black box models, *ACM Computing Surveys* **51**, 5, pp. 93:1–93:42, doi:10.1145/3236009.

Ham, Y. J., Moon, D., Lee, H.-W., Lim, J. D., and Kim, J. N. (2013). Activation pattern analysis on malicious Android mobile applications, in *1st International Conference on Artificial Intelligence, Modelling and Simulation, AIMS 2013* (IEEE Computer Society), doi:10.5555/2605697.2605748.

Ho, C. M. K., Yow, K. C., Zhu, Z., and Aravamuthan, S. (2022). Network intrusion detection via flow-to-image conversion and vision transformer classification, *IEEE Access* **10**, pp. 97780–97793, doi:10.1109/ACCESS.2022.3200034.

Imran, M., Appice, A., and Malerba, D. (2024). Evaluating realistic adversarial attacks against machine learning models for windows PE malware detection, *Future Internet* **16**, 5, p. 168, doi:10.3390/FI16050168.

Keshk, M., Koroniotis, N., Pham, N., Moustafa, N., Turnbull, B. P., and Zomaya, A. Y. (2023). An explainable deep learning-enabled intrusion detection framework in iot networks, *Information Science* **639**, p. 119000, doi:10.1016/J.INS.2023.119000.

Kozák, M., Jurecek, M., Stamp, M., and Troia, F. D. (2024). Creating valid adversarial examples of malware, *Journal of Computer Virology and Hacking Techniques*, pp. 1–15. doi:10.1007/s11416-024-00516-2.

Kuppa, A. and Le-Khac, N. (2020). Black box attacks on explainable artificial intelligence(XAI) methods in cyber security, in *2020 International Joint Conference on Neural Networks, IJCNN 2020* (IEEE), pp. 1–8, doi:10.1109/IJCNN48605.2020.9206780.

Kuppa, A. and Le-Khac, N. (2021). Adversarial XAI methods in cybersecurity, *IEEE Transactions on Information Forensics and Security* **16**, pp. 4924–4938, doi:10.1109/TIFS.2021.3117075.

Lakkaraju, H., Kamar, E., Caruana, R., and Leskovec, J. (2019). Faithful and customizable explanations of black box models, in V. Conitzer, G. K. Hadfield, and S. Vallor (eds.), *Proceedings of the 2019 AAAI/ACM Conference on AI, Ethics, and Society, AIES 2019* (ACM), pp. 131–138, doi:10.1145/3306618.3314229, https://doi.org/10.1145/3306618.3314229.

Lo, W. W., Layeghy, S., Sarhan, M., Gallagher, M., and Portmann, M. (2022). E-graphsage: A graph neural network based intrusion detection system for IoT, in *2022 IEEE/IFIP Network Operations and Management Symposium, NOMS 2022* (IEEE), pp. 1–9, doi:10.1109/NOMS54207.2022.9789878.

Lobascio, L., Andresini, G., Appice, A., and Malerba, D. (2025). Adversarial training to improve accuracy and robustness of a Windows PE malware detection model, in G. Costa, R. Montanari, M. Carminati, and G. Sciarretta (eds.), *Proceedings of the Joint National Conference on Cybersecurity, ITASEC & SERICS 2025, CEUR Workshop Proceedings*, Vol. 3962 (CEUR-WS.org).

Lundberg, S. M. and Lee, S. (2017). A unified approach to interpreting model predictions, in I. Guyon, U. von Luxburg, S. Bengio, H. M. Wallach, R. Fergus, S. V. N. Vishwanathan, and R. Garnett (eds.), *Advances in Neural Information Processing Systems 30: Annual Conference on Neural Information Processing Systems 2017, NIPS 2017*, pp. 4765–4774.

Mahdavifar, S., Alhadidi, D., and Ghorbani, A. A. (2022). Effective and efficient hybrid Android malware classification using pseudo-label stacked auto-encoder, *Journal of Network and Systems Management* **30**, 1, p. 22, doi:10.1007/s10922-021-09634-4.

Marino, D. L., Wickramasinghe, C. S., and Manic, M. (2018). An adversarial approach for explainable AI in intrusion detection systems, in *IECON 2018 — 44th Annual Conference of the IEEE Industrial Electronics Society* (IEEE), pp. 3237–3243, doi:10.1109/IECON.2018.8591457, https://doi.org/10.1109/IECON.2018.8591457.

Melis, M., Scalas, M., Demontis, A., Maiorca, D., Biggio, B., Giacinto, G., and Roli, F. (2022). Do gradient-based explanations tell anything about adversarial robustness to Android malware? *International Journal of Machine Learning and Cybernetics* **13**, 1, pp. 217–232, doi: 10.1007/S13042-021-01393-7.

Meyer, A. P., Ley, D., Srinivas, S., and Lakkaraju, H. (2023). On minimizing the impact of dataset shifts on actionable explanations, in R. J. Evans and I. Shpitser (eds.), *Uncertainty in Artificial Intelligence, UAI 2023, Proceedings of Machine Learning Research*, Vol. 216 (PMLR), pp. 1434–1444.

Mittelstadt, B. D., Russell, C., and Wachter, S. (2019). Explaining explanations in AI, in Danah Boyd and J. H. Morgenstern (eds.), *Proceedings of the Conference on Fairness, Accountability, and Transparency, FAT 2019* (ACM), pp. 279–288, doi:10.1145/3287560.3287574.

Nauta, M., Trienes, J., Pathak, S., Nguyen, E., Peters, M., Schmitt, Y., Schlötterer, J., van Keulen, M., and Seifert, C. (2023). From anecdotal evidence to quantitative evaluation methods: A systematic review on evaluating explainable AI, *ACM Computing Surveys* **55**, 13s, pp. 295:1–295:42, doi:10.1145/3583558.

Noppel, M., Peter, L., and Wressnegger, C. (2023). Disguising attacks with explanation-aware backdoors, in *44th IEEE Symposium on Security and Privacy, SP 2023* (IEEE), pp. 664–681, doi:10.1109/SP46215.2023.10179308, https://doi.org/10.1109/SP46215.2023.10179308.

Pintor, M., Demetrio, L., Sotgiu, A., Melis, M., Demontis, A., and Biggio, B. (2022). secml: Secure and explainable machine learning in python, *SoftwareX* **18**, p. 101095, doi:10.1016/J.SOFTX.2022.101095.

Piras, G., Pintor, M., Demetrio, L., and Biggio, B. (2022). Explaining machine learning DGA detectors from DNS traffic data, in C. Demetrescu and A. Mei (eds.), *Proceedings of the Italian Conference on Cybersecurity (ITASEC 2022), Rome, Italy, June 20–23, 2022, CEUR Workshop Proceedings*, Vol. 3260 (CEUR-WS.org), pp. 150–168.

Raff, E., Barker, J., Sylvester, J., Brandon, R., Catanzaro, B., and Nicholas, C. K. (2018). Malware detection by eating a whole EXE, in *The Workshops of the The Thirty-Second AAAI Conference on Artificial Intelligence, AAAI Technical Report*, Vol. WS-18 (AAAI Press), pp. 268–276.

Reynaud, S. and Roxin, A. (2025). Review of explainable artificial intelligence for cybersecurity systems, *Discover Artificial Intelligence* **5**, 1, p. 78, doi:10.1007/S44163-025-00318-5.

Ribeiro, M. T., Singh, S., and Guestrin, C. (2016). "Why should I trust you?": Explaining the predictions of any classifier, in B. Krishnapuram, M. Shah, A. J. Smola, C. C. Aggarwal, D. Shen, and R. Rastogi (eds.), *Proceedings of the 22nd ACM SIGKDD International*

Conference on Knowledge Discovery and Data Mining, KDD 2016 (ACM), New York, NY, pp. 1135–1144, doi:10.1145/2939672.2939778.

Rjoub, G., Bentahar, J., Wahab, O. A., Mizouni, R., Song, A., Cohen, R., Otrok, H., and Mourad, A. (2023). A survey on explainable artificial intelligence for cybersecurity, *IEEE Transactions on Network and Service Management* **20**, 4, pp. 5115–5140, doi:10.1109/TNSM.2023.3282740.

Rose, L. D., Andresini, G., Appice, A., and Malerba, D. (2024). VINCENT: cyber-threat detection through vision transformers and knowledge distillation, *Computers & Security* **144**, p. 103926, doi:10.1016/J.COSE.2024.103926.

Rose, L. D., Andresini, G., Appice, A., and Malerba, D. (2025). OLIVANDER: A counterfactual-based method to generate adversarial windows PE malware, *Data Mining and Knowledge Discovery* **39**, 5, p. 46, https://doi.org/10.1007/s10618-025-01127-1.

Rosenberg, I., Meir, S., Berrebi, J., Gordon, I., Sicard, G., and David, E. O. (2020). Generating end-to-end adversarial examples for malware classifiers using explainability, in *2020 International Joint Conference on Neural Networks, IJCNN 2020, Glasgow, United Kingdom, July 19–24, 2020* (IEEE), pp. 1–10, doi:10.1109/IJCNN48605.2020.9207168.

Sartor, G. and Lagioia, F. (2020). The impact of the general data protection regulation (gdpr) on artificial intelligence, *European Parliament, Directorate-General for Parliamentary Research Services*, pp. 1–100, https://dx.doi.org/10.2861/293.

Selvaraju, R. R., Cogswell, M., Das, A., Vedantam, R., Parikh, D., and Batra, D. (2020). Grad-cam: Visual explanations from deep networks via gradient-based localization, *International Journal of Computer Vision* **128**, 2, pp. 336–359, doi:10.1007/S11263-019-01228-7.

Seneviratne, S., Shariffdeen, R., Rasnayaka, S., and Kasthuriarachchi, N. (2022). Self-supervised vision transformers for malware detection, *IEEE Access* **10**, pp. 103121–103135, doi:10.1109/ACCESS.2022.3206445.

Severi, G., Meyer, J., Coull, S. E., and Oprea, A. (2021). Explanation-guided backdoor poisoning attacks against malware classifiers, in M. D. Bailey and R. Greenstadt (eds.), *30th USENIX Security Symposium, USENIX Security 2021* (USENIX Association), pp. 1487–1504.

Slack, D., Hilgard, A., Singh, S., and Lakkaraju, H. (2021). Reliable post hoc explanations: Modeling uncertainty in explainability, in M. Ranzato, A. Beygelzimer, Y. N. Dauphin, P. Liang, and J. W. Vaughan (eds.), *Advances in Neural Information Processing Systems 34: Annual Conference on Neural Information Processing Systems, NeurIPS 2021, virtual*, pp. 9391–9404.

Slack, D., Hilgard, S., Jia, E., Singh, S., and Lakkaraju, H. (2020). Fooling LIME and SHAP: Adversarial attacks on post hoc explanation methods, in A. N. Markham, J. Powles, T. Walsh, and A. L. Washington (eds.), *AIES 2020: AAAI/ACM Conference on AI, Ethics, and Society* (ACM, New York, NY), pp. 180–186, doi:10.1145/3375627.3375830.

Sovrano, F. and Vitali, F. (2023). An objective metric for explainable AI: how and why to estimate the degree of explainability, *Knowledge-Based Systems* **278**, p. 110866, doi:10.1016/J.KNOSYS.2023.110866.

Sy, B. K. (2009). Integrating intrusion alert information to aid forensic explanation: An analytical intrusion detection framework for distributive IDS, *Information Fusion* **10**, 4, pp. 325–341, doi:10.1016/J.INFFUS.2009.01.001.

van Lent, M., Fisher, W., and Mancuso, M. (2004). An explainable artificial intelligence system for small-unit tactical behavior, in D. L. McGuinness and G. Ferguson (eds.), *Proceedings of the Nineteenth National Conference on Artificial Intelligence, Sixteenth Conference on Innovative Applications of Artificial Intelligence,AAAI 2004* (AAAI Press/The MIT Press, Cambridge, MA), pp. 900–907.

Wang, M., Zheng, K., Yang, Y., and Wang, X. (2020). An explainable machine learning framework for intrusion detection systems, *IEEE Access* **8**, pp. 73127–73141, doi:10.1109/ACCESS.2020.2988359.

Warnecke, A., Arp, D., Wressnegger, C., and Rieck, K. (2020). Evaluating explanation methods for deep learning in security, in *IEEE European Symposium on Security and Privacy, EuroS&P 2020* (IEEE), pp. 158–174, doi:10.1109/EUROSP48549.2020.00018.

Wu, B., Chen, S., Gao, C., Fan, L., Liu, Y., Wen, W., and Lyu, M. R. (2021). Why an Android app is classified as malware: Toward malware classification interpretation, *ACM Transactions on Software Engineering and Methodology* **30**, 2, pp. 21:1–21:29, doi:10.1145/3423096.

Ying, Z., Bourgeois, D., You, J., Zitnik, M., and Leskovec, J. (2019). Gnnexplainer: Generating explanations for graph neural networks, in H. M. Wallach, H. Larochelle, A. Beygelzimer, F. d'Alché-Buc, E. B. Fox, and R. Garnett (eds.), *Advances in Neural Information Processing Systems 32: Annual Conference on Neural Information Processing Systems 2019, NeurIPS 2019*, pp. 9240–9251.

Zhang, Z., Hamadi, H. M. N. A., Damiani, E., Yeun, C. Y., and Taher, F. (2022). Explainable artificial intelligence applications in cyber security: State-of-the-art in research, *IEEE Access* **10**, pp. 93104–93139, doi:10.1109/ACCESS.2022.3204051.

Şandor, M., Portase, R. M., and Coleşa, A. (2023). Ember feature dataset analysis for malware detection, in *ICCP 2023*, pp. 203–210, doi:10.1109/ICCP60212.2023.10398693.

https://doi.org/10.1142/9789811262043_0006

Chapter 6

Adversarial EXEmples: Evasion Attacks Against Machine Learning Windows Malware Detectors

Luca Demetrio[*] and Battista Biggio[†]

[*] *University of Genova, Italy*

[†] *University of Cagliari, Italy*

In this chapter, we dive into the complex task of testing the security of malware detectors implemented with machine learning techniques. We first introduce the concept of adversarial attacks against learning algorithms, by analyzing the possible threat models formalized as a single framework (Section 6.1). We follow by focusing on understanding how these attacks can be deployed in the domain of malware detection, by introducing the limitations of the current state of the art, and explaining which gaps must be filled to succeed in testing the robustness of machine learning threat detectors (Section 6.2). We conclude the chapter by providing experimental analysis of adversarial attacks against malware detectors by leveraging a publicly-available open-source tool (Section 6.3).

6.1 Adversarial Machine Learning

Machine Learning is becoming ubiquitous in the field of computer security, and both academia and industry are investing time, money and human resources to apply these statistical techniques to address the daunting task of malware detection. In particular, Windows malware is still a threat in the wild, as thousands of malicious programs are uploaded to VirusTotal every day.[1] Modern approaches use machine learning to detect such threats at scale, leveraging many different learning algorithms and feature sets (Anderson and Roth, 2018; Coull and Gardner, 2019; David and Netanyahu, 2015; Hardy *et al.*, 2016; Incer *et al.*, 2018; Kolosnjaji *et al.*, 2016; Raff *et al.*, 2018; Saxe and Berlin, 2015; Trizna, 2022).

While these techniques have shown promising malware-detection capabilities, they were not designed to deal with non-stationary, adversarial problems in which attackers can manipulate the input data to evade detection. This has been widely discussed in the last decade in the area of *adversarial machine learning* (Biggio and Roli, 2018; Huang *et al.*, 2011), a field that addresses the security aspects of machine-learning algorithms under attacks. Hence, we assume the presence of a skilled and resourceful attacker that, depending on their capabilities and knowledge of the target machine learning model, can launch different types of adversarial attacks according to a precise goal (Section 6.1.1). We then explain how to craft evasion attacks, strategies intended to cause the victim model to misclassify input samples at test time (Section 6.1.2), and, before delving into the generation of attacks against malware detectors, we highlight the fundamental challenges posed by applying adversarial machine learning techniques in the malware domain (Section 6.1.3).

6.1.1 Know Your Adversary: Taxonomy of Attacks

To better deal with adversarial attacks against machine learning models, we define three major axes to consider when formalizing the space of possible threats. In particular, we imagine an attacker that threatens a model in order to fulfill a specific goal, by leveraging their

[1] https://www.virustotal.com/gui/intelligence-overview.

knowledge of the victim system and its capabilities. Depending on a combination of these three axes (goal, knowledge, and capabilities), we can craft attacks with ease as shown in Table 6.1, and study how a particular model is robust with respect to these strategies.

Attacker's Goals: The security violations that the attacker can cause include the following: (i) *Integrity violations*, when the attacker is able to cause misclassifications, without compromising its regular functionalities; (ii) *Availability violations* when the attacker is able to compromise the functionality of the model, hence disrupting its regular usage; and (iii) *Privacy violations*, when the attacker is able to access private information about the target model, or to retrieve sensitive information encoded at training time. These security violations can be *targeted* or *untargeted*, whether the attacker wants to cause security violations for a specific set of samples (i.e., a specific user) or not. Lastly, the error caused by these security violations can be *specific* or *generic*, depending on whether the attacker wants to reach a specific result (e.g., misclassify a sample to a desired class), or they are satisfied with every mistake that the target might make.

Attacker's Knowledge: Depending on what the attacker is able to discover about the target model, the strategies that will be applied drastically change. Such knowledge can be split into four crucial assets: (i) knowledge of the training data used to develop the model; (ii) knowledge of the feature representation extracted from the input; (iii) knowledge of which learning algorithm is in place; and (iv) knowledge of the parameters of the model itself.

We refer to *perfect knowledge* (white-box) as the condition in which the attacker possesses all four of these assets, and they can launch the most powerful attacks against the target victim model. From the perspective of security testing of machine learning models, this stands as a lower bound for the performance of the target, as it represents a worst case scenario.

We refer to *partial knowledge* as the condition in which the attacker possesses a combination of the assets mentioned before, but not all of them. For instance, the attacker may know the learning algorithm and the feature representation, but not the model weights and training data. Depending on the combination of known and unknown assets, the attacker is forced to approximate the missing knowledge with ad hoc techniques. When training data are missing, the attacker can leverage the collection of similar data, by labeling them with the known learning algorithm. If the attacker does not know the learning algorithm, the feature representation, or the trained parameters, they can rely on surrogate models that they train on whatever data is available.

We refer to *zero knowledge* (black-box) as the condition in which the attacker has no knowledge of the mentioned assets, and the target is only accessible through queries. In this scenario, the feasibility of adversarial attacks relies solely on the surrogate data and learning algorithm that the attacker can collect and develop, respectively. Hence, robustness can be quantified by the means of either *query attacks*, in which the attacker collects responses from the target and devises a plan accordingly, or *transfer attacks*, where the attacker creates attacks through the use of surrogates that mimic the behavior of the target, and are then tested on the real system.

Attacker's Capabilities: Lastly, the attacker chooses their strategy according to their ability to make an impact on the target model. Such a strategy can be *explorative*, if the attacker can only tamper with test data, while it is *causative* when the attacker can also taint the training data of a model. Such perturbations cannot be applied randomly, and they must preserve the domain constraints that govern the validity of samples. For instance, an image is still valid after the injection of noise, which causes a degradation in quality, rather than corruption of the file. However, more complex objects, like programs or traffic data, must be manipulated so as not to corrupt their original functionality and semantics.

Given this framework for instantiating attacks, we can now compose goals, knowledge, and capabilities to create powerful threats that threaten the security of machine learning products. Before discussing how to produce bypassing samples, we first briefly introduce other relevant attacks that can harm machine learning models, as depicted in Table 6.1.

Sponge Attacks: These attacks cause *explorative availability* security violations by crafting adversarial examples that force the target model to consume more energy (Cinà *et al.*, 2022a; Shumailov *et al.*, 2021). Since neural networks are composed of sequences of neurons that fire when they encounter a pattern they learned at training time, sponge samples maximize such response by activating as many

Table 6.1. Categorization of attacks against machine learning models.

	Goals		
Capabilities	**Integrity** Misclassifications that do not compromise normal system operations	**Availability** Misclassifications that compromise normal systems operations	**Privacy/ Confidentiality** Querying strategies that reveal confidential information about learning models or users
Test data	Evasion (a.k.a. adversarial examples)	Sponge samples	Model stealing/ extraction Membership Inference Model Inversion
Training data	Poisoning (to permit future evasions) e.g., backdoors or neural network trojans	Poisoning (to maximize classification error)	—

neurons as possible. When deployed on dedicated accelerating hardware, sponge samples interfere with their optimization heuristics, thus increasing the energy demand. The latter has a side effect on the economy of the target victim, as it increases its maintenance costs as well. However, these attacks still need to be investigated in-depth since they target specific hardware components, and thus more research is needed to investigate their general applicability (Cinà *et al.*, 2022a).

Poisoning Attacks: These attacks cause both *integrity* and *availability* violations of machine learning models since the attacker can tamper with both test data and the training samples. Hence, the attacker can inject ad-hoc points to either permit future *explorative* evasions of selected samples without altering the behavior of the model for all inputs or degrade the intended functionality of the victim with *causative* strategies, making its use impractical (Biggio and Roli, 2018; Cinà *et al.*, 2022b). Suppose the attacker has *perfect* knowledge of the target. In that case, they can leverage gradient information to optimize samples that cause the most damage in terms of the violation the attacker wants to cause (Biggio *et al.*, 2012). Otherwise, in *limited* or *zero* knowledge scenarios, poisoning samples can be computed on a surrogate model, and then injected inside the training data of the victim (Demontis *et al.*, 2019).

Among these poisoning attacks, we highlight a particular subclass of techniques, the so-called *Backdoor* attacks. These strategies cause *integrity* violations by leveraging perturbations of samples applied at training time. Backdoor attacks focus on crafting *triggers*, specific patterns implanted inside training data that unleash an intended behavior of the model for future *explorative* attacks. For instance, backdoors could systematically produce misclassifications of a particular class of samples, forcing the model to output desired outcomes decided a priori by the attacker (Gu *et al.*, 2019). Also, it has been shown from recent work that malware detectors can also be injected with backdoors at training time (Severi *et al.*, 2021), creating a worrying scenario where detectors become vulnerable to attack only in the presence of specific patterns that unleash the behavior planted by the attacker.

Privacy and Confidentiality Attacks: As the name suggests, these attacks cause *explorative privacy and confidentiality* violations of the victim machine learning model, by exfiltrating sensitive information through querying it with ad-hoc samples. Depending on the assets the attacker wants to gain knowledge of, the techniques applied change accordingly.

Membership Inference Attacks: These strategies try to establish if a particular input data sample has been used at training time (Shokri *et al.*, 2017). The fundamental intuition behind this family of attacks is that neural network models behave slightly differently when dealing with known and unknown data. By exploiting such a difference, the attacker can compute a confidence score indicating the likelihood that the network has already used the samples as training data.

Model Inversion Attacks: These strategies focus on retrieving sensitive information stored inside the target machine learning model at training time, potentially disclosing private information of selected users (Fredrikson *et al.*, 2014, 2015). By querying the target model, the attacker can adjust input samples to be close to the interesting training ones. In this way, the attacker can understand the feature values of relevant data and potentially disclose private information stored inside the model.

Model Stealing/Extraction Attacks: These techniques address the problem of retrieving the parameters of the victim model itself (Tramèr *et al.*, 2016), hence copying it without consuming the resources required for training it from scratch. The latter also economically impacts the target since this family of attacks can retrieve industrially-developed technologies. A company might have invested capital inside its development, and attackers can steal and resell it, making a profit at the victim's expense. Also, this could let attackers avoid the payment of *Machine Learning As a Service* (MLaaS) APIs since they can use the stolen model without interacting with the company that it is offering the service. In the case of malware detection, some preliminary work (Rigaki and Garcia, 2022) study how malware detectors used as MLaaS can be stolen by attackers, hence reversing the detectors to bypass and use them as a proxy for future evasions.

6.1.2 Evasion Attacks

These techniques address the problem of creating samples that bypass detection, hence causing an *integrity violation* at test time, leveraging different levels of knowledge of the target systems. These attacks are commonly known as *evasion attacks*, whose results are the so-called *adversarial examples.* Adversarial examples are normally found by optimizing a perturbation against the target model either via gradient-based optimization, when the attacker has perfect knowledge (i.e., white-box setting, in which the kind of model and its trained parameters are accessible), or via gradient-free optimizers, when the attacker has only limited or zero knowledge of the model (i.e., black-box setting, where the model can be queried using different inputs, and feedback on the corresponding predictions is observable). In the black-box setting, it is also possible to stage *transfer attacks*, which are gradient-based attacks optimized against a surrogate model which also succeeds against the target model. Such attacks are feasible only when the surrogate model provides a differentiable and sufficiently-smooth approximation of the target model, which is clearly neither always available to the attacker nor easy to build (Biggio and Roli, 2018; Demontis *et al.*, 2019). In Figure 6.1, we exemplify the process used to craft adversarial examples, starting from the image of a school bus (classified correctly with

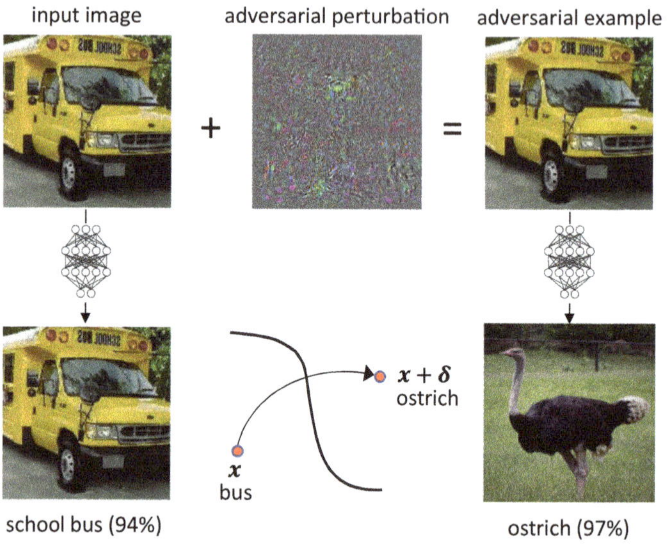

Fig. 6.1. Adversarial examples are crafted by optimizing an input perturbation $\boldsymbol{\delta}$ to fool the target model. In this example, a slightly-perturbed image of a school bus is misclassified as an ostrich.

94% confidence by a state-of-the-art model trained on ImageNet), and showing how it can be perturbed to generate an adversarial example misclassified as an ostrich (with 97% confidence). The latter is computed by solving the following optimization problem:

$$\begin{aligned} \max_{\boldsymbol{\delta}} \quad & L(\boldsymbol{x} + \boldsymbol{\delta}, y; \boldsymbol{\theta}), \\ \text{s.t.} \quad & \|\boldsymbol{\delta}\|_p \leq \epsilon, \quad \boldsymbol{x} + \boldsymbol{\delta} \in [0, 1]^d, \end{aligned} \tag{6.1}$$

where $L(\boldsymbol{x}, y, \theta)$ is a loss function that exhibits lower values when the input sample $\boldsymbol{x}$ (for instance, the input image consisting of d pixels) is correctly assigned to class y by the model (parameterized via $\boldsymbol{\theta}$). The goal is to optimize the applied perturbation $\boldsymbol{\delta}$, to maximize the loss on the perturbed sample $\boldsymbol{x} + \boldsymbol{\delta}$, to produce, with high confidence, a misclassification by the target model. However, this should be achieved while preserving some constraints on the applied perturbation. First, the ℓ_p norm of $\boldsymbol{\delta}$ is typically upper bounded by a small number ϵ, to keep the perturbation size small. Second, the perturbed sample $\boldsymbol{x} + \boldsymbol{\delta}$ is also typically constrained to stay within some bounds, e.g., to ensure that each pixel of the perturbed image lies in the scaled interval $[0, 1]$.

Algorithm 6.1: Generalized gradient-based attack for optimizing adversarial examples.

Input : $\boldsymbol{x}$, the initial sample; y, the original class label; N, the number of iterations; α, the step size; $\boldsymbol{\theta}$, the target model; L the loss function; Π, the projection operator enforcing the constraints in Equation 6.1.

Output: $\boldsymbol{x}^\star$, the solution found by the algorithm

1 $\boldsymbol{\delta}_0 \leftarrow \mathbf{0}$ ▷ `Initialize` δ

2 **for** $i \in [1, N]$ **do**

3 $\quad\boldsymbol{\delta}_i \leftarrow \boldsymbol{\delta}_{i-1} + \alpha \nabla_{\boldsymbol{x}} L(\boldsymbol{x} + \boldsymbol{\delta}_{i-1}, y; \boldsymbol{\theta})$ ▷ `Gradient update(s)`

4 $\quad\boldsymbol{\delta}_i \leftarrow \Pi(\boldsymbol{x}, \boldsymbol{\delta}_i)$ ▷ `Enforce constraints on` $\boldsymbol{\delta}$

5 **end**

6 **return** $\boldsymbol{x}^\star \leftarrow \boldsymbol{x} + \texttt{best}(\boldsymbol{\delta}_0, \ldots, \boldsymbol{\delta}_N)$ ▷ `Return best solution`

When the model under attack is differentiable, adversarial examples can be computed through the application of *gradient-based* optimization algorithms, like Projected Gradient Descent (PGD) (Biggio *et al.*, 2013; Madry *et al.*, 2017), as described in Algorithm 6.1. The algorithm runs until all the predefined iterations are finished, and with each step it updates the manipulation $\boldsymbol{\delta}$ using the gradient of the loss function with respect to the input (line 3). Since the attacker has constraints that must not be violated as reported in Eq. (6.1), the manipulation is hence projected inside the imposed constraints (line 4). The output of the PGD algorithm is the manipulated sample that maximizes the chance of classification error.

6.1.3 Limitations of Current Evasion Attack Strategies

While the formulation described in Eq. (6.1) works well for the image domain, it is not straightforward to extend it to the domain of malware detection, since malware samples are much more complex than images, and the detectors built to spot them leverage complex pre-processing functions that mostly obstruct the computations of gradients.

Functionality-Preserving Manipulations: To begin with, adversarial examples are computed by adding a perturbation to an image, but such is acceptable only in domains where addition is defined. This concept is straightforward to understand in the case of malware samples. Since executable binaries must be compliant with a complex format, the misplacement of a single byte (especially in some important part of the PE header) may well to lead to corruption of the program. To exacerbate the problem, machine learning models leverage distance functions to work properly and to separate data in the intended classes. In the image domain, pixels can be treated as continuous values between 0 and 1, and they can be summed together to obtain other pixel values. If such summation includes an infinitesimal increment, the obtained pixel value also represents a color close to the original one. In the malware domain, where each program is represented as a string of bytes, flipping a single bit might change one opcode or operand in such a way as to change functioning malware into a program that fails to run at all. It is therefore wrong to expect that the summation of two byte values will produce two programs that are very close in either structure or behavior.

Second, constraining the perturbation size using ℓ_p norms may not have any practical meaning for the application at hand. As we pointed out in the previous discussion, since there is no notion of summation and subtraction between byte values, it is not possible to formally define a *continuous* distance function between binaries. (There are many ways to compute a discrete distance function between binaries, given that we can just regard them as strings.)

Proof of Concept Attacks at Feature-Level: When computing adversarial attacks in the image domain, usually the target model to fool is end-to-end differentiable, implying that it is possible to trace the effect on the output directly to each pixel value. Hence, there is a direct correlation between the manipulation of one portion of the image and the model output. However, in the malware detection domain, this is hard to achieve, as malware detectors usually extract complex information from input samples, by the means of aggregating and discarding portions of it. Hence, this process is not end-to-end differentiable, rendering a gradient-based adversarial attack useless.

6.2 Adversarial EXEmples

Since we are interested in generating adversarial evasion attacks against Windows malware detectors implemented with machine learning techniques, we need to re-think the strategy formalized in Eq. (6.1) from the ground up. Our goal can be achieved by either developing complex input-space manipulations whose application to program samples do not break their functionality, and/or adapting existing optimization algorithms to include these constraints while computing the minimization. The result of this new formulation is the production of *adversarial EXEmples*, minimally perturbed Windows malware that evade machine learning detection. To guide the reader in better understanding the concept of adversarial EXEmples, we first describe the data structure used in Windows programs (Section 6.2.1) to describe the constraints of this domain, and we introduce a novel attack formalization (Section 6.2.2). We then present how attackers can create functionality-preserving manipulations of programs stored as a file (Section 6.2.3), and we conclude by customizing optimization algorithms to reflect the change of domain, from images to programs (Section 6.2.4).

6.2.1 Windows PE File Format

The Windows Portable Executable (PE) file format was originally introduced alongside Windows NT 3.1, and it describes how programs are correctly represented and stored as a file on disk. This structure includes several components that all together instruct the Windows Operating System how to map each of them into RAM and where to find the starting point of execution, that is, the *entry point* of the program. For brevity, we report here the most relevant components that will be used in this chapter, while more technical and comprehensive documentation has been released online by Microsoft.[2]

DOS Header and DOS Stub (A): The DOS header contains metadata for loading the executable inside a DOS environment, while the DOS Stub is made up of a few instructions that will print *This program cannot be run in DOS mode* if executed inside a DOS environment. These two components have been kept to maintain compatibility with older Microsoft operating systems. From the perspective of a modern application, the only relevant locations contained inside the DOS Header are (i) the magic number `MZ`, a two-byte signature

[2]https://learn.microsoft.com/en-us/windows/win32/debug/pe-format.

of the file, and (ii) the four-byte integer at offset `0x3c`, that works as a pointer to the actual header. If one of these two values is altered for some reason, the program is considered corrupted, and the OS will not execute it.

PE Header (B): The PE Header contains the magic number `PE` along with other file characteristics, such as the target architecture, the header size, and the file attributes.

Optional Header (C): The Optional Header contains information the OS needs for loading the binary into memory. Among these fields, the Optional Header specifies the (i) *file alignment*, which acts as a constraint on the structure of the executable since each section of the program must start at an offset multiple to that field, and the (ii) *size of headers* that specifies the amount of bytes that are reserved for all the headers of the program, and it too must be a multiple of the *file alignment*. Lastly, the Optional Header contains offsets that point to useful structures, like the Import Table needed by the OS for resolving dependencies, the Export Table to provide functions that other programs can reference, and more.

Section Table (D): This table is a list of entries that indicates the characteristics of each section of the program. Each section entry has a name, an offset to the location inside the binary, a virtual address where the content should be mapped in memory, and the characteristics of such content (i.e., read-only, write-only, executable, and more).

Section (E): These are contiguous chunks of bytes loaded in memory by the loader while parsing the Section Table. To name a few, there is the code of the program (*.text* section), initialized data (*.data*), read-only constants (*.rdata*), and others. To maintain the alignment specified inside the Optional Header, these sections might be zero-padded to match the format constraint. It is clear that, even without executing the program contained inside a file, it is possible to infer some useful information from its headers, imports, exports, and sections.

6.2.2 Evasion Attack Formalization

Creating adversarial EXEmples is, in principle, equivalent to generating regular adversarial examples. However, since the malware domain has much more strict constraints, we need to express them inside the optimization problem, to force the generation of functionality-preserving solutions that can still be run on a Windows machine. This can be achieved by writing the following optimization equation, similar to Eq. (6.1):

$$\begin{aligned} \max_{\boldsymbol{\delta}} \quad & L(h(\boldsymbol{x};\boldsymbol{\delta}), y; \boldsymbol{\theta}), \\ \text{s.t.} \quad & g(\boldsymbol{\delta}) \leq \epsilon, \end{aligned} \tag{6.2}$$

where $\boldsymbol{x} \in [0, 255]^\star$ is a program expressed as a string of byte values, $\boldsymbol{\delta} \in \mathbf{M}$ is the manipulation to inject inside the input sample expressed as a sample of a generic set of manipulations $\mathbf{M}$, y is the original label of sample $\boldsymbol{x}$, $\boldsymbol{\theta}$ are the parameters of the malware detector. In addition, we introduce two new functions that force the optimization algorithm to produce executable results: (i) a manipulation function h, and a constraint function g.

The *manipulation function* $h : [0, 255]^\star \times \mathbf{M} \to [0, 255]^\star$ takes in input a program and a manipulation, and it returns a new program that has been injected with the content described by $\boldsymbol{\delta}$. We will discuss how to construct this function in Section 6.2.3.

The *constraint function* $g : [0, 255]^\star \to \mathbb{R}$ is a function that indicates the size of the perturbation. In the context of a Windows program, this function usually counts the number of byte values that are modified when applying $h(\boldsymbol{x}, \boldsymbol{\delta})$, to mimic the behavior of ℓ_p norms in the image domain.

This optimization problem can be solved using two different families of algorithms, depending on whether the attacker has perfect (white-box) or limited/zero (black-box) knowledge of the target model. These techniques are generally referred to respectively as (i) gradient-based and (ii) gradient-free optimizers (Biggio and Roli, 2018; Demetrio *et al.*, 2021b). We will tackle the formulation of both white-box and black-box algorithms in Section 6.2.4.

6.2.3 Program Manipulations

We discuss here the set of functionality-preserving manipulation functions h that can be used to create adversarial EXEmples according to Eq. (6.2). In the context of the Windows PE file format, there are only a few transformations that can be applied without compromising the execution of the input program. We categorize them either as structural or behavioral, as detailed as follows.

Structural: This family of manipulations affects only the structure of the input program by exploiting ambiguities inside the file format without altering its behavior. We depict a condensed graphical representation of this family of manipulations in Figure 6.2.

(s.1) Perturb Header Fields (Anderson *et al.*, 2017; Castro *et al.*, 2019; Labaca Castro *et al.*, 2019). This technique includes altering section names, breaking the checksum, and altering debug information. These fine-grained manipulations are visually shown in dark gray in Figure 6.2, and they are applied to the PE components B, C and D in Figure 6.3.

(s.2) Filling Slack Space (Anderson *et al.*, 2017; Castro *et al.*, 2019; Kreuk *et al.*, 2018; Labaca Castro *et al.*, 2019; Suciu *et al.*, 2019). This technique manipulates the slack space inserted by the compiler to maintain the alignments inside the file. The corresponding slack bytes (inside E in Figure 6.3) are usually set to zero, and the code of the executable never references them. This technique is graphically shown in light gray in Figure 6.2.

(s.3) Padding (Kolosnjaji *et al.*, 2018; Kreuk *et al.*, 2018; Suciu *et al.*, 2019). This technique injects additional bytes at the end of the file (after E in Figure 6.3), graphically shown in purple in Figure 6.2.

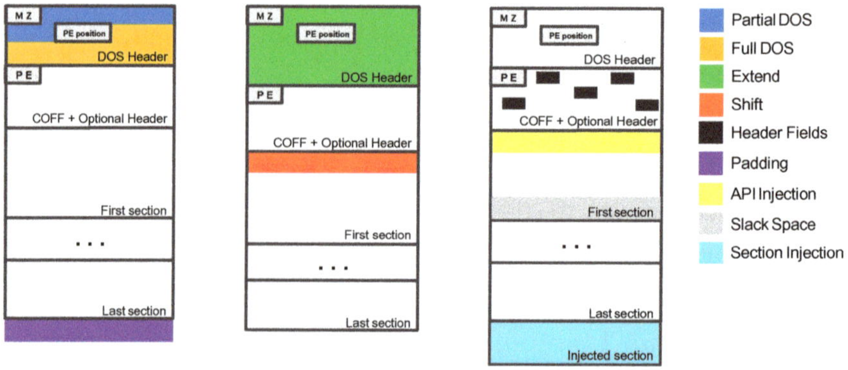

Fig. 6.2. Graphical representation of the locations perturbed by different structural manipulations (shown in colors).

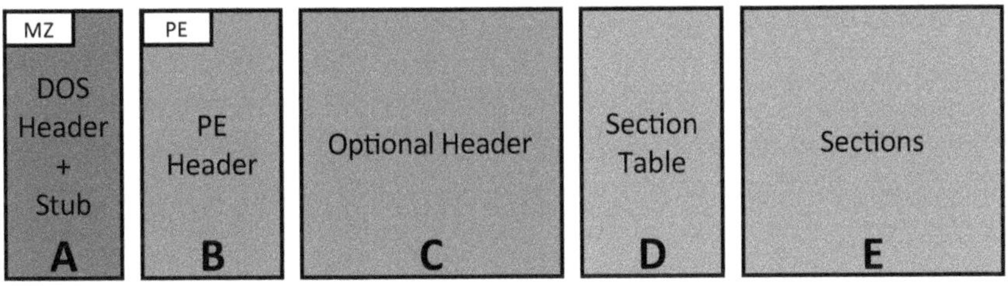

Fig. 6.3. A graphical representation of the Windows PE file format.

(s.4) Manipulating DOS Header and Stub (Demetrio *et al.*, 2019, 2021b). This technique modifies some bytes in the DOS Header (A in Figure 6.3) which are not used by modern programs (Section 6.2.1), and they are graphically shown in blue in Figure 6.2.

(s.5) Extend the DOS Header (Demetrio *et al.*, 2021b). This technique extends the DOS header by injecting content before the actual header of the program (between A and B in Figure 6.3). This technique is graphically shown in yellow in Figure 6.2.

(s.6) Content shifting (Demetrio *et al.*, 2021b). This technique creates additional space before the beginning of a section by shifting the content forward and injects adversarial content in between (i.e., between D and E in Figure 6.3). This technique is graphically shown in red in Figure 6.2.

(s.7) Section Injection (Anderson *et al.*, 2017; Castro *et al.*, 2019; Labaca Castro *et al.*, 2019). This technique injects new sections into the input file by creating an additional entry inside the section table (thus affecting D and E in Figure 6.3). Each section entry is 40 bytes long, so all the content has to be shifted by that amount without compromising file and section alignments as specified by the header. This technique is graphically shown in light blue in Figure 6.2.

(s.8) Import Function Injection (Anderson *et al.*, 2017; Castro *et al.*, 2019; Labaca Castro *et al.*, 2019). This technique injects import functions by adding an appropriate entry to the Import Address Table, specifying which function from which library must be included during the loading process (this affects C and E in Figure 6.3). This technique is graphically shown in light yellow in Figure 6.2.

Behavioral: This family of perturbations can change the program behavior and execution traces while preserving the malware program's intended functionality. For example, these transformations encompass the binary rewriting techniques in Wenzl *et al.* (2019), as discussed below. Throughout the chapter, we will focus more on the previously-described structural manipulations, but we list behavioral manipulation for completeness. Interested readers can find more information about these manipulations in the references (Wenzl *et al.*, 2019).

(b.1) Packing (Anderson *et al.*, 2017; Castro *et al.*, 2019; Labaca Castro *et al.*, 2019). This technique amounts to encrypting or encoding the content of the binary inside another binary and decoding it at run-time. The effect of a packer is invasive since the whole structure of the input sample is modified.

(b.2) Direct (Wenzl *et al.*, 2019). This approach rewrites specific portions of the code, like replacing assembly instructions with equivalent ones (e.g., additions and subtractions with opposite sign).

(b.3) Minimal Invasive (Anderson *et al.*, 2017; Wenzl *et al.*, 2019). This technique sets the entry point to a new executable section that returns to the original code.

(b.4) Full Translation (Wenzl *et al.*, 2019). This approach lifts all the code to a higher representation, e.g., LLVM,[3] since it simplifies the application of perturbations, and it then translates the code back to assembly language.

Parameterization with $\boldsymbol{\delta}$: We have defined the functionality-preserving manipulations that can be used to perturb a Windows executable, so now we need to construct the h function by building a relationship between the injected bytes and the manipulation $\boldsymbol{\delta}$. In the context of the structural manipulation, for the *s.1*–*s.7* $\mathbf{M}$ corresponds to a string of byte values to insert inside the locations identified by the manipulation itself. For instance, the padding manipulation *s.3* can be written using the string concatenation $h(\boldsymbol{x}, \boldsymbol{\delta}) = \boldsymbol{x} \oplus \boldsymbol{\delta}$, while the DOS header manipulation *s.4* can be written as the creation of a new program with specific bytes replaced with

[3]https://llvm.org/.

new values according to the manipulations $h(\boldsymbol{x}, \boldsymbol{\delta}) = \boldsymbol{x}_{0,3} \oplus \delta \oplus \boldsymbol{x}_{60,|\boldsymbol{x}|}$, where $|\boldsymbol{x}|$ is the original length of the program $\boldsymbol{x}$.

6.2.4 Optimization Strategies

Minimizing the problem formulated in Eq. (6.2) can be tackled in different ways, depending on the knowledge gathered on the target system. When the machine learning model under attack is completely known by the adversary, and is differentiable, the attacker can leverage *gradient-based* optimization algorithms. On the other hand, if the model under attack is either non-differentiable (like a Random Forest, or a K-Nearest Neighbor algorithm), or its parameters are unknown (for instance, the model is hosted on a private server), the attack can leverage *gradient-free* optimization algorithms.

Gradient-Based Algorithms: Recalling the concepts introduced in Section 6.1, computing the gradient of a differentiable function implies retrieving the direction of maximum ascent, and by moving accordingly in this direction, it is possible to find a local maximum for the function. Hence, we can leverage PGD (Algorithm 6.1) to compute adversarial EXEmples that maximize the classification error, and bypass detection. However, we need to customize the optimization algorithm to consider the presence of either the manipulation function h, and byte values that are not continuous. To do so, we explicitly assume the presence of a feature extractor function ϕ used by the network that is applied before computing the decision. This step is always necessary in this domain, because of the discrete nature of byte values and their lack of continuous distance metrics. Intuitively, we leverage the signal provided by gradients inside the differentiable space of the model, and then we provide a way to reconstruct an input sample from the perturbations applied, somehow inverting the feature mapping. We illustrate in Algorithm 6.2 how to define gradient descent to produce adversarial EXEmples, as also depicted in Figure 6.4.

First, the optimization algorithm applies an initial perturbation h to the input malware program $\boldsymbol{x}$, obtaining a modified program $\boldsymbol{x}' = h(\boldsymbol{x}, \boldsymbol{\delta})$ (line 3). Since we want to leverage the information retrieved from gradients inside the feature space of the model, the algorithm encodes the manipulated program $\boldsymbol{x}'$ in the feature space

Algorithm 6.2: Gradient-based (white-box) optimization algorithm to produce adversarial EXEmples.

Data: $\boldsymbol{x}$, the initial malware sample; N, total number of iterations; y, the original label; θ, the parameters of the target model.
Result: $\boldsymbol{x}^\star$, the adversarial EXEmple.

1 $\boldsymbol{\delta}^{(0)} \in \mathbf{M}$
2 **for** $i \in [0, N-1]$ **do**
3 $\quad \boldsymbol{x}' \leftarrow h(\boldsymbol{x}, \boldsymbol{\delta}^{(i)})$ ▷ `malware manipulation`
4 $\quad \boldsymbol{z}' \leftarrow \phi(\boldsymbol{x}')$ ▷ `feature extraction`
5 $\quad \boldsymbol{z}^\star \leftarrow \arg\max_{\boldsymbol{z}'} L(\boldsymbol{x}', y; \boldsymbol{\theta})$ ▷ `feature-space optimization`
6 $\quad \boldsymbol{\delta}^{(i+1)} \leftarrow \arg\min_{\boldsymbol{\delta} \in \mathbf{M}} \|\boldsymbol{z}^\star - \phi(h(\boldsymbol{x}, \boldsymbol{\delta}^{(i)}))\|_2$ ▷ `input-space reconstruction`
7 **end**
8 $\boldsymbol{x}^\star \leftarrow h(\boldsymbol{x}, \text{best}(\boldsymbol{\delta}_0, \ldots, \boldsymbol{\delta}_{N-1}))$
9 **return** $\boldsymbol{x}^\star$

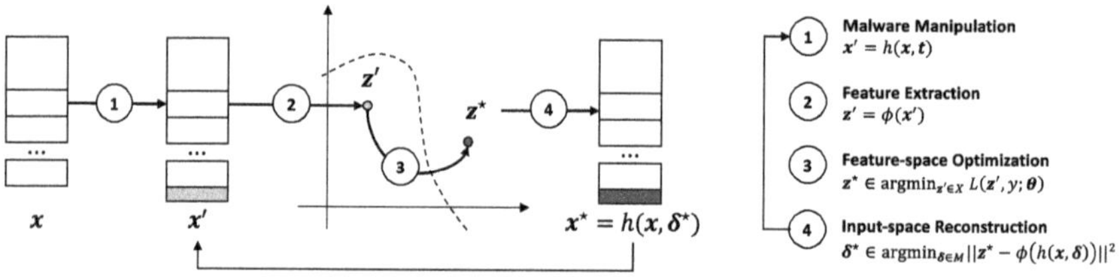

Fig. 6.4. Generation of adversarial EXEmples leveraging gradient-based optimization.

as $\boldsymbol{z}' = \phi(\boldsymbol{x}')$ (line 5). The third step (line 5) consists of modifying the feature-based representation $\boldsymbol{z}'$ of the manipulated input sample $\boldsymbol{x}'$ to maximize the loss function L, using gradient-based updates. It is worth remembering that the feature-based representation $\boldsymbol{z}^\star$ obtained after this step may not necessarily correspond to any input program. For this reason, it is necessary to use proper reconstruction strategies to ensure not only that the reconstructed sample is a valid program, but that it also preserves the intended functionality of the initial malware program $\boldsymbol{x}$. The final step (line 6) optimizes the parameters $\boldsymbol{\delta}^\star$ to generate a functionality-preserving malware sample $\boldsymbol{x}^\star$ whose feature-based representation is as close as possible to the desired $\boldsymbol{z}^\star$.

Hence, attack strategies that need gradients must (i) define how they compute gradient descent in the feature space and (ii) define how they reconstruct samples inside the real input space. For clarity, we report here two strategies that leverage gradients and input reconstruction in different ways.

Byte Gradient Descent (BGP) modify one byte at the time, following the direction of the gradient (Demetrio *et al.*, 2021b; Kolosnjaji *et al.*, 2018), illustrated in Algorithm 6.3. This optimization algorithm is suitable when dealing with end-to-end malware detectors that learn maliciousness from raw bytes without feature engineering. However, since byte values have no distance metrics, the network transforms them using an embedding layer that learns a representation where distance metrics, like ℓ_p norms, can be used (line 1). Due to this transformation, each byte is now a $d-$dimensional vector, and

---

Algorithm 6.3: Byte Gradient Descent (BGD) algorithm, that optimizes one byte at a time

---

Input : $\boldsymbol{x}$, the original malware sample; y, the original label; $\boldsymbol{\theta}$, the parameters of the model, $\boldsymbol{m}$, a mask that filters the bytes to optimize; γ the number of bytes to optimise; N the total number of iterations

Output: $\boldsymbol{x}^\star$, the adversarial EXEmple

1 $\mathbf{E}_i = \hat{\phi}(i), \forall i \in [0, 256]$

2 $\boldsymbol{\delta}^{(0)} \in \mathbf{M}$

3 **for** $i \in [0, N-1]$ **do**

4     $\mathbf{Z} \leftarrow \phi(h(\boldsymbol{x}, \boldsymbol{\delta}^{(i)}))$

5     $\mathbf{G} \leftarrow \nabla_{\mathbf{Z}} L(\mathbf{Z}, y; \boldsymbol{\theta}) \odot \boldsymbol{m}$

6     $\boldsymbol{g} \leftarrow (\| \mathbf{G}_0 \|, \ldots, \| \mathbf{G}_n \|)$

7   **for** $k \in \mathit{argsort}\ (\boldsymbol{g})_{0,\ldots,\gamma} \wedge g_k \neq 0$ **do**

8   **for** $j \in [0, \ldots, 255]$ **do**

9             $\mathbf{S}_{k,j} \leftarrow \mathbf{G}_k^t \cdot (\mathbf{E}_j - \mathbf{Z}_k)$

10             $\widetilde{\mathbf{Z}}_{k,j} \leftarrow \| \mathbf{E}_j - (\mathbf{Z}_k + \mathbf{G}_k \mathbf{S}_{k,j}) \|_2$

11   **end**

12         $\boldsymbol{\delta}_k^{(i+1)} \leftarrow \arg\min_{j:\mathbf{S}_{k,j}>0} \widetilde{\mathbf{Z}}_{k,j}$

13   **end**

14 **end**

15 $\boldsymbol{x}^\star \leftarrow h(\boldsymbol{x}, \mathrm{best}(\boldsymbol{\delta}^{(0)}, \ldots, \boldsymbol{\delta}^{(N-1)})$

16 **return** $\boldsymbol{x}^\star$

---

such is reflected in the gradient too (line 5). To mimic PGD, BGP uses as a step size the number of modified bytes among the ones selected by the manipulation at each iteration. This is done by (i) masking all the other byte values that must not be modified (line 5), and by modifying only the non-zero entries of the gradient, ranked from the highest to the lowest (line 7). To select the value of each embedded byte, we can now iterate among all the possible 255 values and pick up the ones that align with the gradient (from line 8 to line 12). Notice that, since this embedding operation has a one-to-one mapping with the original bytes, we can easily reconstruct samples in the input space by inverting the look-up used to embed the bytes (line 12).

Manipulations Gradient Descent (MGD) fixes random content to inject at the beginning of the optimization, and then it iteratively applies manipulations whose results align to the gradient of the loss function (Lucas *et al.*, 2021), described in Algorithm 6.4. At each iteration, the optimization algorithm draws at random one manipulation from a set of pre-selected ones $\mathbf{H}$, along with random values for it (line 5 and line 6). The original paper uses the

---

Algorithm 6.4: Manipulations Gradient Descent (MGD) algorithm that applies manipulations that aligns with the gradient.

Input : $\boldsymbol{x}$ the original malware sample; N the total number of iterations, $\mathbf{H}$, manipulations to use

Output: $\boldsymbol{x}^\star$, the adversarial EXEmple

1 $\boldsymbol{x}' \leftarrow \boldsymbol{x}$
2 **for** $i \in [0, N-1]$ **do**
3     $\boldsymbol{z} \leftarrow \phi(h(\boldsymbol{x}', \boldsymbol{\delta}^{(i)}))$
4     $\boldsymbol{g} \leftarrow \nabla_{\boldsymbol{z}} L(\boldsymbol{z}, y; \boldsymbol{\theta})$
5     $\hat{h} \leftarrow$ random manipulation from $\mathbf{H}$
6     $\hat{\boldsymbol{\delta}} \leftarrow$ random values
7     $\hat{\boldsymbol{z}} \leftarrow \phi(\hat{h}(\boldsymbol{x}', \hat{\boldsymbol{\delta}}))$
8     $\hat{\boldsymbol{g}} \leftarrow \nabla_{\hat{\boldsymbol{z}}} L(\hat{\boldsymbol{z}}, y; \boldsymbol{\theta})$
9   **if** $\boldsymbol{g} \cdot \hat{\boldsymbol{g}} > 0$ **then**
10         $\boldsymbol{x}' \leftarrow \hat{h}(\boldsymbol{x}', \hat{\boldsymbol{\delta}})$
11   **end**
12 **end**
13 **return** $\boldsymbol{x}'$

---

b.2 behavioral manipulation, which rewrites pieces of code with semantically-invariant ones. Once the optimization algorithm has both the perturbed and source program, it computes gradients with respect to the loss of the attack (line 4 and line 8), and computes the scalar product to check if they are aligned (line 9). If the scalar product is positive, then the randomly applied manipulation potentially maximizes the loss of the attack. Hence, the manipulation is applied (line 10), and the attack continues. In contrast to BGD, MGD applies the input-space reconstruction by design since the sample is always manipulated in input space, and the gradient is checked only to understand if the manipulation had some effect on the loss of the attack.

Gradient-Free Algorithms: While computing gradients is appealing due to their nature of pointing in the right direction, the majority of malware detectors are either deployed in the cloud, or leverage non-differentiable models or not-invertible feature extraction mechanisms. Hence, these systems do not provide any gradient information to the attacker. To overcome this issue, attackers can leverage *gradient-free* algorithms that estimate where to explore the target function in order to retrieve the highest misclassification error.

One naive approach is posed by *transfer attacks*, which refers to adversarial samples optimized against a private model owned by the attacker, whose decision function is similar to the real target of the attack. Once the adversary has concluded their computation, they query the real target with all the samples computed on the copy (Demontis *et al.*, 2019). Intuitively, suppose the decision function of the private and the real model are similar. In that case, evasion is very likely to happen even if the optimization has been computed on a different function. This approach only requires the attacker to either train or own a machine learning model that behaves like the victim, and they hence can compute a gradient-based strategy against it.

On the other hand, to better adapt the computed adversarial perturbation to the victim, it is possible to leverage algorithms that only exploit the output of the target model without requiring any gradient information. These are named *query attacks*, and they update the manipulation after retrieving each answer. An example of a family of gradient-free optimization algorithms is posed by *genetic algorithms*.

Algorithm 6.5: Genetic algorithm to compute adversarial EXEmples without gradients.

Input : $\boldsymbol{x}$, the initial sample; L, the loss function to maximize; P, the population size; Q, the query budget.
Output: $\boldsymbol{x}^\star$, the adversarial EXEmple.

1 $q \leftarrow 0$, $\mathbf{S} \leftarrow \emptyset$
2 $\mathbf{S}' \leftarrow (\boldsymbol{\delta}_1, \ldots, \boldsymbol{\delta}_P), \boldsymbol{\delta}_i \in \mathbb{R}^d$
3 **while** $q < T$ **do**
4 $\quad \mathbf{S} \leftarrow \text{selection}(\mathbf{S} \cup \mathbf{S}', L, \boldsymbol{t})$
5 $\quad \mathbf{S}' \leftarrow \text{crossover}(\mathbf{S})$
6 $\quad \mathbf{S}' \leftarrow \text{mutate}(\mathbf{S}')$
7 $\quad q \leftarrow q + P$
8 **end**
9 $\boldsymbol{\delta}^\star \leftarrow$, best candidate from $\mathbf{S}$ with maximum L
10 $\boldsymbol{x}^\star \leftarrow h(\boldsymbol{x}, \boldsymbol{\delta}^\star)$
11 **return** $\boldsymbol{x}^\star$

Intuitively, this family of algorithms tries to mimic natural evolution by leveraging random mutations and survival to generate better solutions. We describe how to apply a simple genetic algorithm Algorithm 6.5 for the context of adversarial EXEmples. First, the algorithm is initialized by randomly generating a matrix of byte sequences to inject $\mathbf{S}' = (\boldsymbol{\delta}_1, \ldots, \boldsymbol{\delta}_d) \in \mathbb{R}^d, \boldsymbol{\delta}_i \in \mathbb{R}^d$, which represents the initial population of P candidate manipulation vectors (line 2). The genetic optimizer iterates over three steps that ensures the differentiation of the upcoming generation of candidates: *selection*, *cross-over*, and *mutation*. The *selection* step (line 4) applies the loss function L to evaluate the candidates in $\mathbf{S}'$. It then selects the best N candidates between the current population $\mathbf{S}'$ and the population generated at the previous iteration $\mathbf{S}$. The resulting vectors are the candidates associated with the maximum values of L, i.e., the most promising for creating adversarial EXEmples. The *crossover* function (line 5) takes the selected candidates as input and returns a novel set of N candidates by mixing the values of pairs of randomly-chosen vector candidates. The *mutation* function (line 6) changes the elements of each input vector at random, with a fixed low probability. The combination of both *cross-over* and *mutation* ensures that each population has different traits w.r.t. to the previous one, allowing the algorithm to properly choose a new potential solution, i.e., byte sequences, discarding the useless ones, and exploring the space of feasible solutions. After Q queries, the optimizer extracts the manipulation vector $\boldsymbol{\delta}$ corresponding to the maximum value of the objective function F (line 9), which is then used to create and return the optimal adversarial EXEmple $\boldsymbol{x}^\star$ (line 11). To clarify, the attacker could leverage the *s.7* padding manipulation to inject a total of 100KB at the end of the executable. Then, the genetic algorithm would try to assemble permutations of 100KB that decrease the score of the target model by mutating and swapping a few bytes at once.

Injection of Benign Content: The presented genetic algorithm leverages string manipulations that are injected by applying the manipulations described in Section 6.2.3. While in principle this is not an issue, it becomes problematic when the manipulation is altering long byte sequences, enlarging the search space for the optimization algorithm. Focusing again on the example with the padding manipulation, the genetic algorithm would require countless optimization steps to combine most of the possible sequences among the permutations of 100KB. As a side effect, the target classifier is required to compute a lot of queries, and this high usage might raise suspicion. To speed up the process, the attacker can set aside the injection of single bytes one at the time, and favour the injection of pre-computed content extracted from the class of benign software. Intuitively, the more content that is correlated with the legitimate class is injected, the less malicious the detectors will regard the file. For this reason, we can leverage GAMMA (Demetrio *et al.*, 2021a), a genetic algorithm that extracts benign content from regular software and implants it in unused space of input malware with padding or section injection, by also constraining the size of perturbation. GAMMA is formalized as a minimization problem:

$$\arg\min_{\boldsymbol{\delta}} L(f(h(\boldsymbol{x}, \boldsymbol{\delta})), y_t) + \lambda g(\boldsymbol{\delta})$$

where f is a function that returns the output of the target model, y_t is the target label associated with the benign class, g is the constraint function that counts how many bytes are perturbed by $h(\boldsymbol{x}, \boldsymbol{\delta})$, whose magnitude is controlled by the regularization parameter λ. By tuning the value of this regularization parameter, the optimizer will favor shorter or longer byte sequences to inject, hence tuning the amount of perturbation that is injected inside input samples.

6.3 Coding Attacks with SecML Malware

Most of the concepts described in Section 6.2 are available online inside *SecML Malware* (Demetrio and Biggio, 2021), the first Python library for creating adversarial EXEmples with both gradient-based and gradient-free optimization algorithms, and we will leverage this library to provide a brief tutorial on how to instantiate these attacks. This library is based on SecML (Pintor *et al.*, 2022), which offers generic adversarial attacks that can be customized to the domain of choice. The official repository of SecML Malware can be found at https://github.com/pralab/secml_malware, and it already contains tutorials covering the library's basic functionalities. We first introduce how the library can be used to wrap machine learning malware detectors (Section 6.3.1), and we follow by showing how to instantiate and run both gradient-based (Section 6.3.2) and gradient-free (Section 6.3.3) attacks.

6.3.1 Wrapping Machine Learning Malware Detectors

An initial assessment of the performances of machine-learning malware detectors for Windows can be easily handled through SecML Malware. The library offers wrappers to import both pre-trained end-to-end neural networks and well-known detectors proposed in the literature. For instance, we instantiate MalConv, a convolutional neural network (Raff *et al.*, 2018), and we wrap it inside SecML Malware as shown in Listing 6.1. SecML Malware contains a PyTorch implementation of such a model that can first be instantiated, and then passed as input to the wrapper class.

With the invocation of the `load_pretrained_model` method, the pre-trained weights for MalConv are loaded inside the model. Now, the `clf` object contains a SecML Malware model that can be used for computing inference on input programs, as shown in Listing 6.2. Before feeding programs to MalConv, they must be correctly formatted by calling the `bytes_to_numpy` class method that transforms a sequence of bytes into a numerical array, which can then be used by the library through the generic `CArray` data structure.

```
from secml_malware.model.malconv import MalConv
from secml_malware.models import CClassifierEnd2EndMalware

clf = MalConv()
clf = CClassifierEnd2EndMalware(clf)
clf.load_pretrained_model()
print(clf)

"""
CClassifierEnd2EndMalware{'classes': None, 'n_features':
None, 'preprocess': None, 'n_jobs': 1, 'model': MalConv(
  (embedding_1): Embedding(257, 8)
  (conv1d_1): Conv1d(8, 128, kernel_size=(500,), stride
=(500,))
  (conv1d_2): Conv1d(8, 128, kernel_size=(500,), stride
=(500,))
  (dense_1): Linear(in_features=128, out_features=128,
bias=True)
  (dense_2): Linear(in_features=128, out_features=1, bias=
True)
), 'trained': False, 'input_shape': (1, 1048576), '
softmax_outputs': False, 'batch_size': 256, 'loss': '
binary_crossentropy', 'optimizer': None, '
optimizer_scheduler': None, 'epochs': 100, 'plus_version':
 False, 'train_transform': Lambda()}
"""
```

Listing 6.1. Instantiate a MalConv Pytorch classifier and wrap it inside SecML Malware.

```
from secml.array import CArray
with open("petya_ransomware.exe", "rb") as file_handle:
    code = file_handle.read()
x = MalConv.bytes_to_numpy(
    code, clf.get_input_max_length(), 256, False
)
print(net.decision_function(CArray(x)))

"""
CArray(1, 2)(dense: [[0.088773 0.911227]])
"""
```

Listing 6.2. Compute probability scores of a program, given its path on disk.

In this example, we use MalConv to compute the probability of being either benign or malicious for the well-known Petya ransomware.[4] The pre-trained network correctly attributes higher probability to the malicious class. SecML Malware also offers a `predict` method, as shown in Listing 6.3 to get only a single label from each sample.

6.3.2 Gradient-Based Evasion Attacks

We can now code evasion attacks against end-to-end malware detectors, by leveraging the manipulations and optimization algorithms shipped with SecML Malware. The library implements BGD (Algorithm 6.3) as its default optimization algorithm, but MGD can be easily included by extending the base attack class. To create an attack that leverages *s.4*, the DOS Header manipulation, we write the code shown in Listing 6.4.

```
print(net.predict(CArray(x)))

"""
CArray(1,)(dense: [1])
"""
```

Listing 6.3. Predict the label of input malware.

```
attack = CHeaderEvasion(net, iterations=50)
sample, label = CArray(x), CArray(1)
y_pred, scores, adv_ds, f_obj = attack.run(x,y)
print(scores)

"""
CArray(1, 2)(dense: [[9.998403e-01 1.597160e-04]]
"""
```

Listing 6.4. Creation of an evasion attack against MalConv using the DOS Header manipulation.

[4]https://www.cloudflare.com/learning/security/ransomware/petya-notpetya-ransomware/.

```
adv_x = adv_ds.X[0,:]
real_adv_x = attack.create_real_sample_from_adv("
petya_ransomware.exe" adv_x)
real_adv_x = MalConv.bytes_to_numpy(real_adv_x, clf.
get_input_max_length(), 256, False)
print(net.decision_function(CArray(real_adv_x)))

"""
CArray(1, 2)(dense: [[9.998403e-01 1.597160e-04]]
"""
```

Listing 6.5. Reconstruction of the sample as a real malware after the optimization.

In this example, we instantiate the attack to run for 50 iterations on the ransomware used in Listing 6.2, whose original malware probability is 91% (0.91 in the output). After applying the attack, the probability (according to MalConv) falls to roughly 0.015% ($1, 5 \cdot 10^{-4}$ in the output). SecML Malware stores the adversarial EXEmples computed with `attack.run` inside the `adv_ds` object. Since these attacks produce real malware, we can convert the manipulated sample back to its byte representation through the `create_real_sample_from_adv`, as shown in Listing 6.5. Hence, we can compute the probability scores attributed by MalConv of the adversarial EXEmples, which are the same as the ones returned by the attack.

We now leverage SecML Malware to test the robustness of machine learning malware detectors for Windows that have been proposed in the literature, by replicating the results of proposed attacks (Demetrio *et al.*, 2021b). In particular, we show the efficacy of BGD leveraging the *s.4*, the DOS header manipulation, and *s.6*, the Content shifting manipulation against different neural networks: (i) MalConv, which has been previously discussed; and (ii) a smaller deep neural network with either ReLU or linear activations (DNN-ReLU and DNN-Lin) (Coull and Gardner, 2019). All these neural networks have been trained on the EMBER dataset(Anderson and Roth, 2018), which includes 15.62M specimens of Windows goodware and malware. We test the selected attacks on 100 samples, and the results of the gradient-based attacks are reported in Figure 6.5.

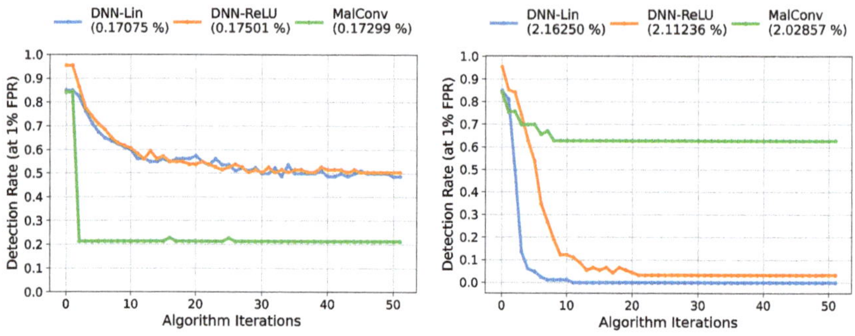

(a) (b)

Fig. 6.5. Detection rate of end-to-end neural networks tested with BGD-*s.4* and BGD-*s.6*. The percentage in the legend refers to how many byte values the BGD optimizer perturbed during the attack. (a) DOS header manipulation and (b) Content shifting manipulation.

```
from secml_malware.models import CClassifierEmber
gbdt = CClassifierEmber("ember_model.txt")
print(gbdt)

"""
CClassifierEmber{'classes': 2, 'n_features': 2381, '
preprocess': None, 'n_jobs': 1}
"""
```

Listing 6.6. Wrapping a pre-trained GBDT inside SecML Malware.

6.3.3 Gradient-free Evasion Attacks

Similarly to gradient-based attacks, we can instantiate gradient-free optimization algorithms with SecML Malware. We will attack a Gradient Boosting Decision Tree (GBDT) trained on the EMBER dataset to show this functionality. We first wrap the GBDT inside SecML Malware, as shown in Listing 6.6.

Before instantiating an attack, we need a wrapper that abstracts from the internals of the target model under attack. In this way, the optimization algorithm only has access to the scores, and no internal information can be retrieved. This is accomplished by leveraging objects inherited from the `CWrapperPhi` class. This wrapper

```
from secml_malware.attack.blackbox.c_wrapper_phi import
CEmberWrapperPhi
from secml_malware.attack.blackbox.
c_blackbox_header_problem import
CBlackBoxHeaderEvasionProblem
from secml_malware.attack.blackbox.ga.
c_base_genetic_engine import CGeneticAlgorithm

wrapper = CEmberWrapperPhi(gbdt)
problem = CBlackBoxHeaderEvasionProblem(wrapper,
population_size=10, iterations=10)
ga = CGeneticAlgorithm(problem)

with open('petya_ransomware.exe','rb') as f:
    code = f.read()
    x = CArray([np.frombuffer(code, dtype=np.uint8)])

y_pred, scores, adv_ds, f_obj = ga.run(x, CArray([1]))
print(scores)

"""
CArray(1, 2)(dense: [[7.973885e-06 9.999920e-01]])
"""
```

Listing 6.7. Gradient-free attack against GBDT.

only exposes a `predict` method that returns the predicted label and, optionally, the probability score.

To create a gradient-free attack, SecML first needs to instantiate the manipulation used by the attack, and then pass it to the genetic optimizer discussed in Algorithm 6.5. Once the optimizer has been set up, the attack can be executed on input samples, as shown in Listing 6.7. In this case, there is no need to preprocess the input sample since the `CWrapperPhi` wrapper will take the feature extraction into account for us, and we can just deal with unmodified samples. As you might notice, this time the attack is not successful. The attack is manipulating bytes inside the DOS header, but the GBDT has a robust feature extraction phase that interferes with the adversarial manipulation.

Hence, we can leverage benign content injection using the GAMMA attack (Demetrio *et al.*, 2021a) discussed in Section 6.2.4. To do so, SecML Malware already offers a built-in implementation of the attack, and it can be instantiated as shown in Listing 6.8.

```
from secml_malware.attack.blackbox.
c_gamma_sections_evasion import
CGammaSectionsEvasionProblem
goodware_folder = 'goodware_samples'
content, _ = CGammaSectionsEvasionProblem.
create_section_population_from_folder(goodware_folder,
how_many=10, sections_to_extract=['.rdata'])

attack = CGammaSectionsEvasionProblem(section_population,
wrapper, population_size=10, penalty_regularizer=1e-6,
iterations=5, threshold=0)

ga = CGeneticAlgorithm(problem)

with open('petya_ransomware.exe','rb') as f:
    code = f.read()
    x = CArray([np.frombuffer(code, dtype=np.uint8)])

y_pred, scores, adv_ds, f_obj = ga.run(x, CArray([1]))
print(scores)

"""
CArray([[0.73634 0.26366]])
"""
```

Listing 6.8. GAMMA section injection against GBDT.

Now the model is attributing a modest confidence to the goodware class, instead of the malware class, thanks to the injection of content associated with benign programs. In particular, we leverage `.rodata` sections of goodware that contain initialized constant strings. By varying the regularization parameter, the size of the injected content varies, as shown in Figure 6.6. In the example, we compute GAMMA attack as shown in Listing 6.8, with different values of the regularizer λ.

Each dot in the plot is produced by repeating the attack with a specific number of queries and the regularization parameter. We used values for the regularization parameter $\lambda \in \{10^{-i}\}_{i=3}^{9}$. As expected, the latter correctly alters the quantity of content that is injected inside the input malware. As a comparison, we also add the performance of random content injection to show that the optimization algorithm is working correctly.

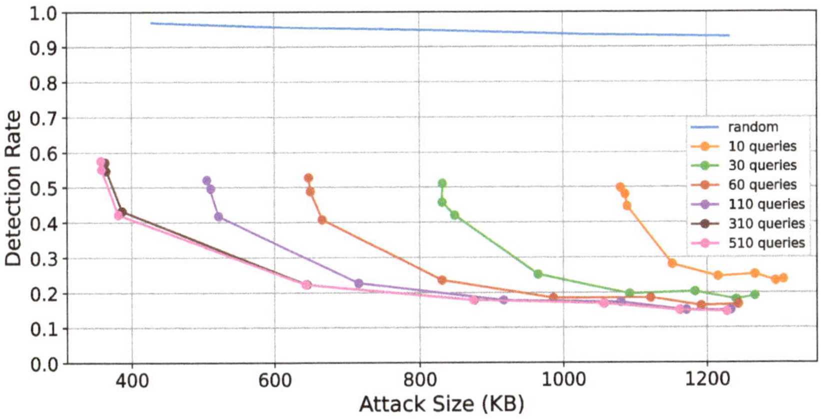

Fig. 6.6. GAMMA attack repeated for different values of queries and regularization parameters.

6.4 Summary

In this chapter, we have bridged the gap between regular adversarial machine learning evasion attacks, which are mostly proposed to target the image domain, and adversarial EXEmples, which are carefully-manipulated Windows programs that bypass detection. We illustrated how the optimization strategy can be formulated to take into account the complexity of this domain, by introducing the concept of functionality-preserving manipulations needed to preserve the sample's malicious nature while executing the attack. We also explained how optimization algorithms should be modified to leverage the presence of both manipulations and non-differentiable classifiers. Finally, we leveraged an open-source library to replicate results from the state of the art by offering a brief tutorial on its usage.

Bibliography

Anderson, H. S., Kharkar, A., Filar, B., and Roth, P. (2017). Evading machine learning malware detection, *Black Hat*.

Anderson, H. S. and Roth, P. (2018). Ember: An open dataset for training static PE malware machine learning models, *arXiv preprint arXiv:1804.04637*.

Biggio, B., Corona, I., Maiorca, D., Nelson, B., Šrndić, N., Laskov, P., Giacinto, G., and Roli, F. (2013). Evasion attacks against machine learning at test time, in H. Blockeel, K. Kersting, S. Nijssen, and F. Železný (eds.), *Machine Learning and Knowledge Discovery in Databases (ECML PKDD), Part III, LNCS*, Vol. 8190 (Springer Berlin, Heidelberg), pp. 387–402.

Biggio, B., Nelson, B., and Laskov, P. (2012). Poisoning attacks against support vector machines, in *Proceedings of the 29th International Conference on Machine Learning*, pp. 1467–1474.

Biggio, B. and Roli, F. (2018). Wild patterns: Ten years after the rise of adversarial machine learning, *Pattern Recognition* **84**, pp. 317–331.

Castro, R. L., Schmitt, C., and Rodosek, G. D. (2019). Armed: How automatic malware modifications can evade static detection? in *2019 5th International Conference on Information Management (ICIM)* (IEEE), pp. 20–27.

Cinà, A. E., Demontis, A., Biggio, B., Roli, F., and Pelillo, M. (2022a). Energy-latency attacks via sponge poisoning, *arXiv preprint arXiv:2203.08147*.

Cinà, A. E., Grosse, K., Demontis, A., Vascon, S., Zellinger, W., Moser, B. A., Oprea, A., Biggio, B., Pelillo, M., and Roli, F. (2022b). Wild patterns reloaded: A survey of machine learning security against training data poisoning, *arXiv preprint arXiv:2205.01992*.

Coull, S. E. and Gardner, C. (2019). Activation analysis of a byte-based deep neural network for malware classification, in *2019 IEEE Security and Privacy Workshops (SPW)* (IEEE), pp. 21–27.

David, O. E. and Netanyahu, N. S. (2015). Deepsign: Deep learning for automatic malware signature generation and classification, in *2015 International Joint Conference on Neural Networks (IJCNN)* (IEEE), pp. 1–8.

Demetrio, L. and Biggio, B. (2021). Secml-malware: Pentesting windows malware classifiers with adversarial exemples in python, *arXiv preprint arXiv:2104.12848*.

Demetrio, L., Biggio, B., Lagorio, G., Roli, F., and Armando, A. (2019). Explaining vulnerabilities of deep learning to adversarial malware binaries, in *Proceedings of the Third Italian Conference on Cyber Security (ITASEC)*.

Demetrio, L., Biggio, B., Lagorio, G., Roli, F., and Armando, A. (2021a). Functionality-preserving black-box optimization of adversarial Windows malware, *IEEE Transactions on Information Forensics and Security* **16**, pp. 3469–3478. https://doi.org/10.1109/TIFS.2021.3082330.

Demetrio, L., Coull, S., Biggio, B., Lagorio, G., Armando, A., Roli, F. *et al.* (2021b). Adversarial exemples: A survey and experimental evaluation of practical attacks on machine learning for Windows malware detection, *ACM Transactions on Privacy and Security* **24**, 4, pp. 1–31.

Demontis, A., Melis, M., Pintor, M., Matthew, J., Biggio, B., Alina, O., Cristina, N.-R., Roli, F. *et al.* (2019). Why do adversarial attacks transfer? Explaining transferability of evasion and poisoning attacks, in *28th USENIX security symposium* (USENIX Association), pp. 321–338.

Fredrikson, M., Jha, S., and Ristenpart, T. (2015). Model inversion attacks that exploit confidence information and basic countermeasures, in *Proceedings of the 22nd ACM SIGSAC Conference on Computer and Communications Security*, pp. 1322–1333.

Fredrikson, M., Lantz, E., Jha, S., Lin, S., Page, D., and Ristenpart, T. (2014). Privacy in pharmacogenetics: An {End-to-End} case study of personalized warfarin dosing, in *23rd USENIX Security Symposium (USENIX Security 14)*, pp. 17–32.

Gu, T., Liu, K., Dolan-Gavitt, B., and Garg, S. (2019). Badnets: Evaluating backdooring attacks on deep neural networks, *IEEE Access* **7**, pp. 47230–47244.

Hardy, W., Chen, L., Hou, S., Ye, Y., and Li, X. (2016). Dl4md: A deep learning framework for intelligent malware detection, in *Proceedings of the International Conference on Data Mining (DMIN)* (The Steering Committee of the World Congress in Computer Science, Computer Engineering, and Applied Computing), p. 61.

Huang, L., Joseph, A. D., Nelson, B., Rubinstein, B. I., and Tygar, J. D. (2011). Adversarial machine learning, in *Proceedings of the 4th ACM Workshop on Security and Artificial Intelligence* (ACM), pp. 43–58.

Incer, I., Theodorides, M., Afroz, S., and Wagner, D. (2018). Adversarially robust malware detection using monotonic classification, in *Proceedings of the Fourth ACM International Workshop on Security and Privacy Analytics* (ACM, New York, NY), pp. 54–63.

Kolosnjaji, B., Demontis, A., Biggio, B., Maiorca, D., Giacinto, G., Eckert, C., and Roli, F. (2018). Adversarial malware binaries: Evading deep learning for malware detection in executables, in *2018 26th European Signal Processing Conference (EUSIPCO)* (IEEE), pp. 533–537.

Kolosnjaji, B., Zarras, A., Webster, G., and Eckert, C. (2016). Deep learning for classification of malware system call sequences, in *Australasian Joint Conference on Artificial Intelligence* (Springer, Springer Cham), pp. 137–149.

Kreuk, F., Barak, A., Aviv-Reuven, S., Baruch, M., Pinkas, B., and Keshet, J. (2018). Adversarial examples on discrete sequences for beating whole-binary malware detection, *arXiv preprint arXiv:1802.04528*, pp. 490–510.

Labaca Castro, R., Schmitt, C., and Rodosek, G. D. (2019). Aimed: Evolving malware with genetic programming to evade detection, in *2019 18th IEEE International Conference on Trust, Security and Privacy in Computing and Communications (TrustCom)* (IEEE).

Lucas, K., Sharif, M., Bauer, L., Reiter, M. K., and Shintre, S. (2021). Malware makeover: Breaking ml-based static analysis by modifying executable bytes, in *Proceedings of the 2021 ACM Asia Conference on Computer and Communications Security*, pp. 744–758.

Madry, A., Makelov, A., Schmidt, L., Tsipras, D., and Vladu, A. (2017). Towards deep learning models resistant to adversarial attacks, in *International Conference on Learning Representations*, arXiv preprint arXiv:1706.06083.

Pintor, M., Demetrio, L., Sotgiu, A., Melis, M., Demontis, A., and Biggio, B. (2022). secml: Secure and explainable machine learning in python, *SoftwareX* **18**, p. 101095.

Raff, E., Barker, J., Sylvester, J., Brandon, R., Catanzaro, B., and Nicholas, C. K. (2018). Malware detection by eating a whole exe, in *Workshops at the Thirty-Second AAAI Conference on Artificial Intelligence.*

Rigaki, M. and Garcia, S. (2022). Stealing malware classifiers and avs at low false positive conditions, *arXiv preprint arXiv:2204.06241.*

Saxe, J. and Berlin, K. (2015). Deep neural network based malware detection using two dimensional binary program features, in *Malicious and Unwanted Software (MALWARE), 2015 10th International Conference on* (IEEE), pp. 11–20.

Severi, G., Meyer, J., Coull, S., and Oprea, A. (2021). {Explanation-Guided} backdoor poisoning attacks against malware classifiers, in *30th USENIX Security Symposium (USENIX Security 21)*, pp. 1487–1504.

Shokri, R., Stronati, M., Song, C., and Shmatikov, V. (2017). Membership inference attacks against machine learning models, in *2017 IEEE Symposium on Security and Privacy (SP)* (IEEE), pp. 3–18.

Shumailov, I., Zhao, Y., Bates, D., Papernot, N., Mullins, R., and Anderson, R. (2021). Sponge examples: Energy-latency attacks on neural networks, in *2021 IEEE European Symposium on Security and Privacy (EuroS&P)* (IEEE), pp. 212–231.

Suciu, O., Coull, S. E., and Johns, J. (2019). Exploring adversarial examples in malware detection, in *2019 IEEE Security and Privacy Workshops (SPW)* (IEEE), pp. 8–14.

Tramèr, F., Zhang, F., Juels, A., Reiter, M. K., and Ristenpart, T. (2016). Stealing machine learning models via prediction {APIs}, in *25th USENIX Security Symposium (USENIX Security 16)*, pp. 601–618.

Trizna, D. (2022). Quo vadis: Hybrid machine learning meta-model based on contextual and behavioral malware representations, in *Proceedings of the 15th ACM Workshop on Artificial Intelligence and Security*, pp. 127–136.

Wenzl, M., Merzdovnik, G., Ullrich, J., and Weippl, E. (2019). From hack to elaborate technique—A survey on binary rewriting, *ACM Computing Surveys (CSUR)* **52**, 3, pp. 1–37.

https://doi.org/10.1142/9789811262043_0007

Chapter 7

Hamm-Grams: An Algorithm for Mining Regular Expressions of Bytes

Derek Everett*, **Edward Raff**†, **and James Holt**‡

**Amazon, Columbia, MD, USA*
†CrowdStrike, Syracuse, NY, USA
‡CrowdStrike, Greensboro, NC, USA

7.1 Introduction

The detection of malware is a problem of the utmost importance. Therefore, designing reliable and robust machine-learning features for malware detection is an ongoing field of research and activity. The need for cheap deployment and training costs is of particular relevance, as malware is increasingly observed in extremely limited compute environments with resources too limited to run parsing. Notable incidents have included industrial control systems (Langner, 2011) and satellites (Van Camp and Peeters, 2022) as targets of malware. Such systems may have as little as 256 KB of system RAM (Lin *et al.*, 2020), requiring especially small models.

n-gram features, which are sequences of n consecutive characters, form a powerful tool in the machine learning toolbox. Combined with linear classifiers such as L_1-penalized logistic regression, n-grams create a formidable and effective baseline and are commonly used in practice. Such models are cheap to train, do not require GPU co-processors, and are small and fast enough to deploy in almost all situations. For static malware detection, n-grams of bytes are commonly used features; however, as n increases, the likelihood of an n-gram re-occurring decreases, as all n tokens from the alphabet Σ must match. If any single entry changes, the feature effectively "disappears", making n-grams brittle when larger values of n are desired.

An example that illustrates one failure case of n-grams for malware detection is the following x86 assembly sequence:

```
push ebp
sub edx, edx
mov ebp, esp
```

which corresponds to the byte 5-gram (in hex) `55 29 D2 89 E5`. The second assembly instruction sets the value to zero and could be equivalently replaced with the instruction `xor edx,edx`, which would change the 5-gram to `55 31 D2 89 E5`. A Hamming distance of one separates these two 5-grams, and many other assembly instructions also have fixed-length equivalent counterparts. Situations like this one are especially likely to occur in register renaming and changes of the function or data addresses that are prevalent even in non-adversarial recompilation. If we could learn to detect the regular expression `55 ? D2 89 E5`, we would have a feature that is robust to these changes.

Thus far, automated methods for constructing regular expressions for use in detecting malware have been hampered by the technical limitations of existing algorithms. For example, regular language induction methods, having been designed for problems in natural language rather than assembly code, cannot be applied directly due to the much larger sequence lengths and sample sizes. Prior approaches have also relied on genetic algorithms and similar search strategies that are not scalable (Angluin, 1982; Angluin *et al.*, 2015). The open challenge is in finding regular expressions in a computationally efficient manner that can readily scale to the data necessary to train modern-day malware detection systems.

In this work, we propose a new method of mining frequently occurring patterns based on the Hamming similarity between fixed-length token sequences. We allow wildcard tokens; a sequence with $\mathcal{K}$ wildcard tokens can match a set of n-grams within a Hamming distance of $\mathcal{K}$. Thus, we term these features *hamm-grams*. As a simple example, the hamm-gram `AB?D` matches both `ABCD` and `ABFD`, but does not match `ABDC`. By restraining ourselves to the space of Hamming similarity, a set of hamm-grams forms a regular language. This guarantees that a search for matches can be done efficiently, that is, in linear time with respect to the input sequence length.

The rest of this chapter is organized as follows. First, we briefly discuss the related work in regular language induction, regular expressions, and n-grams in Section 7.2. Next, we design an efficient algorithm for hamm-gram extraction in Section 7.3. Finally, to demonstrate how our approach provides benefits for both malware family classification and malicious vs benign classification, we perform studies on two publicly available malware datasets, namely the Drebin Android malware family dataset, and the Ember 2018 Windows malware dataset, in Section 7.4.

7.2 Related Work

Regular expressions have been important building blocks of malware signature detection for decades, across file types and platforms (Hahn, 2014; Levchenko *et al.*, 2011; Smutz and Stavrou, 2012; van Baar *et al.*, 2014), and are still used by most modern anti-virus products (Botacin *et al.*, 2021). However, these regular expressions have thus far been constructed by human effort. Reverse-engineering a binary file to identify signatures can take days or weeks for an expert analyst (Votipka *et al.*, 2019; Yong Wong *et al.*, 2021), and so there is great value in the acceleration and automation of this process.

The field of regular language induction has benefited from significant study (Angluin, 1982; Angluin *et al.*, 2015; Coste and Nicolas, 1997; Dupont *et al.*, 1994; Kudo and Shimbo, 1988), but the methods that have been developed are not applicable to malware detection. Those methods often require a fixed subset of languages and a corpus of *known* positive and negative samples, and incur hard-to-quantify computational complexity and slow inference. In our case, the set of possible exemplars is all observed n-grams, on the order of 10^{12} unique substrings in large corpora, which is orders of magnitude beyond the scales (10^3 or less) for which regular language induction methods are feasible.

The method we propose uses algorithmic tools from regular languages to build deterministic finite automata (DFA) to efficiently search for matches to all stored hamm-grams. Moreover, we restrict our regular expressions to the space of hamm-grams to create a computationally feasible approach. This approach extends the literal characters by a symbol that can match any single literal character (which we denote throughout by "?") and requires each expression to have a predetermined fixed length. As a result, this subset DFA can be implemented by a prefix tree (Trie) extended to allow child nodes to be wildcards.

n-grams have been popular features since the first works applying machine learning to the malware problem (Kephart *et al.*, 1995), and have remained popular in both machine learning and security venues (Drew *et al.*, 2016; Jang *et al.*, 2011; Kolter and Maloof, 2004; Shareghi *et al.*, 2019) with significant effort to reduce the cost of n-gram extraction (Ceska *et al.*, 2007; Curtin *et al.*, 2026; Gupta *et al.*, 2024; Raff *et al.*, 2025; Raff and McLean, 2018; Raff and Nicholas, 2018a). Prior attempts to build static features with more flexibility than n-grams have not become popular due to reduced accuracy. The study Walenstein *et al.* (2007) proposed "n-perms", where a byte-sequence was sorted to a canonical order to reduce specificity. As an example, `CBA`, `BCA`, and `ABC` would all be considered equivalent n-perms because they are all identical to `ABC` after being sorted. Others have attempted to reduce n-gram specificity by first disassembling an executable to apply domain knowledge, e.g., Shabtai *et al.* (2009) proposed reducing instructions like `mov eax,42` to just the instruction mnemonic `mov`; Masud *et al.* (2008) proposed reducing the operands to a reduced set of tokens denoting the type, for example, `mov eax,42` would become `mov.register.constant` to denote that the first and second arguments were a register type and a constant type. However, subsequent works applying these techniques to larger industry-sized corpora have found that simple byte n-grams were more accurate (Zak *et al.*, 2017). In contrast, our work develops a method that finds hamm-grams without any extra domain knowledge. Other challenges in malware detection, like measuring effect size and label confidence, are beyond the scope of this chapter (Joyce *et al.*, 2021, 2022, 2025; Patel *et al.*, 2023).

7.3 Complex LSH Method and Properties

Creating hamm-grams from a candidate collection of n-grams first requires a way to bin n-grams of small mutual Hamming distance together. Otherwise, an algorithm would require a number of comparisons that scales at least quadratically in the total collection size. This binning will be achieved by developing a rolling hash function that is locality-sensitive by Hamming distance. The approach will be given in Section 7.3.1, and we show analytically that it corresponds to the Hamming distance in Section 7.3.2. In Section 7.3.3, we confirm experimentally that this rolling LSH accomplishes our goals. Once n-grams have been hashed such that similar n-grams collide, we employ an agglomerative clustering method for mining hamm-grams from the buckets, and this is described in Section 7.3.4.

7.3.1 Description of Complex LSH

Consider sequences of length m,

$$[s_0, s_1, \ldots, s_{m-1}], \tag{7.1}$$

where s_i are drawn from a finite alphabet $\mathcal{A}$ of T characters. Let our *tokenizer* $\mathcal{T}$, defined such that

$$\mathcal{T} : \mathcal{A} \rightarrow \{e^{i\psi_0}, e^{i\psi_1}, \ldots, e^{i\psi_T}\}, \tag{7.2}$$

be a bijective function that maps every element of the alphabet to a unique complex number with unit modulus. It follows that each sequence can be uniquely represented by a sequence of tokens:

$$[\mathcal{T}(s_0), \mathcal{T}(s_1), \ldots, \mathcal{T}(s_{m-1})] \equiv [t_0, t_1, \ldots, t_{m-1}]. \tag{7.3}$$

Consider breaking each sequence into n-grams:

$$[t_0, t_1, \ldots, t_{n-1}], \ldots, [t_{m-n-1}, t_{m-n}, \ldots, t_{m-1}]. \tag{7.4}$$

We require a locality-sensitive hashing algorithm that is sensitive to the Hamming distance (Hamming, 1950) between n-grams and can be computed in *sub-linear* time in n. The algorithm we developed that fulfills these needs is described as follows.

First we fill a vector $\boldsymbol{w}$ of size n with powers of unit-modulus complex number a,

$$\boldsymbol{w} \equiv [a^1, a^2, \ldots, a^n], \tag{7.5}$$

where

$$a \equiv e^{i\phi}, \tag{7.6}$$

and ϕ is sampled from Uniform$[0, 2\pi]$. This is convenient for taking powers:

$$a^r = e^{ir\phi}, \tag{7.7}$$

from which it follows that

$$a^{-1} = e^{-i\phi}. \tag{7.8}$$

In the following, we use the notation $\boldsymbol{v}_{[i:j]}$ to denote the slice of a vector $\boldsymbol{v}$ beginning at v_i and ending at v_{j-1}. Consider the dot product between our weight vector $\boldsymbol{w}$ and our tokens,

$$h_p \equiv \boldsymbol{w} \cdot \boldsymbol{t}_{[j:j+n]} = a^1 t_j + a^2 t_{j+1} + \cdots + a^n t_{j+n-1}. \tag{7.9}$$

Further, note that the dot product between the weight vector and the adjacent window is given by

$$\boldsymbol{w} \cdot \boldsymbol{t}_{[j+1:j+n+1]} = a^1 t_{j+1} + a^2 t_{j+2} + \cdots + a^n t_{j+n}. \tag{7.10}$$

Using that

$$a^{-1} h_p - t_j = a^1 t_{j+1} + a^2 t_{j+2} + \cdots + a^{n-1} t_{j+n-1}, \tag{7.11}$$

it follows that

$$h_u \equiv \boldsymbol{w} \cdot \boldsymbol{t}_{[j+1:j+n+1]} = a^{-1} h_p - t_j + a^n t_{j+n}. \tag{7.12}$$

Thus, we've shown that the updated complex hash h_u (the dot-product between the adjacent window and the weights) can be computed with complex multiplication and addition involving only the previous complex hash h_p, the excluded token t_j, and the new token t_{j+n}. This computation scales as $\mathcal{O}(1)$ with respect to the vector length n, and therefore will be efficient enough to be applied to every n-gram in each file.

In Figure 7.1, we've provided an illustration that explains at an intuitive level how the hash we have devised is locality-sensitive under the Hamming distance. As an example, we consider computing the hash on the 3-grams of English letters, `fax`, `fox`, and `ace`. Each of the three letters is assigned (randomly) a unit vector in the complex plane, which are denoted $\mathcal{T}(\text{f})$, $\mathcal{T}(\text{o})$, and so on for all letters considered. Now, according to Eq. 7.9, the complex value assigned to the 3-gram `fox` is $a^1\mathcal{T}(\text{f}) + a^2\mathcal{T}(\text{o}) + a^3\mathcal{T}(\text{x})$, and similarly for the others.

Because a and all of the complex values assigned to the letters are unit-length vectors, their products are also unit-length vectors. Therefore, in each sum we have unit-length vectors added tip-to-tail. Now, it should be clear why `fox` and `fax` are more likely to be mapped to complex values that lie closer together, and therefore more likely

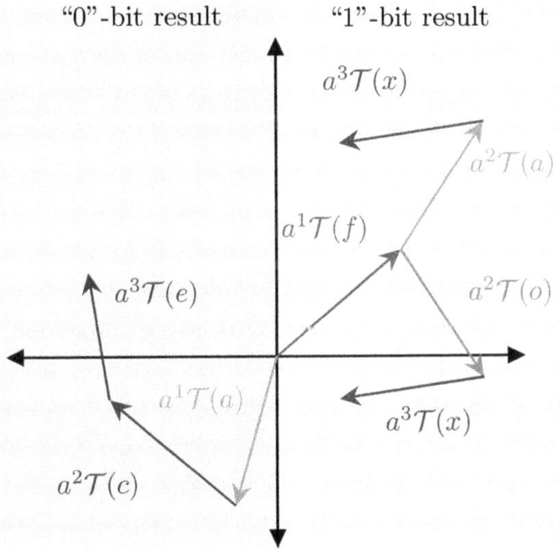

Fig. 7.1. An example of how the complex hashing function tends to put similar sequences into the same hash bucket, illustrated on 3-grams of English letters: `fax` and `fox` which get a "1"-bit for their hash, and `ace` which receives a "0" bit for its hash. Each $a^i\mathcal{T}(\cdot)$ applies a new rotation and fixed step size. The accumulation of such operations results in similarly shaped trajectories that differ in expectation as a function of how many steps in the sequence differ, i.e., the Hamming distance. It is thus more likely for two sequences with low Hamming distance to end up in the same half of the plane, e.g., fax and fox are both on the right hand side and receive a "0" bit in this example.

to fall within the same half-plane. This example also illustrates that although `fax` and `ace` both have the character `a`, because they occur at different positions in the sequence, they get multiplied by differing powers of a and are mapped to different vectors in each sum.

Finally, once the complex hashes h_i have been computed for all possible windows, a bit hash-code b_i can be assigned to each according to the truth value of the following statement:

$$b_i \equiv (\mathcal{R}\{h_i\} > 0). \tag{7.13}$$

This entire process can be repeated M times with independently and randomly sampled angles ϕ to define an M-bit hash code. In the following sections, we demonstrate both by analytic considerations and experiments that the hash code we have developed is locality-sensitive under the Hamming distance.

7.3.2 Semi-analytic Approximation

In this section, we demonstrate that the hashing algorithm described above is locality-sensitive with respect to the Hamming distance (rather than the Jaccard distance (Jaccard, 1912), for example). To do so, we derive certain approximate analytic results under the assumption of uniformly random sequences. To that end, we consider again the expression for the dot product between a random weight vector $\boldsymbol{w}$ and a particular tokenized n-gram,

$$\boldsymbol{w} \cdot \boldsymbol{t} = e^{i[\phi+\psi_0]} + e^{i[2\phi+\psi_1]} + \cdots + e^{i[n\phi+\psi_{n-1}]}. \tag{7.14}$$

Since both the weight-vector phasors $e^{ij\phi}$ and the token phasors $e^{i\psi_j}$ are drawn from circularly symmetric distributions, it follows that their product $e^{i(j\phi)}e^{i\psi_{j-1}} = e^{i[(j\phi)+\psi_{j-1}]}$ is also a uniform distribution over the ring of unit modulus (Tse and Viswanath, 2005). Therefore, Eq. (7.14) is equivalent to a sum of the form

$$Z_n \equiv \sum_{j=1}^{n} e^{i\theta_j}, \tag{7.15}$$

where $\theta_j \sim \text{Uniform}[0, 2\pi]$. This sum has familiar and useful properties (Weisstein, 2026), which we briefly review. We note that the following results are derived in the approximation $n, k \gg 1$, and we use the notation $\langle \cdots \rangle$ for expectation values.

Lemma 7.1 (Properties of Z_n). *The random walk $Z_n = \sum_{j=1}^{n} e^{i\theta_j}$, where $\theta_j \sim \text{Uniform}[0, 2\pi]$, satisfies the following properties:*

$$\langle Z_n \rangle = 0, \quad \langle |Z_n|^2 \rangle = n, \quad \langle \mathcal{R}\{Z_n\}^2 \rangle = \langle \mathcal{I}\{Z_n\}^2 \rangle = n/2.$$

Furthermore, for large n, the distribution of $x_n = \mathcal{R}\{Z_n\}$ is approximately

$$x_n \sim \mathcal{N}(0, n/2).$$

Proof. The distribution is circularly symmetric, and therefore

$$\langle Z_n \rangle = \langle \mathcal{R}\{Z_n\} \rangle = \langle \mathcal{I}\{Z_n\} \rangle = 0. \tag{7.16}$$

Moreover,

$$\langle |Z_n|^2 \rangle = \left\langle \sum_{i=1}^{n} \sum_{k=1}^{n} e^{i(\theta_j - \theta_k)} \right\rangle \tag{7.17}$$

$$= n + \left\langle \sum_{j \neq k}^{n} e^{i(\theta_j - \theta_k)} \right\rangle = n \tag{7.18}$$

Since by definition,

$$|Z_n|^2 = \mathcal{R}\{Z_n\}^2 + \mathcal{I}\{Z_n\}^2, \tag{7.19}$$

it follows by symmetry that

$$\langle \mathcal{R}\{Z_n\}^2 \rangle = \langle \mathcal{I}\{Z_n\}^2 \rangle = n/2. \tag{7.20}$$

The sum Z_n is equivalent to a random walk in the complex plane with unit-length steps. The resulting approximate probability distribution in the limit of large-n is usually attributed to Lord Rayleigh (1905). In the continuous limit, the problem is equivalent to a diffusion equation, which yields a probability density given by the multivariate Gaussian. Therefore, denoting $x_n \equiv \mathcal{R}\{Z_n\}$, we can approximate the probability density for x_n by

$$x_n \sim \mathcal{N}(0, n/2). \tag{7.21}$$

□

Lemma 7.2 (Probabilistic Relation for Hamming Distance). *Let x_c and Δx be the real parts of the sums of random walks for vectors differing by Hamming distance k. The probability that $|\Delta x| > |x_c|$ is given by*

$$p = \frac{1}{\pi} \tan^{-1}\left(\sqrt{\frac{\bar{k}}{1-\bar{k}}}\right), \quad \text{where } \bar{k} = k/n.$$

Proof. Now consider the complex hashes (before we take the sign of the real part) of two vectors $\boldsymbol{t}$ and $\boldsymbol{t}'$ which differ by exactly k tokens; that is, the two vectors are separated by a Hamming distance equal to k. Let t_c be the subvector of length $n-k$ which is common to both $\boldsymbol{t}$ and $\boldsymbol{t}'$, and $\boldsymbol{w}_c$ the corresponding subvector (according to index) of $\boldsymbol{w}$. Similarly, let $\boldsymbol{t}_d$ and $\boldsymbol{t}'_d$ be the subvectors of k elements which are unique to $\boldsymbol{t}$ and $\boldsymbol{t}'$ respectively, and $\boldsymbol{w}_d$ the corresponding subvector (according to index) of $\boldsymbol{w}$.

To more easily estimate the probability that their bit hash codes differ, we note that it is equivalent to the following probability: Sample three random walks starting from the origin, one of length $(n-k)$, and two of length k. Suppose, without loss of generality, that the walk of length $(n-k)$ yields a positive real value x_c. What is the probability that exactly one of the two walks of length k yields a negative real value Δx with a magnitude larger than x_c? If p denotes the probability that the first walk yields a negative real value with a magnitude larger than x_c, from the independence of the two random walks, it follows that $1-p$ gives the probability that the second walk does not. Therefore, altogether the probability we seek is given by $2p(1-p)$, with a factor of two counting the two possible situations (either the first or second walk may be the one that yields the negative real value).

To solve for p, we note that

$$p = \frac{1}{2}\mathcal{P}(|\Delta x| > |x_c|), \tag{7.22}$$

where $x_c \sim \mathcal{N}(0, (n-k)/2)$ and $\Delta x \sim \mathcal{N}(0, k/2)$. The factor of $1/2$ accounts for the fact that a larger magnitude alone is not sufficient, but it must also have opposite sign (two possibilities which are equal by symmetry). The probability distribution of the absolute value of a zero-mean normal random variable is given by the half-normal distribution with zero location parameter, therefore $|x_c| \sim \mathrm{HN}(0, (n-k)/2)$ and $|\Delta x| \sim \mathrm{HN}(0, k/2)$. The cumulative distribution function for the half-normal distribution with zero location parameter and scale parameter σ is given by

$$\mathcal{P}(|\Delta x| < a) = \mathrm{erf}\left(\frac{a}{\sqrt{2}\sigma}\right). \tag{7.23}$$

Let

$$I \equiv \mathcal{P}(|\Delta x| < |x_c|) = \int_0^\infty da \mathcal{P}(|\Delta x| < a)\rho(|x_c|). \tag{7.24}$$

We have the result that

$$I = 1 - \frac{2}{\pi}\tan^{-1}\left(\frac{\sqrt{k}}{\sqrt{n-k}}\right). \tag{7.25}$$

It follows that

$$\mathcal{P}(|\Delta x| > |x_c|) = \frac{2}{\pi}\tan^{-1}\left(\frac{\sqrt{k}}{\sqrt{n-k}}\right), \tag{7.26}$$

and therefore that

$$p = \frac{1}{\pi}\tan^{-1}\left(\frac{\sqrt{k}}{\sqrt{n-k}}\right) = \frac{1}{\pi}\tan^{-1}\left(\sqrt{\frac{\bar{k}}{1-\bar{k}}}\right), \tag{7.27}$$

where we have defined $\bar{k} \equiv k/n$. □

Theorem 7.1 (Collision Probability). *The probability of a hash-code collision given Hamming distance k is*

$$\mathcal{P}(\text{coll.} \mid H_d = k) = 1 - 2p(1-p),$$

where p is as given in Lemma 2. For $\bar{k} \to 1$, the asymptotic behavior is

$$\mathcal{P}(\text{coll.} \mid H_d = k) \approx \frac{1}{2} + \frac{2}{\pi^2}\frac{1-\bar{k}}{\bar{k}}.$$

Proof. The probability decays with a long tail as the scaled Hamming distance increases. Specifically, consider the Taylor expansion of $\tan^{-1}(z)$ as $z \to \infty$:

$$\tan^{-1}(z) = \frac{\pi}{2} - \frac{1}{z} + \text{(Higher Order Terms)}. \tag{7.28}$$

Therefore, denoting

$$z \equiv \sqrt{\frac{\bar{k}}{1-\bar{k}}}, \tag{7.29}$$

we have that

$$p \approx \frac{1}{2} - \frac{1}{\pi}\sqrt{\frac{1-\bar{k}}{\bar{k}}}. \tag{7.30}$$

Therefore, for values of $\bar{k}$ close to one, and keeping only leading order terms,

$$\mathcal{P}(\text{coll.}|H_d = k) \approx \frac{1}{2} + \frac{2}{\pi^2}\frac{1-\bar{k}}{\bar{k}}. \tag{7.31}$$

□

We see that the derived approximations obey the expected asymptotic limits, with identical sequences being assigned the same bit code with probability one, while maximally different sequences have a purely random 50% chance of being assigned the same bit (there are two possible bits). In practice, we use M-bit hash codes, and the probability of an M-bit collision will decay much more rapidly. This is observed in the experiment described in the following section.

7.3.3 Experiments on Random n-grams

As an experimental test of our complex LSH scheme, we generate 100 independent random experiments. In each experiment, we first create 10 random weight vectors (giving our final bit hash-code space dimensionality 2^{10}), create 1000 random ($n = 100$)-grams by sampling an alphabet of 256 unique tokens, as well as creating Hamming neighbors by swapping exactly H_d tokens with random alternates. The collision probabilities are shown in Figure 7.2 as a function of Hamming distance. The 95% credible interval over random experiments is shown assuming a Gaussian distribution. We see that the probability of collision of all ten-bit hash codes decays rapidly as a function of (normalized) Hamming distance.

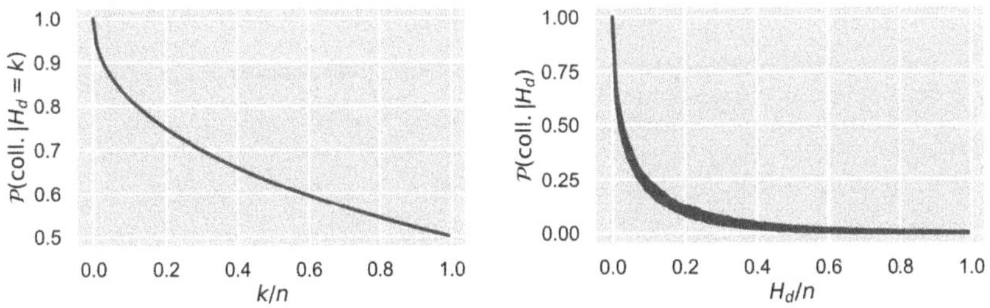

Fig. 7.2. (Left) Approximate probability of two n-grams having a single-bit hash code collision given that they differ by Hamming distance k. (Right) 95% credible interval for collision probability between pairs of ($n = 100$)-grams as a function of normalized Hamming distance H_d/n.

7.3.4 Extracting Hamm-Grams

We have now established the algorithm by which we can run a rolling hash function over a sequence of bytes such that byte sequences with small Hamming distance are more likely to collide into the same hash bucket. Using this new hash, we extend the KiloGrams approach to extract commonly occurring hamm-grams.

The KiloGrams algorithm (Raff *et al.*, 2019) used a rolling hash function to find the top-k hashes by frequency of n-grams, ignoring collisions. A second pass over the data would then use the Space Savings data structure to find the true top-k n-grams by ignoring any n-gram that did not have a top-k hash. Because the vast majority of n-grams are singletons, and the true top-k are selected with high probability, it allowed them to find the true top-k n-grams with high probability for almost arbitrary values of n.

Selecting the top-k hamm-grams is non-trivial, as finding a minimum set of hamm-grams (n-grams with wildcard tokens) is computationally intractable. We instead devise a procedure to build possible hamm-grams after the second pass, followed by a third pass which performs matching against the training corpus, sorts regular expressions by number of matches, and keeps only the top-k.

As shown in Algorithm 7.1, the first two loops over all documents in a corpus $\mathcal{C}$ run a modified KiloGram algorithm, collecting the most frequent hashes, and then saving all n-grams that reside in the top-k buckets. Agglomerative clustering with a fixed stopping condition is used to create hamm-grams from the n-grams within each bucket. This can be implemented in sub-cubic time (in the number

Algorithm 7.1: Hamm-Gram Extraction

Input: rolling hash function $h(\cdot)$, corpus of $\mathcal{C}$ documents, desired number of frequent hamm-grams k

```
T ← new integer array;
foreach document x ∈ C do
    /* First pass: find top-k hashes                              */
    foreach n-gram g ∈ x do
        q' ← h(g);
        T[q'] ← T[q'] + 1;
    end
end
T_k ← QuickSelect(T, k);                              // top-k hashes
S_H ← k different buckets, each corresponding to a top-k hash;
foreach document x ∈ C do
    /* Second pass: save n-grams in top-k buckets                 */
    foreach n-gram g ∈ x do
        q' ← h(g);
        if q' ∈ T_k then
            Insert g into the bucket corresponding to q';
        end
    end
end
foreach bucket of n-grams S ∈ S_H do
    /* Cluster n-grams within each bucket                         */
    while n-grams remain in S which can be merged do
        Apply agglomerative clustering on n-grams in S;
    end
end
Build a prefix tree of all saved hamm-grams;
F ← new map of final hamm-gram counts;
foreach document x ∈ C do
    /* Third pass: count matches and rank hamm-grams              */
    foreach character c_i in document x do
        if a match is found then
            Record the match;
            Update F with the count of matches;
        end
    end
end
return top-k hamm-grams from F ranked by number of matches
```

of n-grams within the bucket) by an implementation using priority queues (Manning, 2008). Two hamm-grams are candidates for "merging" if wildcards can be placed in a new expression until it matches both expressions without exceeding the predetermined budget of wildcards. Among all candidates, the two hamm-grams of the smallest Hamming distance are merged. This process is iterated until there are no mergeable hamm-grams left. In addition, because the Hamming distance is defined as an integer, any pair found to have a Hamming distance of zero can be immediately merged without calculating the remaining distances. In practice, these immediate merges result in an average-case runtime that is significantly better than the worst-case scenario.

7.4 Hamm-Gram Results on Malware

7.4.1 Results on Drebin Android Malware Family Task

We demonstrate and compare the performance of the top-k hamm-grams and top-k n-grams on the Drebin (Arp *et al.*, 2014) Android malware family classification dataset. We have first taken a subset of the twenty malware classes in the dataset which have at least forty samples, resulting in a dataset of twenty classes totaling 4661 samples. In each experiment performed, we kept either the top-(k=5e2) or top-(k=5e3) grams. We begin by examining the learned n- and hamm-gram features, measures of information they carry regarding the malware family, and how well these features cluster into groups. Then we compare the performance of Logistic Regression models trained and these features.

Finally, we trained and tested Logistic Regression classifiers on random training/testing splits of the n-gram and hamm-gram features for various gram sizes n, for ten random experiments each. These results are shown in Figure 7.3. In the first case, we keep the top-(k=5e3) features. In this case, we see both n-gram and hamm-gram features achieving balanced accuracies of greater than 95%. These accuracies are considerable given the challenge of having only a few examples per malware family for training. In the second case, we keep only the top-(k=5e2) features. In this case, we see that for

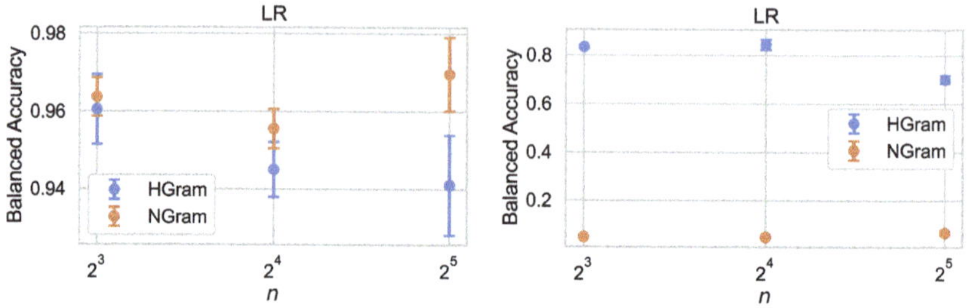

Fig. 7.3. Balanced accuracy scores of Logistic Regression classifiers trained on the top-(k=5e3) (left) or top-(k=5e2) (right) features, as a function of gram size. The standard deviation over ten random experiments is shown as vertical bars.

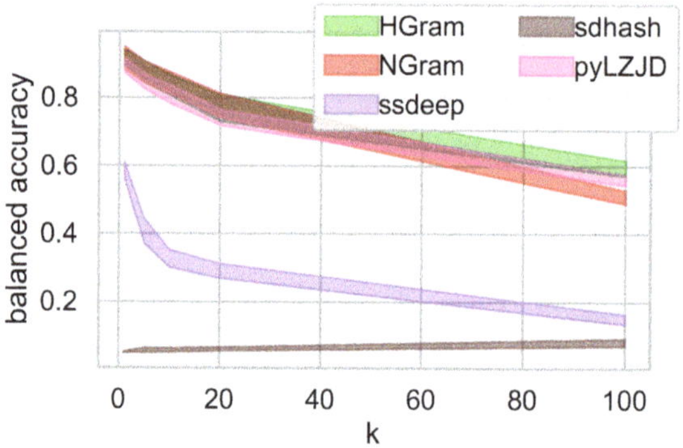

Fig. 7.4. Comparison between hamm-gram features and three additional hash baselines: ssdeep, sdhash, and LZJD.

all gram sizes (n), hamm-grams significantly outperform ordinary n-grams. For (n=8)-grams, the balanced accuracy is barely better than random guessing, while for size 8 hamm-grams the balanced accuracy is already better than 80%, a significant improvement, especially considering the difficulty of learning to classify twenty families of malware with as few as 40 examples of each. Thus, we see that hamm-gram features can provide significant advantages in cases where model computations are memory- and/or latency-constrained.

Additionally, in Figure 7.4, we compare hamm-grams against three similarity hashing methods: ssdeep (Kornblum, 2006), sdhash (Roussev, 2010), and LZJD (Raff and Nicholas, 2018b). ssdeep is a fuzzy hash that runs hash functions on fixed-size segments of the data. sdhash is a fuzzy hash that uses Bloom Filters to generate similarity scores. LZJD creates Lempel-Ziv dictionaries and measures file similarity in terms of the Jaccard distance between their vocabularies. Each of these methods is intended to work when some small number of bytes distinguish one specimen from another, and are suitable for malware data. However, they are harder to deploy in many situations because the k-NN strategy requires storing all data and several orders of magnitude more computation than logistic regression. We also used the hamm-gram and n-gram feature vectors and k-NN classification under cosine distance. As can be seen, our hamm-gram features are significantly better than ssdeep and sdhash, two industry-standard tools, for similarity search. Hamm-grams perform at a level comparable to PyLZJD and n-grams for nearest-neighbor search on this dataset, but a hamm-gram LR classifier outperforms LZJD. This further shows the value of our approach in building malware family detectors that have more robustness to natural changes that occur as malware spreads and modifies, while being faster and lighter in weight, making hamm-gram classifers feasible to deploy on endpoints in a network.

7.4.2 Examples of Learned Hamm-Gram Features for Drebin

Our empirical results demonstrate that the hamm-gram approach significantly improves the accuracy when only a smaller number of features can be considered due to computational constraints. This claim was expanded by exploring the top-k features produced by each algorithm. Most notably, the normal n-gram approach suffers from extreme feature redundancy that reduces the effective information available to the underlying algorithm. In this section, we specifically examine certain explicit features learned on the Drebin corpus.

A prominent failure case of the standard n-gram features on the Drebin dataset are various alterations of the pattern `SHA1-Digest: ???`, each occupying a place in the top-k features. On the other hand, the hamm-gram model with size 16 found this RegEx itself as a feature, freeing up space for other semantically different features. By conflating these highly redundant n-grams, our hamm-gram approach creates more capacity in the final top-k list for informative features that are both wild-card free (i.e., a normal n-gram that would not have been kept otherwise, because common and semantically redundant n-grams would have kept it out of the feature selection stage) or that actively use the wild-card capability.

Another example containing wild cards deals with variants of the byte sequence <FONT C????>.html where the "?" indicates a wild card. In this case, it found a RegEx feature identifying a malicious family that uses fonts as a vector for malware. In each sample in the corpus, the font has a different name that always begins with a "C", and is four or five characters long. This pattern was identified by our hamm-gram approach. Normal n-grams do not find this feature, since the created font names are each unique.

7.4.3 Results on Ember 2018 Malware Classification Task

In this section, we report on a comparison between Logistic Regression models trained and tested on the EMBER 2018 dataset (Anderson and Roth, 2018) using either the top-k n-gram features or top-k hamm-gram features. The EMBER 2018 dataset consists of Windows Portable Executable (PE) files, 600,000 training samples, and 200,000 testing samples, split evenly between malicious and benign samples.

Table 7.1 shows the standardized partial AUC scores for logistic regression models using either the top-k n-gram features or top-k hamm-gram features, for $k = 10^4$. We show the standardized partial AUC because high false positive rates are unacceptable in deployed malware detection scenarios. These models were trained using LIBLINEAR with a Lasso penalty hyperparameter which was optimized on validation data by Optuna. We see that the model with

Table 7.1. Standardized Partial AUCs for different features sets and sizes, on EMBER 2018 dataset, for liblinear model with k=1e4.

Feature	n	**AUC(FPR < 0.001)**	**AUC(FPR < 0.01)**
n-gram	8	0.580	0.737
n-gram	16	0.557	0.703
h-gram	8	**0.605**	**0.770**
h-gram	16	0.585	0.736

Table 7.2. Standardized Partial AUCs for different features sets and sizes, on EMBER 2018 dataset, for liblinear model with k=1e5.

Feature	n	AUC(FPR < 0.001)	AUC(FPR < 0.01)
n-gram	8	0.684	0.857
n-gram	16	0.600	0.785
h-gram	8	**0.746**	**0.893**
h-gram	16	0.694	0.852

Table 7.3. Partial AUCs for different features sets and sizes, on PDF dataset, for liblinear model with k=1e4.

Feature	n	AUC(FPR < 0.001)	AUC(FPR < 0.01)
n-gram	8	0.957	0.991
n-gram	16	0.944	0.985
h-gram	8	**0.985**	**0.994**
h-gram	16	0.978	0.991

hamm-gram features of length 8 (and with a wildcard budget of 2), is the best-performing model. Additionally, the model with hamm-gram features of length 16 (and with a wildcard budget of 4) performs comparably to the best-performing n-gram model.

In similar fashion, Table 7.2 shows the standardized partial AUC scores for logistic regression models using either the top-k n-gram features or top-k hamm-gram features, for $k = 10^5$. Again, we see that the model with hamm-gram features of size 8 (with a wildcard budget of 2), has the strongest performance, and the model with hamm-gram features of length 16 (and with a wildcard budget of 4) performs similarly to the best performing n-gram model.

7.4.4 Results on PDF Classification Task

In this section, we report comparisons on a dataset of 100K train and 10k test malicious and benign PDFs scraped from VirusTotal. The comparison in Table 7.3 yields similar conclusions, with hamm-gram features of size 8 performing the best on the task, better than n-gram features of size 8 or 16. Additionally, the hamm-grams of size 16 perform as well as the best n-gram model ($n = 8$).

7.5 Conclusion

In this chapter, we have proposed a novel algorithm for mining *hamm-grams*, common regular expressions of bytes, utilizing a newly developed Locality Sensitive Hash. We have demonstrated that hamm-grams provide significant increases in model performance on an Android malware classification task and on large malware detection tasks for Windows Portable Executables and PDFs. Finally, we have demonstrated examples of mined hamm-gram features where allowing wildcards was essential to discovering a meaningful underlying concept in the data.

Bibliography

Anderson, H. S. and Roth, P. (2018). EMBER: An open dataset for training static PE malware machine learning models, *ArXiv e-prints* arXiv:1804.04637 [cs.CR].

Angluin, D. (1982). Inference of reversible languages, *Journal of the ACM* **29**, 3, pp. 741–765, doi:10.1145/322326.322334, https://doi.org/10.1145/322326.322334.

Angluin, D., Eisenstat, S., and Fisman, D. (2015). Learning regular languages via alternating automata, in *Proceedings of the 24th International Conference on Artificial Intelligence*, IJCAI'15 (AAAI Press, Washington, DC), pp. 3308–3314.

Arp, D., Spreitzenbarth, M., Hubner, M., Gascon, H., Rieck, K., and Siemens, C. (2014). Drebin: Effective and explainable detection of android malware in your pocket. *NDSS* **14**, pp. 23–26.

Botacin, M., Domingues, F. D., Ceschin, F., Machnicki, R., Zanata Alves, M. A., de Geus, P. L., and Grégio, A. (2021). AntiViruses under the microscope: A hands-on perspective, *Computers & Security* **112**, p. 102500, doi:10.1016/j.cose.2021.102500, https://linkinghub.elsevier.com/retrieve/pii/S0167404821003242.

Ceska, Z., Hanak, I., and Tesar, R. (2007). Teraman: A tool for n-gram extraction from large datasets, in *2007 IEEE International Conference on Intelligent Computer Communication and Processing* (IEEE), pp. 209–216, doi:10.1109/ICCP.2007.4352162, http://ieeexplore.ieee.org/document/4352162/.

Coste, F. and Nicolas, J. (1997). Regular inference as a graph coloring problem, *Workshop on Grammatical Inference, Automata Induction, and Language Acquisition (ICML'97)* citeseer.nj.nec.com/coste97regular.html.

Curtin, R. R., Lu, F., Raff, E., and Ranade, P. (2026). Intermediate n-gramming: Deterministic and fast n-grams for large n and large datasets, in *Proceedings of the AAAI Conference on Artificial Intelligence*, Vol. 40 (arXiv), http://arxiv.org/abs/2511.14955.

Drew, J., Moore, T., and Hahsler, M. (2016). Polymorphic malware detection using sequence classification methods, in *2016 IEEE Security and Privacy Workshops (SPW)* (IEEE), pp. 81–87, doi:10.1109/SPW.2016.30, http://ieeexplore.ieee.org/document/7527757/.

Dupont, P., Miclet, L., and Vidal, E. (1994). What is the search space of the regular inference? in *Proceedings of the Second International Colloquium on Grammatical Inference and Applications*, ICGI '94 (Springer-Verlag, Berlin, Heidelberg), pp. 25–37.

Gupta, S., Lu, F., Barlow, A., Raff, E., Ferraro, F., Matuszek, C., Nicholas, C., and Holt, J. (2024). Living off the analyst: Harvesting features from yara rules for malware detection, in *2024 IEEE International Conference on Big Data (BigData)*, pp. 2624–2634, doi:10.1109/BigData62323.2024.10825735, https://ieeexplore.ieee.org/abstract/document/10825735, iSSN: 2573-2978.

Hahn, K. (2014). *Robust Static Analysis of Portable Executable Malware*, Master Thesis, HTWK Leipzig.

Hamming, R. W. (1950). Error detecting and error correcting codes, *The Bell System Technical Journal* **29**, 2, pp. 147–160, 10.1002/j.1538-7305.1950.tb00463.x.

Jaccard, P. (1912). The distribution of the flora in the alpine zone. 1, *New Phytologist* **11**, 2, pp. 37–50.

Jang, J., Brumley, D., and Venkataraman, S. (2011). BitShred: Feature hashing malware for scalable triage and semantic analysis, in *Proceedings of the 18th ACM Conference on Computer and Communications Security - CCS* (ACM Press, New York, New York, USA), ISBN 9781450309486, pp. 309–320, doi:10.1145/2046707.2046742, http://dl.acm.org/citation.cfm?doid=2046707.2046742.

Joyce, R. J., Amlani, D., Nicholas, C., and Raff, E. (2022). MOTIF: A large malware reference dataset with ground truth family labels, in *The AAAI-22 Workshop on Artificial Intelligence for Cyber Security (AICS)*, https://github.com/boozallen/MOTIF.

Joyce, R. J., Everett, D., Fuchs, M., Raff, E., and Holt, J. (2025). ClarAVy: A tool for scalable and accurate malware family labeling, in *Companion Proceedings of the ACM on Web Conference 2025*, WWW '25 (Association for Computing Machinery, New York, NY, USA), pp. 277–286, https://dl.acm.org/doi/10.1145/3701716.3715212.

Joyce, R. J., Raff, E., and Nicholas, C. (2021). A framework for cluster and classifier evaluation in the absence of reference labels, in *Proceedings of the 14th ACM Workshop on Artificial Intelligence and Security (AISec '21)* (Association for Computing Machinery), doi:10.1145/3474369.3486867, arXiv: 2109.11126v1.

Kephart, J. O., Sorkin, G. B., Arnold, W. C., Chess, D. M., Tesauro, G. J., and White, S. R. (1995). Biologically inspired defenses against computer viruses, in *Proceedings of the 14th International Joint Conference on Artificial Intelligence — Volume 1*, IJCAI'95 (Morgan Kaufmann Publishers Inc., San Francisco, CA, USA), pp. 985–996, http://dl.acm.org/citation.cfm?id=1625855.1625983.

Kolter, J. Z. and Maloof, M. A. (2004). Learning to detect malicious executables in the wild, in *Proceedings of the 2004 ACM SIGKDD international conference on Knowledge discovery and data mining - KDD '04* (ACM Press, New York, New York, USA), pp. 470–478, doi: 10.1145/1014052.1014105, http://portal.acm.org/citation.cfm?doid=1014052.1014105.

Kornblum, J. (2006). Identifying almost identical files using context triggered piecewise hashing, *Digital Investigation* **3**, pp. 91–97.

Kudo, M. and Shimbo, M. (1988). Efficient regular grammatical inference techniques by the use of partial similarities and their logical relationships, *Pattern Recognition* **21**, 4, pp. 401–409, https://doi.org/10.1016/0031-3203(88)90053-2, https://www.sciencedirect.com/science/article/pii/0031320388900532.

Langner, R. (2011). Stuxnet: Dissecting a cyberwarfare weapon, *IEEE Security & Privacy* **9**, 3, pp. 49–51, doi:10.1109/MSP.2011.67.

Levchenko, K., Pitsillidis, A., Chachra, N., Enright, B., Félegyházi, M., Grier, C., Halvorson, T., Kanich, C., Kreibich, C., Liu, H., McCoy, D., Weaver, N., Paxson, V., Voelker, G. M., and Savage, S. (2011). Click trajectories: End-to-end analysis of the spam value chain, in *Proceedings of the 2011 IEEE Symposium on Security and Privacy*, SP '11 (IEEE Computer Society, Washington, DC, USA), pp. 431–446, http://dx.doi.org/10.1109/SP.2011.24.

Lin, J., Chen, W.-M., Cohn, J., Gan, C., and Han, S. (2020). Mcunet: Tiny deep learning on iot devices, in *Annual Conference on Neural Information Processing Systems (NeurIPS)*, Vol. 15, pp. 11711–11722, Neural Information Processing Systems Foundation, Inc, San Diego, CA.

Manning, C. D. (2008). *Introduction to Information Retrieval* (Syngress Publishing, Rockland, MA).

Masud, M. M., Khan, L., and Thuraisingham, B. (2008). A scalable multi-level feature extraction technique to detect malicious executables, *Information Systems Frontiers* **10**, 1, pp. 33–45, doi:10.1007/s10796-007-9054-3, http://link.springer.com/10.1007/s10796-007-9054-3.

Patel, T., Lu, F., Raff, E., Nicholas, C., Matuszek, C., and Holt, J. (2023). Small effect sizes in malware detection? Make harder train/test splits! *Proceedings of the Conference on Applied Machine Learning in Information Security.* https://arxiv.org/abs/2312.15813.

Raff, E., Curtin, R. R., Everett, D., Joyce, R. J., and Holt, J. (2025). Zipf-Gramming: Scaling byte n-grams up to production sized malware corpora, in *Proceedings of the 34th ACM International Conference on Information and Knowledge Management*, CIKM '25 (Association for Computing Machinery, New York, NY, USA), pp. 5988–5996, https://doi.org/10.1145/3746252.3761551.

Raff, E., Fleming, W., Zak, R., Anderson, H., Finlayson, B., Nicholas, C., and Mclean, M. (2019). Kilograms: Very large n-grams for malware classification, *arXiv preprint arXiv:1908.00200.*

Raff, E. and McLean, M. (2018). Hash-grams on many-cores and skewed distributions, in *2018 IEEE International Conference on Big Data (Big Data)* (IEEE), pp. 158–165, doi:10.1109/BigData.2018.8622043, https://ieeexplore.ieee.org/document/8622043/.

Raff, E. and Nicholas, C. (2018a). Hash-grams: Faster n-gram features for classification and malware detection, in *Proceedings of the ACM Symposium on Document Engineering 2018* (ACM, Halifax, NS, Canada), http://doi.acm.org/10.1145/3209280.3229085.

Raff, E. and Nicholas, C. (2018b). Lempel-ziv jaccard distance, an effective alternative to ssdeep and sdhash, *Digital Investigation* **24**, pp. 34–49.

Rayleigh (1905). The problem of the random walk, *Nature* **72**, 1866, pp. 318–318, doi:10.1038/072318a0.

Roussev, V. (2010). Data fingerprinting with similarity digests, in *Advances in Digital Forensics VI: Sixth IFIP WG 11.9 International Conference on Digital Forensics, Hong Kong, China, January 4–6, 2010, Revised Selected Papers 6* (Springer, Berlin Heidelberg), pp. 207–226.

Shabtai, A., Moskovitch, R., Elovici, Y., and Glezer, C. (2009). Detection of malicious code by applying machine learning classifiers on static features: A state-of-the-art survey, *Information Security Technical Report* **14**, 1, pp. 16–29, http://dx.doi.org/10.1016/j.istr.2009.03.003, http://www.sciencedirect.com/science/article/pii/S1363412709000041.

Shareghi, E., Gerz, D., Vulić, I., and Korhonen, A. (2019). Show some love to your n-grams: A bit of progress and stronger n-gram language modeling baselines, in J. Burstein, C. Doran, and T. Solorio (eds.), *Proceedings of the 2019 Conference of the North American Chapter of the Association for Computational Linguistics: Human Language Technologies, Volume 1 (Long and Short Papers)* (Association for Computational Linguistics, Minneapolis, Minnesota), pp. 4113–4118, doi:10.18653/v1/N19-1417, https://aclanthology.org/N19-1417/.

Smutz, C. and Stavrou, A. (2012). Malicious PDF detection using metadata and structural features, in *Proceedings of the 28th Annual Computer Security Applications Conference* (ACM, New York, NY), pp. 239–248.

Tse, D. and Viswanath, P. (2005). *Fundamentals of Wireless Communication*, Wiley series in telecommunications (Cambridge University Press, Cambridge, UK), https://books.google.com/books?id=66XBb5tZX6EC.

van Baar, R., van Beek, H., and van Eijk, E. (2014). Digital forensics as a service: A game changer, *Digital Investigation* **11**, pp. S54–S62, doi:10.1016/j.diin.2014.03.007, http://www.sciencedirect.com/science/article/pii/S1742287614000127.

Van Camp, C. and Peeters, W. (2022). A world without satellite data as a result of a global cyber-attack, *Space Policy* **59**, p. 101458, https://doi.org/10.1016/j.spacepol.2021.101458, https://www.sciencedirect.com/science/article/pii/S0265964621000503.

Votipka, D., Rabin, S. M., Micinski, K., Foster, J. S., and Mazurek, M. M. (2019). An observational investigation of reverse engineers' processes, in *USENIX Security Symposium*, USENIX Association, San Francisco, CA.

Walenstein, A., Venable, M., Hayes, M., Thompson, C., and Lakhotia, A. (2007). Exploiting similarity between variants to defeat malware, in *Proceedings of the Black Hat DC Conference*. https://blackhat.com/presentations/bh-dc-07/Walenstein/Paper/bh-dc-07-walenstein-WP.pdf.

Weisstein, E. W. (2026). Random walk–2-dimensional, https://mathworld.wolfram.com/RandomWalk2-Dimensional.html.

Yong Wong, M., Landen, M., Antonakakis, M., Blough, D. M., Redmiles, E. M., and Ahamad, M. (2021). An inside look into the practice of malware analysis, in *Proceedings of the 2021 ACM SIGSAC Conference on Computer and Communications Security*, CCS '21 (Association for Computing Machinery, New York, NY, USA), pp. 3053–3069, https://doi.org/10.1145/3460120.3484759.

Zak, R., Raff, E., and Nicholas, C. (2017). What can n-grams learn for malware detection?, in *2017 12th International Conference on Malicious and Unwanted Software (MALWARE)* (IEEE), pp. 109–118, doi:10.1109/MALWARE.2017.8323963, http://ieeexplore.ieee.org/document/8323963/.

https://doi.org/10.1142/9789811262043_bmatter

Index